THE ANTECEDENCE of the FEMININE

Fourth Novel in the Series
The Siddhi Wars

By
CURTIS MITCHELL

Cover art by John McManus, *Untitled, Goddess Series, 2020*

Copyright © 2025 by
Flying Key Ventures, Inc.
All rights reserved.

Permission to reproduce in any form
must be secured from the author.

This is a work of fiction. Names, characters, businesses,
places, events and incidents are either the products
of the author's imagination or used in a fictitious manner.
Any resemblance to actual persons, living or dead,
or actual events is purely coincidental.

Please direct all correspondence
and book orders to:
Flying Key Ventures
PO Box 505
Hampstead MD 21074

flyingkey@earthlink.net

Library of Congress Control Number 2025913295

ISBN 978-0-9907067-6-2
eISBN 978-0-9907067-7-9

Printed in the United States of America

For She Who Loves me

"All phenomena are ephemeral, except Death.
Death is not a phenomenon, although dying is.
Death is inevitable, but dying is not immutable."

–The Prophet of Conscience

Table of Contents

1) The Lama and the Molecules of Malice 1
2) What Do You Need from Me? 5
3) Angelica 10
4) The Priests of De Murgos 14
5) Chantana and the Prophet 17
6) Jennifer and Julius 21
7) Matthews in Italy 27
8) The Secret 35
9) The Confessions of Emmalia Aura 38
10) The Molecules of Malice 45
11) The High Council 49
12) The Compound Attack 54
13) Angelica's Sorrow 62
14) The Towers of Marini 64
15) De Murgos 70
16) Dentata 74
17) The Prophet 78
18) Nazeem 80
19) Shambhala 82
20) The Men's Rebellion 92
21) The Mechanic 94
22) Emmalia in Town 100
23) The Blue Hag 102
24) Machismo 106

25) Shopping across North Africa	111
26) Matthews and Venge	114
27) Stonehaven	121
28) Regina's Assignment	124
29) The Antecedence of the Feminine	127
30) Emmalia's Defense	130
31) Kerkyra	135
32) Stonehaven Talk on The Truth	142
33) Maithuna	148
34) Wekka	154
35) Stonehaven Talk on Ecstasy	158
36) Washing the Stone	161
37) Stonehaven Talk on Conscience	168
38) Escape from Egypt	172
39) Dragon Island	177
40) Stonehaven Talk on The Mystery	181
41) Ah, So	185
42) The Djinn in Kerkyra	187
43) The Witness of Chantana and the Prophet	192
44) The Lama's Demise	199
45) Touching the Dragon	201
46) Parting Company	205
47) De Murgos at the Red Stone Temple	209
48) Setting up Stonehaven	212
49) Dragon Stirring	216
50) Stonehaven Maithuna	219
51) Dragon Wakes	226
52) On the Mountain	232
53) Off the Rock	239
54) Return to Kerkyra	242
55) Return to Bree	246

56) THE NEOMYTHIC AGE 248
57) THREE PRIME NUMBERS 251
58) BITER 254
ACKNOWLEDGMENTS 257

1

THE LAMA AND THE MOLECULES OF MALICE

On his way back to the Bardo, the transitional state between death and rebirth, carrying within him the remains of the Black Kite, the Lama's ghost stopped, as was traditional, to visit with the Gate Keeper. They were old friends, the Lama having been back and forth through the Gate many times, even before his somatic death. The Lama would bring good liquor and hashish and tall tales of his adventures. The Gate Keeper had long ago taken to calling the Lama "Rabbit" and would thump the ground with his foot rapidly when the Lama would appear, delighted at the prospect of new stories, especially the stories of the Lama's adventures and misadventures with sex and fighting.

For some reason, the Kundalini Buffer had never formed thoroughly in the Lama, no doubt traceable to the power of Indeterminacy, as in not everything always works out the way one might expect. If nothing else, it had given him extraordinary access to the Truth at an early age, for example, the power of psychometrics—the ability to tell the true history of an object by holding it in his hand. And, knowing the Truth of a thing set him off on a life the trajectory of which was tangential, if not perpendicular, to the lives of his fellow humans.

Alive, he had been inordinately fecund, with at least two dozen children, and had seen to the material support of all those "wen" (the term the feminine members of the Order adopted to replace the derivative word "women") who needed it and asked for it. For this visit he was accompanied by the ghost of one of his daughters, Angel, otherwise known as A—a child he had not known he had. Her ghost had devolved, that is, reverse-aged from the old wen whose heart he had taken from Regina's grasp. It was the only way her healing could begin, to go back before the traumas of her abuse, and the Lama was keeping her about the age of ten, a time before her mother had died, when she had been happy, curious, and innocent.

The Gate Keeper's house was a yurt on the edge of the abyss. The Gate itself usually resided under the firepit in the center of the yurt. While the Gate Keeper's Priestess played with Angel, the Gate Keeper and the Lama sat on either side of the firepit and discussed recent events.

"You know," the Gate Keeper began, scraping away a spot among the coals to reveal the blackness below, "you cannot take what you are carrying through the Gate with you. We must deal with it here, otherwise it will follow your daughter."

"It is greatly diminished from the time it escaped until now."

"Yes, and your daughter is greatly diminished, too."

Covering the black hole with coals, the Gate Keeper said, "Give it," gesturing to the Lama with his palm. "Spit it out. Spit it into the fire, it will be contained."

The Lama made some gestures over his solar plexus, then, raising one hand from the palm of the other, he brought the hand to his mouth and spit out a blob of blackness into his hand. He laid it out on the fire, spreading it out till it laid flat. The fire in the coals pulsed and licked around the edges.

"Oh, my. This is not good," the Gate Keeper said.

"What?" responded the Lama.

"Where is the rest of it? It was many times this size when it came through the Gate, following you."

"It was falling apart. Shedding little pieces everywhere. This is what was left when I was finally able to rip it from her."

"Her?" the Gate Keeper nodded toward Angel.

"Yes. It had attached itself to her Master, rode him, shedding all the while, until she killed him, then what was left attached itself to her."

"What happened to what it shed?"

"I do not know."

"Let's look then, shall we?" the Gate Keeper inquired, pulling a bowl of water over between them. He took the ragged piece of the kite from the fire and dropped it into the bowl. The water bubbled and steamed, hissing like snakes. The piece spread out and sank, attaching itself to the sides of the bowl. The Gate Keeper passed his hand over the bowl. The water became dark. They peered into the darkness.

They saw a man, a true magician without a Conscience, weaving the black cloth then imbuing it with his hatred of a life that had not given him the chance to rise to power and hold others in thrall to him. They heard his glee when he put it over his head like a shawl, and it held there, like a kite that trailed him everywhere. They saw it pass from man to man, landing finally on a man who pretended to convey the Lama's teachings. And there, in a string of images of sexual and physical abuse, it came to rest on A.'s Master.

Then they saw A. and her Master striding down a sidewalk, a thin cloud of dark particles trailing in their wake, some clumping along the ground, others wafting on the breeze. A man following them inhaled one. His face contorted in hatred, then a small pop was heard, and his face returned to a vacuous normal. Continuing to watch the street after the couple had turned the corner, they watched as a man left a coffee shop and inhaled a particle. His face, too, contorted in rage. He turned and re-entered the shop, shouting "You bitch!" They heard glass breaking.

They continued to watch as the day turned to evening. A group of soldiers from the nearby airbase came down the sidewalk, kicking up a cloud of particles as they entered a bar.

A few hours later they emerged again, loud, drunk, aggressive. They returned to a car, piled in and drove to the base. At the Gate there were two MP sentries, feminine and masculine. They stepped out, asked for ID, and a man got out from the back seat and grabbed her, forcing her back into the shelter. The car emptied, men bursting through the door behind the couple, overpowering the male guard, restraining him, forcing him to watch.

They bent the wen over the desk, used a knife to cut her belt and pulled her trousers down. Holding her down, three of them took turns with her. One turned to the other man holding down the male MP, asked him if he wanted a turn. He shook his head and said, "No, I want this one." He smashed the man's face onto the desk, drawing blood, cut the man's belt, pulled down his trousers and took him there, from behind also, the others helping to hold him down on the desk, facing the opposite way to the wen.

The Gate Keeper waved his hand over the scrying bowl, sighing, "I have seen enough."

"We're in big trouble here," the Lama said quietly.

"Yes," the Gate Keeper said slowly. "We are."

"Must it all be collected?"

"Either that or destroyed. The first victim simply burned through the malice, and it troubled him no more. But it seems that for the soldiers, the molecules stuck to them and drove their rage to rape. Not good."

"Very not good."

"You have your work cut out for you, Lama."

The Lama sighed. "Yes." Turning to the Priestess he said, "Can you take her home? I am told her mother is waiting for her."

The Priestess smiled and nodded. Taking Angel's hand, they vanished.

The Gatekeeper swiped the kite rag from the bowl, squeezed the water out of it, and cast it into the fire. They watched the ball of it unfold as it burned, leaving not even any ash.

The world felt lighter for a moment.

2

WHAT DO YOU NEED FROM ME?

Quinn drifted, trying to understand, first by sensation, how he had changed. He both was, and he wasn't—and not in the way that he was only what he was, and that he wasn't everything else that he wasn't. It was a kind of new sensation, a diffuse sensation of being both what he was (whatever that was) and what he wasn't, at the same time. Two sensations, interpenetrating materials that were mixed but were not combined. He struggled to sense them separately and couldn't. He could only sense them both and simultaneously, no matter what part he focused on, so he had given that up and worked on sensing the whole of himself—not just an awareness in a container, but as a container perhaps entirely composed of awareness.

In this diffuse state he found he could hear and see anything anywhere, but only if he focused somewhere. And that focus would keep him from the larger awareness, although something from there, something from anywhere, could grab his attention from behind, so to speak, and force him to pay attention there. It became his work to set internal thresholds for what could grab his attention, otherwise he'd be all over the place, literally it seemed to him, bouncing, or perhaps driven, from one flower in the moment to another. He couldn't do life as a butterfly.

In his drifting, the primary sensation was one of being under water, but it was a water he could breathe. He would feel a push or a pull in different directions, like small waves. Sometimes the waves were singular pulses that would land on him like the touch of a fingertip. In his mind, he looked to see the source of the touches, the impulses, and the waves. He could see back down these lines, these vectors of psychic pressure to their source. They were the prayers of his supplicants, applicants for his attention, beggars for his blessing, and beseechers of his intervention. The applications came singly or in bundles, braided around ropes of light, cords of light, that connected him to his Temples and his holy places, places where his predecessor had manifested.

Seeing, hearing, and feeling what they felt pulled him toward a deeper darkness, where the Shadows of their desires also dwelled, pitiful attempts to hide their motives from him. He knew it would drive him either to madness or the Void, so he distanced himself from it all, holding himself in isolation in the Light, choosing only certain times to make himself available to importunity, and then following only those cords that piqued his curiosity.

He chose to basically ignore the prayers of the venal and the vile among his devotees. He was the God of Destruction after all and the Cult of the Destroyer comprised the bulk of those. The only destruction he was interested in was the destruction of Evil, but he knew that was short-sighted and resolved only that he would ignore them for now, until he could figure out a way to use their desires to make them into better men.

It was the other cult in his domain, the cult of Salakta, that interested him; Salakta, the Goddess of Ecstatic Tantra. He was expected to appear in the masculine practitioners, and enhance them as he gazed through their eyes to behold the Beloved, the Goddess embodied in the feminine practitioners. Salakta he knew, of course. Salakta was She Who Comes, the True Creator, the Mind of All Life on Earth

She wanted him to do it all, of course—make the wen happy and make the men better men. And what he wanted was Her.

In his drifting he felt Her draw near. She took his hand and pulled him upward and toward Her. He sensed his head breaking through a surface and he was under a starlit sky. She tugged his hand toward Her, and he saw Her silhouetted by a fire burning on a beach in front of a thatch lean-to. They walked up to the fire, naked, hand in hand.

There were two stiffly woven baskets on the side of the fire near the lean-to. She opened one and threw him a towel and took one for herself. Toweled off, She took a blanket from one, spread it on the sand, and put out bowls of wood and corked bottles of water on it. She passed him a shawl, draped one over her shoulders, spread her towel on the basket and sat down.

The shawls were embroidered with gold thread that flashed warmly in the firelight.

She sighed. "Where do you think you were, out there in that ocean?"

"I don't know. It was warm, and vaguely comforting. I could practice learning how to hear those who call upon me. Or not hear them, as the case may be."

She barked a laugh. "You were in the subliminal zone."

"What? Where am I now?"

"You are in the liminal zone, out of, and above that ocean. That ocean," she said, nodding to it, "is the zone of feelings, the ocean of emotion, as it were."

"And what is above us?"

"Another zone."

"What is below the subliminal?"

"The zone of the Sea of Grief. What is above us is a hidden zone, the zone where the power of the Hidden Lands is derived."

"What zones? Why zones?"

"Everything has a density, since everything is material. Just like in a solution, substances of different densities settle out in zones, heaviest lowest, lightest highest."

Although he'd never been to the Hidden Lands, he'd heard of them. "How do you keep them hidden at a lower zone?"

"Phase shifting."

"Huh?"

"I will explain later. I wish to speak with you about what we are doing. I know you have a preference for working with the devotees of Salaktism, and I have a proposal for you about that. And I also need you to work with the Skreevist men. Many of them have seen you, and I need you to separate them from De Murgos. You and your brothers must turn them from their privileged attitude towards wen. Use them to help me end the rape culture. Many of them are ambivalent about it already and are suspicious of De Murgos. And they want to be better men toward their spouses and mothers and daughters. Start at the Temple on Wallid, and we will spread it from there, you and I.

"And here is my proposal. I know that you are loathe to occupy the mind of another. And, yet, among the devotees of Salakta, it is traditional that in their coupling they hold space for you and I to enter. Our presence is the foundation of their alchemy. It amplifies the impact of Ecstasy on the world. I will find ten thousand wen. You find ten thousand men. And we will bring them together, generating the power we need to heal the wounds between them. Let us generate a light so bright the flash of it will blind De Murgos."

He thought about it, felt into it, and understood. "Yes, I will do that with you. I will not impose myself on the men of the Order, however. I understand their refusal to be occupied, and I respect it. It is what I would always choose."

"I understand."

"I will include some of the men from the Order in the ten thousand."

"I understand. I will enjoy them," She said, grinning wickedly.

Then She said, "Good. We shall arrange it that they are all engaged at the same time."

"Now," he said, "I have a question for you. So why am I with you. No, not the question I need the answer to. Why are you with me?"

"I have need of you."

"For what? The Alchemy?"

"No, silly. I need you for something else."

"What, you're not immortal? What could you need me for?"

"Of course I'm not. I am ageless, not deathless. Nothing that lives is immortal, all can, and all does, die."

"Wait, what?"

"You heard me. But I will always have another iteration, so long as there is Life, so long as there is Indeterminacy."

"What could you need me for?"

"This," She said. "You are different. You are sufficiently different from all the other men. Even if what I set in motion is what conceived you, you are different. How many other men alive are there who know the golden whirlwind?

"I don't know."

"You could find out. But moreover, how many men are there on the planet, are there within me, my life, who have known it twice?"

"I don't know."

"But you could, and you choose not to."

"Not so much a choice as it is something I haven't considered."

"And why not? What happened to the young man who dared to ask questions?"

"Honestly? It was pretty much beaten out of me."

"But not by me."

"No, not by you…No, you restore me."

"I need difference. And I have been waiting for you."

She held out Her hand to him. When he took it, She stood up and took the two steps over to him, settling on his lap. She put one hand on his heart, touched her forehead to his, and they sat there, breathing in synchrony.

He swelled into Her other hand. Grasping him, She raised up and poised him at Her entrance.

She whispered, "You are the Thoondah. I am the Rock and you are the Splitter. You must split me…You must split the rock that I AM."

She lowered Herself onto him. And of that difference, the difference that She needed, She conceived.

3

Angelica

The Temple of Wasastami, a goddess of writing, music, and the healing arts, had been closed by the High Priests of Skreeva almost a decade ago. The Priestesses of the Temple had been allowed to remain, but new recruits were forbidden. The Priests of Skreeva had erected a moat of alienation fire, which stopped tourists when they got close to the door. The Priestesses were permitted in public only on High Holidays, when they were allowed to hold an orchestral demonstration for the public in the water garden that formed the entrance walkways to the temple. The water gardens were an attraction in themselves, with underwater sculptures of aquatic beasts, even a hippopotamus. Stone herons and ibis stalked the shallows. The double doors of the temple were guarded by twin dragons, carved from the volcanic lava of the island.

A few days after the destruction of the Temple of Skreeva by the Order, Regina, Moon Halter, High Priestess, and a daughter of the Lama, had departed for England, saying she'd be back as soon as she could.

The High Priestess Jasmine had been the Maker of the Green Tetrahedron that activated the statues of the Concubines and served as a beacon in calling down the Temple of the Mountain King onto the Temple to Skreeva. The opening in the floor of the Temple of the

Mountain King was centered on the raised dais that held the collection of Queen Old Woman stones, symbols of the Goddess, taken by the Priests from old temples and held collectively in the back courtyard of the Temple of Skreeva. The Temple of the Mountain King had been dedicated to the Spirits of the Land, older than the Windu worship, now usurped by De Murgos masquerading as Winjeetniya, the unitary power behind the Trinity of Skreeva and his brothers.

Jasmine and her Consort Guiles had their duties at the Yoga School in town but spent as much time as they could at Regina's compound with the Priestess Angelica and her Consort Corey. Onadaya, as a local Islander, worked closely with the newly committed novices Tenara and Napat, introducing them to the Principles and Practices of the Order.

Two weeks after the destruction of the Temple of Skreeva by the Temple of the Mountain King, Angelica met with Jasmine in front of the entrance to the Temple of Wasastami. Jasmine wanted Angelica to meet the dragons, sentient now and patient, that guarded the doors of the Temple.

The High Priests had not yet rescinded the commands that had closed the Temple of Wasastami, but the chaos at the Temples of the Three Brothers, Drahma, Wishnu, and Skreeva, after the destruction of the Temple of Skreeva, had led to a complete absence of the watchers enforcing the High Priest's restrictions on the movement of people through the gate to Her Temple.

After strolling through the water garden, taking their time to explore along the crosswalks and admiring the carved water beasts below the surface and the pools filled with lotus, Jasmine and Angelica sat shoulder to shoulder on the carved benches at the edge of the water garden, as close as they could get to the doors. "The Priestesses know we are here now, and they are watching us," Jasmine said.

Angelica replied, "I can feel their eyes on me, but I can't tell where they're watching from." Jasmine smiled and said, "Yes, they have been hidden for a long time. I have a task for you, if I may."

"Before you arrived," Jasmine started, "The dragons could only awake for a moment. Now they can awaken any time someone approaches, and they are remembering their time before, when they regarded anyone who came to the door, allowing those whose intentions were appropriate and stopping those whose weren't. The wall of fire the High Priest erected around the Temple has lessened, but it has still not gone out. I wanted to see if, together, we could put it out."

The ring of fire around the Temple was low, and blue colored flames lapped lazily toward the sky. Approaches to the flame would cause a flare, but it was weak compared to the wall of flame that would have risen up in prior times and so scarcely showed any inhibiting power to those that approached.

In her time carrying the Dragon, Angelica had learned a good bit of their language. Jasmine, reading her mind, said, "Try it. Say something in Dragon."

Angelica sighed. She put her hands over her womb, still feeling the absence of her friend, her burden, but reassured by the gift, the imprint of the dragon egg that had been left with her, waiting until she, or the world, needed it. She sighed. "Ho gved stedets," she said.

The dragons on either side of the staircase opened their eyes, rolled them once, and focused on Angelica and Jasmine. "Ing gved stadaht," they replied, in voices so low and rumbly they were felt deep in the belly, more than they were heard in the ear.

Anglica felt a burst of joy rip through her. She jumped up, clapping her hands and went to them. As she neared the ring of fire it flashed up at her, and she jumped back, hands raised in front of her. "Whoa," she said, braking to a halt.

Jasmine laughed. "Let's see what we can do, honey." She stepped out beside Angelica and held her hands in a mudra, palms up, just below her solar plexus. As Angelica watched, Jasmine became suffused with emerald-green light that emanated from her, and into her hands emerged the green tetrahedron. She leaned forward and placed it in the middle of the fire. The whole ring flared up, but neither stepped back. They stood there, holding hands, joined in a bond of love that, had it burned, would have been a hotter fire. The green light from the tetrahedron spread over the encircling fire, and where the green went the fire sputtered, and went out.

They stepped over the magical char and Angelica kissed first one dragon, then the other on the snout. Both dragons' lips pulled back in grins, and the outline of their form started to waiver, as if they were trying to move. Angelica put her hands on each snout and whispered,

"Shh, shh. Gradaina wu aitan." And the dragons' images stilled. "Wotani hhrekbu," she said, and the dragons nodded. Their heads turned to each other, and they touched snouts, blubbered their lips, and sighed.

The doors of the Temple opened inward, and there stood an old woman, long white hair bound in a braid, eyes wide. She spoke in Nahasi, "Welcome sisters. We have been waiting for you to return. Where is the young one Napat?"

Jasmine replied, "She is safe. With us."

One of the dragon heads snorted.

"Ah, let me introduce you." She turned to her left. "This is Left," she said, and turning to her right, she said, "This is Right." Her smiling face became serious as she looked at the two wen standing on the steps. "We have waited a long time for the fire to be put out, and to be able to open these doors in this way, to open the Temple again," she said, looking at Jasmine. "And we have waited lifetimes since the spell was cast, for these to wake up," she said, peering at Angelica, who bore the gaze for a moment then looked down. "We know who you are, She tells us," the Elder wen said, pointing up and smiling. "I am Balanni. Would you like to come in for some tea?"

The wen looked at each other and smiled.

Behind them, swans landed in the pools of the water garden.

4

The Priests of De Murgos

A few weeks after the destruction of the Temple of the old Skreeva by the Temple of the Mountain King, the gods Drahma, Wishnu, and the new Skreeva appeared simultaneously before each of the Orders of Priests, while they were having their weekly meetings in their respective Temples. They appeared as the Trimerase—one body, three heads, six arms—descending in front of the High Priests of each Temple.

Drahma spoke, "We are here as the Truth, Truth Born, Truth Told, Truth Faded. Each of these is necessary for manifest reality. As you know, there are some Truths that live forever, some only for the duration of a Life. Understanding Deepens, Understanding Ascends.

"Understand, then, that in this world, not everything is True. We are here representing the Original Truth, Our Truth. And Our Truth is that We were not made by Winjeetniya, the god of white flames. We were created by Salakta, through whom We were made, and with the Faces of Her She assigned to abide with us, you all were created.

"Salakta is your True Creator, and We helped make you from Her."

Then Wishnu spoke. "We are here to remind you of the Truth. We are here to remind you that a man ought not to disrespect and make little of those of Her faces she has assigned to be here. You ought not to disrespect the women and make them less than yourselves. For they are Her representatives also, and by disrespecting them, we disrespect Her. She is the Antecedent One. She came before us, and in everything we do, we shall put her First, and put the consideration of women first."

A wave of force blew through the assembled—men leaned back, as if a stiff wind blew from the Trimerase into the crowd. Then there was silence.

Into that silence, Skreeva spoke. "We must be determined, then, as men, to make this change, this change to what we believe and what we teach, manifest and maintained today, destroying the Old thinking for the Lie that it is. And we shall be equals again from today, my brothers and I. No temple shall be larger than the other. No coffer shall be more full than the other. And you shall all be equal in initial status, distinguishing yourselves from each other by your works.

"We must become better men than we have been. No more shall we take from the Feminine when we want to. No more shall we beat the Feminine, and lord it over them. No more shall we drive them into the streets when they grow old."

A cloud of golden light appeared in front of the Trimerase, and they separated out from each other into three separate beings. In front of each of them the golden cloud formed with their Consorts, Brakshni, Wasastami, and Darvatiye, seated in front of the gods, and smiling at the Priests.

"We are devoted to our Consorts, and we stand behind them as their Consorts. In each of our Temples there shall be a house for Them."

Off to the side, moved there by the power of the manifestation, stood the High Priests of each Temple, some kneeling, some with their heads bowed, trembling. They felt their world crumbling around them, fear rising, they looked to each other in panic, and when the vision of the three sacred pairs faded, amid the ensuing uproar, they began arguing about what to do. The High Priest of all three Temples, the one known as Vicious, went to the corner of the courtyard in the Temple of Skreeva and invoked their replacement god, Winjeetniya.

As usual when Winjeetniya/De Murgos appeared, he told them not to look upon his face, even when he was wearing the mask that made it appear that he had a face. The priests told him what had just transpired. He examined the chaos among the Priests, listened to what the Priests were saying to each other in the commotion. He leaned forward and touched the High Priest in the center of his forehead. "Find the women and the dragon who did this. You have the power. When you do, we shall destroy them. And erect my throne again, so that I may sit among you."

In the corner where they gathered, there was a small pile of the molecules of malice, tracked in by tourists mostly. The gathering there kicked the pile up into a cloud and the group inhaled the dust. Even Winjeetniya took some into himself. The malice tasted good, and thus fed, lingered in their bodies and souls. Winjeetniya smiled at the feeling, smiled at his hatred of wen and dragons, and even his hatred of those who worshipped him.

5

CHANTANA AND THE PROPHET

Chantana, High Priestess of Wallid, had initially thought she would send The Prophet of Conscience home after the destruction of the Temple, but while working with him, she holding together the network of Queen Old Woman stones while he used the network to infuse the island's dreamscape with the impulse to do the right thing (to stay inside) she began to feel something different toward him than her usual aversion to smelly white people. Even when he sweat profusely, as they had both been doing sitting back-to-back when they first did a practice session for the work, he didn't smell rancid, he smelled sweet. She could also feel his love for her. She had originally thought it was the typical infatuation that she'd dealt with her whole life when it came to half of the men, but she felt no fear of her from him either, which is how the other half of men considered her, they were terrified. "No, this one is different," she'd thought.

Even though compelled by the Goddess, she had used him the first night he stayed at her compound, and her attitude toward him remained utilitarian.

For his part, he was smitten by her from the first moment he'd set eyes on her, but he thought it would be inappropriate to approach her with his passion, for he regarded her as a Sacred Person, and he knew she would never violate the expectations her people had of her by a public dalliance with a white man.

Nevertheless, while they were eating on her audience platform with the curtains drawn, by the end of her meal she began to detect the presence of She Whom she Served, first around her, then within her. And as it had the first time, she felt Her begin to build a sensation of heat in her root flower, which spread to the second flower, then concentrated halfway between those at the Jewel in the Arch. The Jewel started to buzz in an annoying way. Suddenly the buzz became an itch she couldn't allow herself to scratch.

Then she felt the Goddess move in her, and she set aside her bowl of rice and curry, stood up, walked over to stand in front of him, pulled her robes apart and stepped forward, planting her feet on either side of his thighs. He glanced up, saw her fierce face glaring at him, then watched her eyes shift as her lips curled into a fierce smile. With one hand she held her phulva open to his gaze and trembled as he breathed on her. With the other hand on the top of his head she pulled his face toward her.

He kissed her there, upon her Jewel, and she trembled again.

But this was different than the first time. The first time had been under stress, under the duress of their imminent magical action, a magical act of war. This time, it was under the magical impulse of Sacred Erotic Beauty.

In the glow of satiation caused by their mutual feeding on each other's energy and alchemical infusions, on the edge of sleep they both realized at the same moment and came awake with a start, that Chantana was pregnant. Her moon was due the next week, but she felt none of the precursor symptoms. His read of her was of an integrated whole, and added to it was another palpable level of psychic energy, as if connected to an additional purpose than the purposes toward which they dedicated and devoted their lives.

"Is it true?" she asked.

"I think so," he answered.

"What shall we do?"

"We shall do as She wishes, I suspect," he replied, pointing upwards.

"Yes, that's true. But how then shall we do it? I have an important role for my people. What will they think? What if it becomes known that the child's father is a white man?"

"I think it is not so much that the child's father is a white man, but that it is me, this white man."

"Oh, no. I don't know which might be worse in the minds of the people."

"Really? You agree?"

"Yes, at least for now. I have not been doing Water Ceremonies for the people for a week now. I must resume them this week. You must go. Go to your mother's compound. There are no troublesome Priests or Meemons there."

"Really? I must go? When?"

"Tonight, after darkness falls."

He sat up, all feelings from the glow of the Beauty starting to dissipate. "This hurts," he said quietly, putting one hand over his solar plexus and the other over his heart.

"Oh, no," she said. "I have hurt you. Do not be hurt. I am not rejecting you. I am protecting you. And this one here," she said, putting her hand low on her belly.

He closed his eyes and opened his mind's eye, seeking Her. He found Her sitting by Her reflecting pool. She smiled hugely at him and nodded her head, yes. "She is happy for us," he said. "She agrees that this is best." He paused and drew a breath. "But I do not want to be away from you. Or the child."

"You shall not be. But you cannot be here, at least for a little while, maybe longer. I will come to you. I will come to Wiley, to your home. And visit for extended times. You will be a part of this child's life."

Into her pause he said in Nahasi, "Nahasi, your language, will be the child's first language. Because it is banned, we will have to teach Windonesian next. Only then my language..."

"Once the child learns the words in Nahasi we will teach them the other two. We will speak all three in sequence, teaching them as they learn. When they are older we will have Nahasi day, Windonesian day, and English day. The child will be smart. The child will learn."

He had a vision of what she was describing. It seemed to him a true vision of the long run, a future he could live into. He smiled and turned to her, taking her in his arms, and he kissed her as he laid her down.

They embraced, and they embraced again. He sighed into her neck and whispered, "When shall you come see me again?"

"In a week," she sighed back. "I can hardly wait to feel you pressed against me, pressed within me, again."

After tea at first light, he was on his scooter and gone by sunrise.

6

JENNIFER AND JULIUS

High Priestess Jennifer Amida almost declined to have her hair straightened for this assignment. She had been obsessed by the details and wondered at the implications. She was also distressed that she was not allowed to share the nature of the Secret with her newly assigned Consort, Julius. She was tall for a wen, but he was taller. And big, a naturally muscled mass of a man, his upper arm as big as her thigh. She'd had an instinctive reaction to his size, an adrenaline/fear reaction, but she was conscious of it, and suppressed it, breathing. And she was surprised when she breathed into it, her perception cleared and she saw him not just as a large man, but also as an enormously calm man. She also realized she could probably outrun him.

She had been looking forward to having her hair tighten and curl heavily near the coast of the Mediterranean Sea and had been traveling with the curls that way for weeks. It would take so much less care. She'd pick it out and tie it back. She'd keep it tucked up behind her under her shawls or whatever traditional clothing she might have to wear. Then the order came down that she was to straighten it because it would look expensive in a way that better fit their cover story. They even gave her the contact information for hairdressers that would do her hair if she needed it, as they traveled along the coast.

She had just had it done in Marseille before their first week away together, a time to practice their cover stories. His story was that he was the second son of a wealthy importer in France (they both spoke excellent French) building his own import business. She was to be his wife and the buyer for the new business, as she spoke better Arabic. Their trip along the northern coast of Africa was supposed to be a scouting trip and would involve buying small consignments of goods and shipping them back to an address in Marseille.

That week away they were supposed to shop locally, make purchases according to a list (not import goods, but necessities), and they were then to bring these to a small town in the mountains for further transport to a Priestess on retreat there. Jennifer had met her once at Stonehaven, her name was Emmalia. She was studying to become a Madeleine, on a Retreat to learn some of the Secrets of the Path of Solitary Cultivation and to cultivate her Siddhi powers.

They went to the contact address to leave the items on the list, mostly foodstuffs, but also some hardware, such as flashlight batteries and lantern wicks. When they arrived the contact person was not at home, so they waited, their car parked near the gate into the small yard. While they were waiting, someone pulled up behind them on a moto-cross bike with a crate strapped to the rear end of the seat,. wearing riding leathers and a helmet with a completely opaque dark face shield.

She got off the bike, took off her gloves, and removed her helmet. Long, dark red hair tumbled down. She shook her head and ran her fingers through it. She looked at Julius and Jennifer, sitting in the car in front of her. Her eyes narrowed. She set the helmet on the seat, went to the gate, and knocked. She was tall, as tall as Jennifer.

When the gate went unanswered, her disappointment, as watched in the rearview mirrors of their car, was obvious.

Jennifer turned to Julius. "Do you think she's who the supplies are for?"

Julius turned to her, "I can't tell. She looks American, though."

They both jumped when she spoke through the open driver's side window, leaning on the door frame, having snuck around to the side when they weren't looking at her. "True enough," she said. "And who might you be?"

Julius, immediately in warrior-mode, leaned back into his seat and forced his hands to stay slack and ready, rather than making fists. Jennifer opened her door and quickly jumped out, putting the car between herself and the American.

"I'm Jennifer. This is Julius," she said.

The American looked over the roof of the car and smiled. "Hi Jennifer." Then she reached into the car and patted Julius on the shoulder. "Hi Julius." She let her hand linger there, assessing the size of it. "I'm Emmalia." She flashed Jennifer the "O-V" hand sign of the Order.

Jennifer caught it, and flashed it back, suddenly smiling. "Is this your place?"

"No, it's not. I'm here to pick up supplies, and drop off something that needs to be mailed," Emmalia said, moving around the back of the car toward Jennifer.

Julius got out of the car and came around behind her.

"Who's place is it?" Jennnifer asked.

"An Elder's. A retired High Priestess and her Consort. They're the caretakers for the cabin where I'm staying."

"Vacation?"

Emmalia shook her head, still smiling, but said nothing. "Come on in. I have to drop this off, and I'm sure they'll be home soon."

"We have some supplies for someone; dried foods, batteries, and such."

"Those'd be for me, probably." Emmalia worked the latch and pushed the gate open, and entered, signaling the others to follow. When the gate closed behind Julius, Emmalia stopped, then backed up, making contact with Jennifer, then pushing her back against Julius. She took a manila envelope from her jacket and threw it on the ground to the side. She took a step forward, turned around and leaned forward, holding Jennifer in place with one hand while she unzipped her leather jacket with the other. She fished one breast out from behind the leather and squeezed, pinching the nipple. She moaned and looked up and smiled at them.

She unsnapped and unzipped her leather pants, pushing them halfway down her thighs, and slid her hand between her legs, and moving it, light as a butterfly on the jewel in the arch.

She dropped to her knees, undid Jennifer's belt and zipper and pulled her pants down to her knees. Jennifer leaned back into Julius, thrusting her phulva forward under Emmalia's lips.

Emmalia inhaled and breathed out the whisper, "Ah, Worship," and kissed her there. She reached between Jennifer's legs and stroked Julius's erection through his pants. Julius began to breathe harder. Jennifer reached forward, putting one hand on Emmalia's head, guiding her, guiding her in, against her while she reached back with her other hand and undid Julius's belt. Emmalia pulled down his pants and shorts, freeing his erection. She stroked him with one hand, then pulled it down and between Jennifer's legs. The head of it emerged under Jennifer's phulva far enough that Emmalia could put her mouth on it, too. Sighing with contentment at the beauty of what she beheld, she sighed, and said, "Exquisite Worship." She worked both with her mouth and each one with one hand, using the thumb of her left on Jennifer's jewel and the palm of her right to hold Julius in place from below.

Emmalia stayed with it until Jennifer orgasmed first, sliding her opening back and forth on the top side of Julius, both hands on Emmalia's head now, bucking her hips against Emmalia's face, crying out, and raining into Emmalia's open mouth. Both Emmalia and Jennifer started laughing at the same time; Emmalia choked trying to laugh and swallow at the same time. She managed to swallow and laughed harder, pulling her face back, standing up and kissing Jennifer, feeding her back some of herself. Jennifer choked on her laughter, too, which made them both laugh harder.

After a short time, the Elder and her consort returned. The others did not hear the gate squeak open. The couple closed the gate and stood there watching the others—Emmalia riding Julius cowgirl style, Jennifer standing at her head, her feet on either side of Julius's head, using her hands and Emmalia's hands and face to come again, raining on both, laughing between each ejaculation, and growling during each.

Emmalia could tell Julius was nearing completion, and she slipped him out of her, working him with a hand until he finished on his belly. Emmalia sat back and motioned Jennifer to join her, and together they feasted on and shared his gift. Still laughing. Then they paused, processing the alchemy, faces radiating bliss, and when they finished, they opened their eyes and gazed at each other, smiling and with Love.

The Elder coughed politely as they finished. Startled, they looked around, saw the couple standing there, watching. Emmalia jumped up, naked, and hugged the Elder then her Consort, giving his erection a little squeeze that no one but Jennifer saw. They both laughed again.

The Elder said, walking toward the front door, "If you're finished, come on in. I'll put some tea on."

With everyone dressed and sitting around the kitchen table with tea, and some bread and butter, Emmalia produced the envelope and asked the Consort to make a copy on the home printer/scanner system. When he was finished Emmalia took the original and put it in the envelope.

"Please mail this to the address on the envelope." It was addressed to Madeleine at Stonehaven. The Elder waved away the cash Emmalia offered her, saying, "It's taken care of."

Saying goodbye outside the gate on the sidewalk, Emmalia hugged and kissed them both, thoroughly. Jennifer asked if Emmalia would like them to follow her up to her cabin, and she said she would, but that their car would never make it, and she'd hate to see them break it up on the trail. Then she promised that if they ever saw each other again, they would have some fun. "Some fun!" she said, putting her helmet on, kick starting the bike, checking the tie-downs covering the supplies in the crate. She pulled a U-turn, driving off through the seasonal dust, and disappeared.

They stood listening until the sound of her engine faded away.

Later, after Jennifer and Julius had driven off back to the coast, the Elder turned to her Consort, and smiled her 'come hither' smile at him, holding out her hand. He took it, and she led him to the bedroom, where they disrobed each other, gently and slowly, murmuring sounds without words to each other.

He sat her down on the bed and stepped back. They regarded each other—the skin sagging at the knees and elbows and under the chin, the crepe-iness surrounding the long lines, the creases in their faces.

They had been together a long time, and both had lived longer than they'd expected.

As she gazed at him, his erection appeared. All she had to do was gaze. It always amazed her. It amazed him, too, she knew. She felt herself dampen, and she reached out to him, pulled him close, and lay back on the edge of the bed. He stood between her thighs, bent his knees slightly, and entered her, slowly, slowly, letting her adapt to him, unfold around him. In one long, slow, delicious thrust he entered her completely, and leaned forward into her arms and she wrapped her legs around him. She sighed, and trembled and as he watched, all the lines and creases of her face smoothed away. She flushed with pleasure.

He leaned in and whispered in her ear, "Are you happy?"

She grinned hugely, nodded her head, and whispered back, "Yes."

7

MATTHEWS IN ITALY

Matthews had been shocked the morning Regina appeared outside the stone wall that marked the boundary of the Compound in the Invisible Lands. Brighid had been keeping him, and he had been keeping to Brighid. She had wanted to imprint in him indelibly, giving him as many vivid and intense memories of Beauty as She could, not wishing to bind him to Her exactly—She neither wanted nor needed a slave—but to place the imagery of Beauty so centrally and deeply in his Soul that he would find himself near paralyzed with Grief at the thought of not returning. She had reason for him to return.

They had been having sex in the doorway, Brighid's back against the frame, Mathews' pack waiting in the yard where he'd tossed it when She'd grabbed him by the back of his pants and pulled him back toward Her.

Regina's fierce whistle came echoing across the yard just at his final peak. He groaned, he shouted, he leaned in and kissed Brighid fiercely. She kissed him back.

"I will return to you," he whispered hoarsely, then, gazing into Her eyes, he said it again, steadily and seriously, "I will return to you."

She smiled. "I believe you."

He withdrew and turned away, feeling torn, and picked up his pack. He walked across the yard to the gate, looking down, a serious expression on his face knowing he had to go, and not able to want to go.

Brighid put Her foot up against the opposite frame and Her dress fell back, revealing both thighs, dazzling in the light from the morning sun. She hooked Her outer arm around under Her belly, as if She was holding it from below. Regina got the message. "I'm happy for you!" she shouted.

On the other side of the gate, he spread his wings.

"What are you doing?" she asked, mildly incredulous. "You can't fly out of here. We have to walk."

"Oh," he said, and shrugged. "Lead the way."

Stepping out, she shook her head wondering for the thousandth time how anybody could master Magic if they weren't born to it. Much to her surprise, Matthews heard her thought and spoke aloud. "I don't know," he said. "Maybe mastery is too much to expect. Would you take minimally competent?" adding a goofy quality to his tone of voice.

She reached up and smacked him on the back of his head before stepping away off the knoll and back toward the village below.

Two days later Matthews found himself in Italy south of Badia along the crest of a mountainous ridge. He was standing in the ruins of the tallest, northernmost one of four castles, or at least their towers, approximately in a row along the ridge. Below him, and nearest, was what appeared to be a restaurant, fairly large, with parking for at least one hundred cars. Beyond that was a village of a few houses and a large building that could have been a warehouse at one point. Beyond that, was a large, occupied village, with a restored castle at the top, approached by spiraling roads and footpaths to an open gate. Further along, there were two more towers, both with piles of rubble at their bases, the furthest had what appeared to be a stout arm, extending out from the side, that had perhaps been used with a pulley to bring supplies to the top. His guides were a resident couple, the Priestess Selena and her Consort Joey, whose name she apparently used only with distaste.

Selena was explaining the view. "You see, here we are the first ridge of country back from the beach. You can see the sea off in the haze. In ancient times there were pirates, and they would land and sack the villages down there where the people farmed. The village chiefs met in Council and decided to build a tower here, where we're standing, and keep watch for the pirates. When they spotted ships, they would send messengers on horseback down to the villages below. People had time to retreat, and they would come here. That way the pirates would get only vegetables and water. Sometimes they'd take fruit, or grain, or oil. They didn't even bother to burn the houses. They knew that the people would come back, and they'd come raiding again.

"When the pirates shifted their perspective to the prospect of gold, it didn't take long to realize that the people needed protection, and accommodation, so they built the castle and the walled village. The fort and the tower beyond it were a part of the defenses for the village and castle.

"Of course, in time the Order bought all this land you see here, including the castle and the village."

"Is everyone here in the Order?" Matthews asked.

"No. Many houses in the village were occupied when the Order found this place. Local people still live there, and the Order secretly supports them indirectly, as long as they, and those to whom inheritance will pass, wish to stay. Initially, the Order was primarily interested in the Castle. The High Priestess is held by them to be the Matriarch of a very wealthy extended family."

Joey, old enough now to realize that he no longer liked the diminutive form of his name but not old enough to curb his enthusiasm for certain subjects, said, "You see that down there? That restaurant? In the Sixties that was a night club. It was also a cover for a prostitution ring. The Order used to use it as a Training Facility, right Selena?"

Selena sucked on her teeth through her lower lip, a cute quick expression of distaste.

Joey, blithely taking the sound as confirmation, "And see, down the road there, around the bend, that building with the big roof? That was called the Dormitory, where the Trainees would take their customers. They called them 'marks' in those days."

"Eventually," Selena took over, "The police became aware of the operation, and the Order shut it down. Too many drunks driving off the road and down the mountain."

"Yeah," Joey took back control. "There was some wild parties down there, I've been told. A lot of the older Priestesses and High Priestesses took a turn through here."

"And what of it?" Selena asked. "Marini is a Sacred Place."

"I know, I know. I just wish I could have been here for it," Joey whined.

"So you could do what? Change the bed sheets?"

"No. I could have been a bouncer or something," he grinned, flexing his shoulders and making his trapezius muscles pop.

"Good thing, too," a new voice stated. Everyone jumped, startled, and turned to the voice.

It came from an Elder, low toned and melodious. Her hair was thick and white, in a plait down her back. She wore a gray dress, cut low at the bodice, exposing her tan, with a blue jean jacket over it, and strapped sandals.

"When we open the Castle to tours, he is on Gate Duty," she said, with an accent that seemed both Italian and Scandinavian. Matthews fell in love with her voice immediately.

Selena introduced them, inclining her head. "High Priestess, this is Matthews, from Stonehaven. Matthews, this is the High Priestess of Marini, Freya."

Matthews bowed slightly, and Freya inclined her head. She held out her hand, palm down. Matthews took it and bent to kiss it. A spark leapt from her hand to his lips. He heard her voice in his head, saying, "Good boy."

Matthews looked up, grinning, in time to see her matching grin before she turned and looked down the valley. "May I ask you a question?"

She nodded.

"Where did you come from? We can see everywhere down from here."

She tilted her head to the side, as if listening to something. She smiled and said, "Thank you Selena. I'll take it from here."

Selena and Joey nodded, turned and walked away from the top level down the ruins of the staircase. Freya stepped up alongside him and slipped her arm under his while they watched until the couple made it to the parking lot of the closed restaurant, got in their car and drove away.

There was a low wall surrounding the small plaza where they stood, the ruins of the foundation of the tower that had once stood there. Freya guided him to the wall on the side away from the coast and said, "Look," she said, pointing to the next plaza down.

He scanned the floor, and near an edge of the lower wall a bush had taken root and leaned over, its leaves making a patch of shade. In the shade he saw a dark, square shaped hole, with a paving stone lying on the ground next to it. "There?" he asked. "You came from there?"

She smiled at not having to point it out to him. She tugged his arm. "Come. Come with me."

They descended the stair and went to the opening in the floor. From the pocket in her jacket, Freya produced a flashlight and shined it into the hole. Matthews looked in and saw a spiral staircase descending about twenty feet to a flat surface. "Go on," Freya told him. "I'll get the cover." When they were both inside she said, "Here, hold the light." The ease with which she moved the cover meant she was either exceptionally strong or the stone was made of some lighter material. He realized there were iron brackets in the ceiling. She picked up a piece of steel hanging from a cable attached to the bracket and slid it through the brackets under the cover. "OK," she said. "Down we go."

Holding the light Matthews eased his way down. He had to duck as his head came under the steps above him. "Shorter men," she said.

He reached the bottom, holding the light so that she could see. She thanked him and took the light. She shined it around until a hole about four feet high was illuminated. "Down there," she said. Matthews groaned and got down on his hands and knees. "Follow me," she said.

The tunnel had an easy slope downwards. In the light he could see that it ended in a larger space, a room in which he hoped he could stand up. Right before they emerged in the room, he noticed that the rock on the walls had changed color—from gray to an almost white color. He touched it. It was smooth and some of it came away in his fingers and felt like sand.

They emerged into the room, and he could stand up, looking around in wonder. There was a table in the room with a candle on it that she lit, turning off the flashlight. She saw him touching the stone in wonder. "Tuff," she said. "Volcanic tuff. It's easily carved and requires no additional support. The cap rock we just came through is much harder, that's why the tunnels were so small."

Looking around Matthews saw an arched tunnel leading on. "Where does it go?"

"Down under the restaurant to the Castle. There's a whole complex under there, originally dug into thousands of years ago. Initiation and other Ceremonies have been held there, depending on the cult of the day, from the worship of the Diosa to the Mysteries of Mithra and the Roman Soldiers. The tunnels connect to the other two towers as well. There is more space down here than in the buildings above us. There is water down here, and food and wine storage, in addition to the Sacred Rooms and the Sanctuary. The pirates were never successful in taking the Castle, and eventually they just stopped trying. They'd ravage the vegetable gardens, fill their water barrels, and go."

"How lo...?" He was going to ask 'how long would it take to see it all. She anticipated this and spoke before he finished.

"Weeks," she said, smiling. Then, "Not telepathy. It's just what everybody asks." She sat on the edge of the table, one foot on the ground.

She gazed at him. He stopped looking around and looked at her. "Take your clothes off," she said. He smiled at her and stood still.

She explained. "I saw Quinn once at Stonehaven before you came. I want to see exactly how much like him you look." She smiled again. "Take your clothes off," she said again, her voice a little more firm but only implying that, if she wanted, she could use the Voice and he would obey.

More helpless in his own mind than he actually was, Matthews obeyed.

"Come closer," she said when he was naked. He came forward. She held up the candle, studying his torso. "Turn around," she said. She studied his back, reaching out and then touching the places where his wings would emerge. She shivered, they looked like long scars on either side of his spine. She brushed both shoulders, as if to wipe away dust, or rain. "Face me," she said.

He turned around again, and she reached out and took his phallus in her free hand. "Show me," she said. She breathed on it, and it stirred. With only the sensation of her palm cradling him, he grew along her hand.

She got down on her knees, leaving the candle on the table so it illuminated them both in sharp profile. She kissed the tip of him, and drew him into her mouth, then she drove her mouth over him. She pulled back, and regarded the beauty in her hand. "Almost," she said. "But just as beautiful."

He smiled and said, "Thank you." Then, "He's larger than me, over all."

She pulled up her dress and sat completely on the table. She guided him in toward her. She asked, "How long does it take you to recover?"

He grinned and said, "Twenty minutes."

"Good," she said. Then she guided him into her. "I shall need you again later tonight. When the moon rises, we shall fly, yes?"

"Yes, we shall fly."

The table was at the perfect height for Matthews. On his first penetration he bent his knees so he could slide up the inside front of her, rubbing over the gland behind her Jewel. When he reached the top she shivered into her first orgasm, moaning with pleasure.

She wrapped her legs around him, holding him to her, holding him still until her shaking subsided. "Again," she said, "Just like that."

By the eighth time he had done it 'just like that' her eyes rolled back in her head and she fell away into bliss. Her scissors grip with her legs around his hips relaxed and he slowly lowered her legs, so that both feet touched the floor. He held still, mounted, hilted, within her.

In a few minutes, he smiling at her the whole while, motionless, she sighed and opened her eyes to gaze at him. More than one awareness gazed out from those eyes at him. The light in the room turned green. In a throaty voice She said, "Thank you."

She sat up, removing him from Her so slowly the pleasure of it made him pant. She laughed, nodding at his control. She pulled up Her legs and turned about, laying Her head over the edge of the table before him. "Feed me," She said.

It didn't take long, she knew the strokes of command. He filled her mouth with this part of his essence. It tore from him, shouting, back hunched, wanting to pull away from ecstasy but She would not let him go, holding him in Her until She finished draining him, all his spasms and shouting falling to stillness and silence.

He could hear Her process the alchemy. She sat up, facing away from him, and swallowed. Her braid hung down the center of Her back. He reached out, pushed it aside, and kissed the back of Her neck. He sensed Her smile.

She leaned back into him with her head, forcing him to step back, so he held her up in his arms from behind. Her face turned to him, she smiled up at him with only one awareness and he kissed her. When their lips separated he said, gently, "So who are you? Are you Freya, the Norse face of She Who Comes?"

She said, "Yes." And "No." and laughing, she spun around, slid off the table, smoothed her dress, grabbed the flashlight and said, "Let's go. It's lunchtime in the Castle. I want to introduce you around." Then, heading for the arched doorway she said, "Get dressed and blow out the candle when you leave. Follow the wall with your hand. I'll wait for you farther on."

Then he was alone. Pulling his pants up. Still grinning.

The night was cloudless, the moon half-full and waxing. Freya had taken Matthews to the top turret lookout on the castle. She was wearing a full-length cape and nothing underneath. "I've been told you can fly on your back. Is it true?"

"Yes," he replied both patiently and smiling.

"Good," she said. "Then I shall be on top. I trust no one to carry me."

"As you wish," he said, still smiling.

"As I wish, hmm?" She sat on a parapet, spread her legs, and in that near compelling tone of voice she said, "I require worship."

He went to his knees and saw one of the most beautiful sights in his life. As he watched she showed him the Fleur de Vie. He leaned forward, tongue out, and she withdrew it, laughing. Then she fell backward off the parapet. He leapt over the parapet and, as he watched, the cloak stiffened, as if it was a wingsuit and suddenly, instead of falling, she was sailing away from him, grinning hugely. He couldn't understand it. His brain told him, "Magic," at which he shrugged and dove after her.

When he caught her he said, "Thank you."

She said, "Don't thank me yet."

8

THE SECRET

Nadahlia Al-lat was kneeling at the small three burner stove, changing the gas bottle in preparation for making supper for her father and brother. She was upset and weeping, not wanting to look at her mother when she was being addressed. She asked, "Once again, please explain it to me, why I have to go."

"Because, as I have said, soon it will become dangerous here. I am going to try to make arrangements to send your brother with you, although I have not told him yet."

"And you know this danger is coming how?"

"You know how. And you have seen it yourself," her mother replied, showing her the palm of her hand, where the oracle would appear. "Have you ever known what you see there to be untrue?"

"Oh, I know what I saw. But that doesn't mean it will happen. It is too terrible, and I have done nothing wrong. Nor will I," she asserted. "Besides, I keep your secret from the Meemons."

"But it doesn't matter whether you have done anything wrong or not! You know this, too! And don't threaten me. The Sight is not the only secret in my possession."

Chastened, and in a quiet voice, she responded "I cannot understand how that can be. Why will they come for me when I have done nothing wrong?"

"You will understand it soon enough." Her daughter turned to look at her, with a pleading expression that hurt her heart. She saw her face in her daughter's, remembering the despair that she'd felt when she'd learned of the Secret. She'd sent the message that she needed help through the old woman in the market at the shoe stand. The old woman was the only one who knew the Secret she had confessed. The old woman let on that she had always known, and that she was paid to watch over her, although she did not say who paid her. She'd heard back already from The Help what would be done to rescue her daughter, but she was deeply afraid for her son. The Help had sent back instructions that there was something they needed him to do. They said they would protect him, but did not say how. She was to come back to the market when she was summoned and receive further instructions.

Her brother Nazeem came through the door, carrying his mud boots and jacket. He put the boots on the carpet and hung the jacket on a hook embedded in the wall. He was smiling.

"Greetings, brother!" Nadahlia called.

"Greetings, Nazeem!" their mother called. "Where is your father?"

"A customer came in late in the day. You know how it is in this business."

She nodded and told him to wash his hands and face in the basin she brought him and placed on a low table near the door.

In their village on the outskirts of Wekka it was sometimes less expensive to use the mud brick that it was the family's business to make, pouring mud into wooden forms, waiting until it dried a little in the merciless sun, then pulling the forms off to let them finish drying. It would be more expensive to use concrete for a small construction. The father had a gasoline powered mixer, and it was his job to run it while Nazeem used an old wheelbarrow to carry the mix to the forms. The dirt they used was free for the hauling from the bigger construction sites closer to the center of the city.

But the time was coming when the business would close. Concrete and cinder block would continue to get less expensive and easier to deliver. Nazeem had no prospects and was thinking that he could go to Europe and work as a laborer there, sending money home.

When Nazeem smiled at his mother the white flash of his teeth reminded her of his father so much it made her heart hurt. The old woman's plan had involved both of her children, and she thought it meant she would never see them again. The old woman had said she could go with them, but that meant she had to leave her husband. And, although he was sometimes mean and aggressive with her, she did not want to leave him.

9

THE CONFESSIONS OF EMMALIA AURA

Dear Madeleine,

She is with me often, you know. I have only to think of Her now, and She Comes. And, as you also know, I have been instructed to engage in ritual every full and new moon, ritual to feed the spirits of the land here, and to feed the world. Alas, because my station, my assignment, is so remote I am often without a Consort, and hence am practicing the path of solo cultivation as instructed. While there is a part of me which longs for the comfort of company, there is another part, a more true and central part of me, that longs foremost for ecstasy—in particular the ecstasy that union with Her brings, and following Her instruction while She abides in me.

I am writing to you, High Priestess, to keep my word to stay in touch with you about how things are proceeding with me, while I am away on assignment.

I have to take a moment to describe to you the beauty of this place, as I do not know if you have been here. It is a one room cabin set in the mountains north of Nice. The southern exposure is windows, set at an angle to each other. Imagine a long bay window with a dozen panels in it rather than three or four. There are built-in low benches or seats running along the walls below the windowsills. On the central table, I have set up my altar. The kitchen area and the bed—a large covered four poster, hung with heavy curtains—are set in the back, bed on the east side, kitchen and sitting area on the west by a large open stone fireplace with hooks on swivels to hold pots into the flames. Sometimes it is still chilly here and I have taken to lighting fires for heat and comfort. The kitchen stove is a combination stove, burning either wood or gas. I imagine it has to be so, as deliveries of gas seem to be made only by mule—I'm kidding. But I know a four-wheeler, like the one I found here in the woodshed, could make the trip. There is also a moto-cross style two-wheeler. Both are in running condition; I checked. The lighting here is interesting. There are two propane lamps on the wall that use little socks like a white-gas lantern. And there are two white gas lanterns and several kerosene lamps. No electricity! The water here gravity fed, it seems, from a pipe somewhere up the mountain, and into a gravity feed tank. It is cold, and clear, and tasty.

Here, high up on the shoulder of this mountain, a lot has been cleared for a yard, and grass planted, with raised beds of flowers and flowering trees around the periphery, and at one end there is a shrine. It seems old, three weathered statues set into a niche, perhaps three-quarter sized, their features worn by weather to indistinct. Judging by the clothing it seems to me it is a mother, with two children in front of her to the sides, her arms resting protectively on their shoulders to the outside. When you stand directly before the scene, the mother is looking off to the northwest while the children seem to be looking directly at the viewer. There is a stone plate set in the ground at their feet with writing carved in it. It says, in French, Latin, and Greek, as near as I can make out, "I rested here."

I could see where flowers had been laid at their feet, perhaps food and water in bowls. I have cleaned these and make the same offerings. With this full moon have come small white flowers in the grass and I picked a few and placed them there. I sense great presence at this spot, and great power.

As you know this past month was the time of the Pink Moon, the April moon, and my instructions were to conduct the ceremony as I have been shown, and to do it twice, once the night prior to the night of the full moon proper, and once on the night after the full moon. The two experiences were dramatically different in the instructions and in the consequent manifestation of the ecstasies.

The moon was very bright, rising through the high window to the left, bathing me and the altar both in brilliant silver-white light. I had found a low sided bowl in the kitchen and brought it over to the altar with me.

I placed the phalluses on the altar, at least an hour before. I prepared the pad before the altar. I bathed and shaved. I put the shawl over my shoulders and sat, naked from the waist down. I lit the three candles, one for each of Her faces in the moon cycle, Maiden, Mature, Crone, the visible cycles of the moon. I left the black candle for the new moon unlit. I lit incense. The copper bowl was on the altar and a bowl with lower sides, along with the skulls of ram, buck, and boar. I meditated. I sang, and then spoke the invocation. I asked Her to come and guide me in what She wanted me to do. I acknowledged the Moon, and Her power over life on earth.

I picked up the larger phallus and held it up to the moon. Then I put it in my mouth and massaged the roof of my mouth with it. I did this until my breathing started to change, and my body started to vibrate, resonating from the sensation on the roof of my mouth. What I used to do was take the saliva from my mouth on my hand and rub it between my legs. These times I used coconut oil, rubbing it on the smaller phallus, too. I blew the candles out.

I lay on my back, working with the phallus to get heated up. Slowly I brought it into me, slowly, in and out. Once I was more energized, I got up on my knees, bringing the copper bowl between my knees. I put the phallus in me as far as it would go, then moved it around slowly. When my breathing changed again, speeding up, I started to move it rapidly in and out. I took it out at times and massaged all around my phulva, and just inside at the g-spot, which triggered more response. Then I put it back inside me and started to move it faster. I would get just to the point of orgasm, take the phallus out, use my hand on the Jewel and that would usually make me rain into the copper bowl. I did this a number of times. Once I started raining, I could feel that She was in me. It used to be that She watched, but now She is in me when I rain.

I leaned forward and put my head on the altar. When my knees gave out I removed the copper bowl and put the lower bowl under me and lay down on my back, knees up, feet on the floor. Now that I was sensitized, my breathing slowed down and sped up, getting deeper. I moaned and cried out at the peaks of the rain releases.

I began vibrating, resonating, like a struck tuning fork. I took the phallus out and slapped myself, softer, then harder. It would almost make me orgasm, and then I would insert just the tip. That little bit of friction would make me rain. I could feel the lips of my phulva growing, engorging. Eventually just a couple slaps would trigger a rain event. Finally, I would put the phallus in me, and orgasm that way for a while. She said to me, "Together we will feed the world."

I spread my arms out and fed the world, energy pouring through my hands. Then I repeated the cycle. Sometimes I would stop and pour the rain from the low sided bowl into the copper bowl. I did this for a while. At some point I moved the bowl away, and started massaging myself, putting fingers in me, manipulating the g spot. When I would rain, I would use my hand to pull it up my body, circling around my breasts. I would take the phallus and use it again, withdrawing right before orgasm. I brought the rain to my third eye, my lips, and massaged it into my face.

Sometimes I would slap myself with my hand. It got to the point where I would simply orgasm without stimulation, I would just rain. She had me draw a circle in my palms with the rain, extend my arms and feed the world.

A column of golden light appeared within me, starting at the root and shooting out through my crown chakra, pulsing with the waves of orgasm. I came back to the phallus, very slowly, then I withdrew it and used my hand to finish.

At some point I laid on the floor with my hands out and brought that golden light to my hands, pulsing it out into the world at the same time it poured out of my crown. My legs started to shake, then my whole body began to shake.

And then there was a movement in me that bid me sit up, with my palms on my thighs. Then I listened to hear if She tells me anything. Sometimes She does, sometimes She doesn't.

The moon was still shining through the window. The shaking continued in me, coming through me in waves.

I wrapped myself in my heavy long wool shawl and took the

bowl out to the south lawn. I held it up to the moon and thanked the Goddess. I got down on my hands and knees and poured it into the earth. I thanked the Earth.

I came inside, poured some water in the bowl, and went back outside to offer it to the Goddess, then I poured the rinse into the earth, not to waste a drop.

The entire ceremony took perhaps an hour and a half.

I heard Her voice as I returned to the cabin. "Now that was solo cultivation," She said to me. I can feel you laughing as you read this.

I went to sleep with the rain drying on me. I didn't sleep much. I woke up every two hours, and I would get up. I felt the need to bathe in the moonlight.

The next day I felt good, not as tired as I thought I'd be. There was work in the gardens, and my reading and journaling. My root vibrated all day, almost a buzzing sensation. I was surprised, but not uncomfortable. When I felt tired, I went to sleep and fell easily. Although I slept the night through, my dreams—storms, wen running and hiding. Wen and men fighting other men in the dark. Fleeing on horseback. Grieving for the lost, and the dead. I had thought it would be a springtime flowers and breezes night, but it was not. In my meditation the next morning, I sent a voice of inquiry to Her, and She replied, "Early spring has been a good time to flee. Wen and children die in the winter." And I understood. If you don't have to flee too far, there is still time to plant a garden before summer.

On the night after the full moon, I proceeded as before. The sequence was much the same as the night before full. With the slapping I became engorged, using my hands more, with one hand out, channeling the ecstasy out into the world. I had my Jewel pinched between my fingers, pulling it up, pulling the hood back. I would massage the g-spot, one finger, and that would make me rain, and between rains, I would have simple orgasms while the gland refilled.

I was even more sensitized than I was two nights prior. When I would open my eyes and look at the moon there were lines of light that I could see, rays pouring down onto me. I worked with my hand, doing the same ritual of painting my body with the rain. First my breasts, then with the next rain my face, then with the next, drawing the circles in my hands.

Since I was working with my hands, and I was so swollen and wet, I felt an impulse and I started to explore my anus. I inserted my middle finger, and while I was pressing on my phulva with my hand, I orgasmed. She guided me to pick up the phallus and, rolling slightly to my side I inserted it behind, slowly with my left hand, until I reached a stopping place. I moved the phallus around, very slowly, my other hand with fingers on my jewel, or in me.

Once again, I don't know why, the phallus was in me and I drew it out very, very slowly and then just as it popped out and I went into a deep, intense orgasm, arching my back, making guttural moaning sounds and I just rained, squirting more than once.

I went back to this maybe four or five times. I would think OK, this is done, and then She would move me to do it again. And with the deep orgasm, arching my back, hard breathing, heavy moaning. It happened every time. Each time that I came like that, my arms would be out and I would be aware of feeding the world.

Even when I stopped with the phallus and my hand, arms out laying on my back, feeding the world. Once I felt a puff of air, I don't know from where, hit me between the legs, and that made me orgasm. I worked the draw, still orgasming, still I was feeding the world, raining sometimes, feeding the world, top chakra open. The light this time, instead of gold, was blue green.

The quality of those anal orgasms was not light, not sparkly, not a sparkly rain. It's like I was in a dark cave. It was dark, not in a sinister way but in a way that was completely different, almost opposite to the sparkly orgasms of two nights past.

My expectations had been that all the orgasms would be sparkly things, but not this time. I sat up, and I was still being taken by these orgasms and raining. I would think I was out of the ritual space, and then the wave would move through me and I'd have to rain again, simply sitting there, raining on the floor, with no stimulation.

This happened while I was sitting up, looking at the moon, thanking the Goddess. I fumbled around relighting the candles, including the black candle for the coming new moon, but my hands were so wet. I stopped orgasming but I kept shuddering and my thighs kept shaking. I had a hard time standing up because my legs were shaking so much.

I put my poncho on, took the bowl, went outside and held it up to the moon, and the four directions, got to my knees and poured it into the earth. I took the rinse water and used it to bless the statues in the shrine. I shivered all over while the water poured.

Then I went to bed, except for the fact that I couldn't fall asleep. Finally, I asked the Goddess to let me sleep, and shortly after, I did. I could feel the energy slow down, the activation settling in me.

That night had a different quality. One of the aspects of it is that I pushed my body pretty hard. Those anal orgasms were so intense, gut wrenching, not like despair or anything like that, but literally my viscera, my guts had been wrenching in spasm. In addition to the physical, I was very far out there in liminal space, sacred space and time. It didn't scare me, but it was a level of surrender that I was not familiar with. It's one thing to go out and trip around the stars, but it's a whole other thing to feel like I was pinned to the earth. Part of what this seems to be is understanding, part of it is acceptance and surrender to what She wants, and trying to understand if "that which says 'I' in me" was even there. It seemed like my self-awareness was elsewhere, and some more basic kind of awareness was paying attention and forming memories.

The next day my root chakra vibrated intensely all day long. Writing this to you triggers this vibration, starting with the tingling, unlike other days when the vibration is mostly in the morning. I am still getting whole body shudders from time to time.

I feel I am evolving, connecting to the eight orgasms in due time. I shall write again at the next full moon. Bless me, will you? For the New Moon Ritual.

The wind today was distinctive, blowing in fiercely, and it continues to make the trees dance. I am in a different state of consciousness today. I feel I have been blessed, that I am in some kind of state of grace.

Oh, and I have a feeling that I know who it was that rested here with her children. I will sit at the shrine and see if I can journey to her, or at least to whom she was.

Your loving student,
Emmalia

10

THE MOLECULES OF MALICE

In the weeks since A had died and the Lama's ghost had confiscated what was left of the black kite, the particles it had shed in the months before her demise had broken down to the molecular level, small enough to be unseen and easy to inhale.

When the molecules entered someone's system, it would trigger a neurological spasm when the molecule encountered a nerve. The electrical charge would destroy the molecule but in that explosion the person would experience a spasm of malice. Anything that someone hated, or even disliked, could be the target, the recipient of that malice, projected toward the image of that thing in the person's mind's eye.

If the discharge occurred on the right nerve, for example the vagus nerve, the person might experience a cascade of rage, anger, or fear and terror as the imagery rose up in them. If they held still long enough, the spasm would pass, and the person was left to their own imagination, the malice fading from them like a cloud-shadow on a sunny day.

Some people, more conscious than others, would remonstrate with themselves and keep any impulses to action or speech in check. Others would swear at themselves under their breath. The most common reaction, however, was to swear at the object of their malice. Still others would act out, yelling at someone they were angry at or resented, and others resorted to violence.

Over time, the majority of the malice became directed at the feminine. It became the source of ever more misogyny, in every culture, and soon it was everywhere.

The command went out to the Order: no Priestess is to go anywhere in public unaccompanied. Soon the command was modified—no Priestess was to go anywhere without a Consort. This wasn't just a gender-based discrimination—many Priestesses had women for Consorts. It was because of the training that all Consorts received. Not just trained to do violence, Consorts were trained in maintaining a high degree of awareness of their environment, able to spot trouble at a distance, giving time to prepare.

Additionally, the Madeleines were all active, journeying to trouble spots, scrying the corners where the malice dust would accumulate, looking into the futures of everyone in the Order, seeking through time to add to everyone's safety—just like Consorts were seeking through space, the Madeleines worked through time. Intuition skills, highly honed, led to many catastrophes being avoided.

The Priestesses and Consorts were not immune to the impact of malice. Even if they held no predisposition to malice, even if they held malice toward none, the feeling would flash in them during the molecular discharge. This was another reason for the prohibition on traveling alone—a discharge was often more easily observable by one's companions than it was observable in oneself.

The new training protocol for how to deal with the molecule was simple. Direct the malice toward De Murgos. Fling it from wherever you thought it was, and let it go.

In some places the rise in violence of people toward each other in public was so severe, that patrols of members of the Order pretending to be regular people were authorized, with a permission from the High Priestess to intervene in violence when it was encountered.

Scientists in the Order began looking for ways to alter and protect against the molecule. They worked on every strategy such as masks, protective gear, chemical sprays that could neutralize the molecule's function, and a kind of vacuuming system that would collect the molecules and compress them in one space—a dangerous but promising idea.

The Madeleines worked on a strategy of developing psychic search techniques to identify accumulations of the molecule. They used empathetic resonance, feeling into the malice then using their scrying abilities to find the location. Once they had that, they could direct the Divine Light provided by the Goddess to burn the molecules with Love. In many cases, this could not be done remotely. Transmitting Love to something as antipathetic as the molecules, telepathically, turned out to be nearly impossible and teams had to be sent to emanate the Love, the resonant opposite of the malice, proximal to the accumulation.

Everywhere the public was aware of the increase in violence but had no idea why and were helpless to do anything about it. Everyday science had no framework in which to comprehend a chemical that functioned like a virus, but instead of physical symptoms it produced emotional symptoms that led to physical symptoms, such as the spasm of physical violence toward another person. But most people were accustomed to the idea of violent and aggressive men. In many places the culture supported the violence, especially against wen.

And to She Who Comes, this was unacceptable and She was willing to promote violence in response, finally, to stop it, even if it meant risking exposure to the world. She was certain that the time was near when She would be revealed.

The difficulty was that the Order wasn't strong everywhere. Their Training Centers were concentrated mostly in the West, in functioning democracies where the people were generally free to move about and the financial markets were such that the immense sums of money controlled by the Order could be hidden from scrutiny. Fortunately, through the ownership of certain hotel chains, they were able to have representatives in most of the major cities of the world. Management was by members of the Order, including security, and the hotels were always a source of intelligence about the state of affairs on the ground.

She had become aware of the Lama's ghost traveling through these other lands. He was collecting molecules. He was eating them, trapping them within himself. At the same time She observed that he was working with his alchemical illuminations, She could see the light of him, the field of him, and the illuminations were increasing the size and brightness of his emanations, strengthening his ability to trap and hold the darkness of the malice.

He was traveling through the cities of Western and Central Asia, collecting the malice from the corners where the wind of passing feet had drifted them together into clumps. She could see the grimace of distaste as he would pop them into his mouth and swallow.

Sometimes he would encounter small gangs of men, joined in common purpose by the malice searching for a victim, some feminine soul upon which to vent their rage. He would follow them, reaching his ghost arm into whatever space the men held onto the molecules. He'd extract the clumps, and consume them, deflating the impending violence. Sometimes She would watch him closely, sending Her love to him, helping maintain the walls of his alembic, the vessel of his distillation, distilling the malice into its purest form. He could feel Her when She did that, and he would turn and smile at Her.

He told Her, "Your love buys time, more time until I become Malice itself." He was alchemizing the darkness, turning it into light but in time it became clear that there was more malice than he could consume.

11

The High Council

During her trip to the Invisible Land in the Highlands to drag Matthews from the Goddess Brighid's arms, the High Priestess Regina Moonhalter received the summons to a meeting of the High Council of the Order of the Fleur de Vie. She spent the night in the Hidden Lands for the first time, in the home of Calley and her sister Brighid, affectionately called Bree, having visited many times since she was a child when she was able to see through the veil that shielded the land from mortal eyes. It was a measure, perhaps, of a change in the nature of her mortality, sleeping dreamlessly in safety for the first time in more nights than she could count. She Who Comes, the True Creator and the Mind of All Life on the Planet, appeared in the room where she slept. The quiet light of Her woke Regina, and she threw on a robe and went to sit with Her near the fire.

Regina reached out to Her and touched Her hand. The radiance dimmed a little, and Her outline became more solid. They smiled at each other, then the smile turned into a huge grin. The contemplation, the images of all that had happened since the last time they sat together, and the feelings of it all, washed through them. The image of the destruction of the Temple of Skreeva on Wallid rose in the air between them.

They started laughing, and when the laughter subsided Regina said, looking away into the fire, "Victory."

The True Creator quietly responded, "Victory."

After a pause, the Goddess said to Regina, "The unforeseen is arising."

Regina responded, "In a world dedicated to Indeterminacy not everything can be foreseen. We get used to it."

The Goddess said, "Yes." She almost said "Yes, but..." and didn't, feeling the sense of acceptance of that Truth arise from Regina, realizing that the sense of expectancy that it could be different existed only in Herself. She smiled, instead.

"Tell me," Regina said.

"When your father left the Bardo, the black kite escaped behind him. It attached itself eventually to your sister's Master. As he degenerated, it too, began to fall apart, leaving little bits of itself everywhere. The pieces cling to men. Sometimes wen, but mostly men. The bits make them malicious. And violent. What is foreseeable is that the men will revolt. Any place they see power, equality, or freedom, they will see usurpation and move to reclaim an imagined prerogative. And any sense of the Antecedence of the Feminine will become impossible for them."

"Most of the wen in this world have no power. They are neither equal nor free."

"It will be worse for them. It is time for the High Council to meet and to develop a strategy for the Order's response. We will meet tomorrow at the Hall, I am calling all of them."

"All of them?"

"Yes. The Archetypes and the Elementals. The High Priestesses and the Madeleines. I am looking forward to seeing you there. Come dressed for your Seat," She smiled, "the Seat of Flowers. And stay here, it will be easier for you to join us."

Brighid entered Regina's room carrying a stool and set it between the two next to the fire. "What are you planning, Mother?"

The Council Hall was circular, ranks of seats, each row raised a little above the others below, with sixteen aisles like spokes on a wheel joining at the hub, a circular raised dais in the middle with four thrones, back to back, and a carving of golden flowers on a tall stalk rising from the center, the top bloom opening to the above with a carving of the abstract flower symbol of the Order. The outer walls of the Hall were glass, with roll down shades for lighting control. The view through the glass was of ocean on all sides.

As Council members arrived, some entered through the double door at one side, others simply manifested in their seats in clouds of sparkling light. She Who Comes manifested in a cloud of golden light, taking her seat on the Fleur de Vie bloom at the top of the Axis Mundi staff, the High Priestesses of the Quadrants seated around her. Regina took her seat in the front row of the Flowering Plants section. Flowers sprouted and bloomed all around her, the flowers changing in their own time. The Priestesses of the different species arrayed themselves behind her.

Calley arrived and took Her seat in the Elementals section, Brighid arrived and took Her place in the Archetype section, next to Wasastami. Both looked at Regina and smiled. The High Priestess of Wallid arrived, somewhat surprised and disoriented, this being her first time at Council, and was seated in the Orders section. Jasmine and Angelica appeared and were seated in the Witness Section next to each other. Jasmine took her hand and held it.

The section for the Madeleines filled. They had been busy up until the last moment telepathically creating consensus on what was to be said. Eventually, 1616 wen took seats.

Their Consorts stood in ranks at the periphery of the circle. 1616 men sat, sat on their heels, kneeled, or stood behind them. This is not to imply that all of these relationships were heterosexual, no. But every Priestess and High Priestess who had earned the right to sit in the Council was given a masculine gendered person to be their assistant, that is, their Consort, to serve them in the manner they deserved to be served.

A report on the destruction of the Old Temple to Skreeva on Wallid was given by Jasmine. Regina spoke on the installation of the new entity, a mortal man formerly known as Quinn the Twice Enlightened, or Thundercock the Rock Splitter, or as the Boddhisatva of Assholes, in the new role of Skreeva, the God of Destruction. Then the High Madeleine stood and shared the visions they'd recorded of the Black Kite shedding, including the assault in the Guard Shack. Then they showed a few Molecules of Malice accumulating in some of the men in a remote village in Windia, documenting how it led to an assault on two wen from a different tribe. It showed the men stripping them naked, beating them with sticks, and driving them to the far edge of a field outside the village where they were gang raped and beaten to death. Similarly, they telepathically showed the Molecules accumulating in the dust of another village in Wuzlimland. The memory then went on to show the stoning death of an unmarried pregnant teenager. The Council Hall was stunned to silence by the brutality.

The Madeleine spoke, "The Molecules of Malice you have seen come from the shedding of the Black Kite and have now spread globally. A single Molecule can be destroyed simply by an infected person resisting the thoughts and feelings the toxic Molecule engenders in them. But if someone, or a group of people, carry more than that, resistance becomes almost impossible, and the people will turn on each other. Mostly, it is men that turn on wen, and the Malice takes the forms of physical and sexual violence. Sex is more lethal for us now and rather than leading us to Life, it more often is leading us to Death."

Regina looked up and saw near the ceiling the ghost of her father, the Lama. He was smiling at her. He nodded his head at her, affirmatively. She stood up and waited for recognition. The Madeleine nodded at her and she spoke, "We know that this substance collects itself together, and can be contained. We know that it can be destroyed. We should develop plans to accomplish both these goals. What we need is a strategy to protect ourselves from the violence, and to protect the people from this violence, as well. For decades we have trained ourselves and our Consorts in the martial arts, and in the arts of self-defense. We must do more than that. In order to protect the people, we should consider more proactive strategies, even if we must operate from the shadows. We know that there are men everywhere who resent the progress the Feminine has made, little though it may be in some places. This resentment means that any man who holds it is vulnerable to the Malice. Left unchecked, the resentment will create a reactionary force—a Men's Rebellion—against the progress we have made to reassert the Antecedence of the Feminine. I do not think we can prevent the Rebellion. But we can shape it, we can use it, and by drawing it out, we can assure that it will most efficiently meet its inevitable end."

The Priestesses, High Priestesses, and the Goddesses all trilled and applauded and whistled.

When the acclamation subsided Regina continued, "War is coming. This battle, the Battle against the Rebellion, the battle to end the oppression of the Patriarchy, end the repression of the Feminine, this battle we will win. Then we shall win the final battle beyond that. Victory may not be guaranteed, but I believe we will get him off the Rock if we prepare now, and begin to fight back, cornering the enemy so that destruction will be swift and simple, and with the fewest casualties possible. This is what I have to say."

The High Priestesses of the Quadrants seated in the middle now stood, each in turn and said the word, "War."

She Who Comes rose from Her flower throne and stood suspended in the air. She turned slowly once in a circle regarding everyone in the Council, smiling at them. She spoke one word, heard evenly throughout the Hall, "War."

The Council echoed Her. "War!" they shouted.

Then She spoke the mantra at the center of their living art, "Sex and Death!"

"Sex and Death!" 1616 voices shouted back, some screaming their rage.

Then She disappeared.

12

THE COMPOUND ATTACK

The High Priest, known commonly as Vicious, ended his morning meditation, a commune with his god Winjeetniya, a contemplation in which sometimes the god spoke to him, at other times he became lost in the white cloud of the god's imaginal substance. He always ended with a sense of conviction as to his purpose and the rightness of his service to this one, the one who claimed to be behind the curtain of the Trimerase, the three god-brothers who shared one body with three heads and six arms. He had always believed deeply in the subjective experience of his connection with Winjeetniya. How could he not? He experienced the presence of that light with feelings of love and forgiveness. How could he not believe? The faces of creation, maintenance, and destruction were only the faces of fragments of a natural law that only love could have created. His rational mind agreed with his feelings.

Winjeetniya loved women too, but only when they obeyed men, which was congruent with his sense of masculine superiority. The feminine could never be allowed to arrogate to itself any kind of equality, let alone superiority. He recalled the times when he was a child that his father would rant about the inferiority of the feminine, how could they be allowed to vote when they couldn't even know their own mind? How could they be considered clean enough to enter the Temples when they bled?

Men did not bleed and were therefore clean.

Secretly, he was terrified of blood. He believed that all men were secretly terrified of blood. He was baffled by the mystery of the wound that bled but did not kill. He was terrified of the power of the vagina to cure itself.

He believed he could smell menses in a woman, especially the tourist women who came to his temple, His temple! Winjeetniya's Temple! And he resented, no, hated, that the laws of the land allowed them to trod their filthy feet upon his sacred stones. He had never understood that it might have signified something else, something Sacred, and he was unwilling to consider that it might.

He had recruited several dozen men who were disaffected by the new face that the Destroyer, Skreeva, was showing them. He was showing them the power of the Tantra, which he abhorred. He rejected the notion that Ecstasy was to be found with the feminine. Ecstasy, properly speaking, was only to be obtained in the pure, and purified, contemplation of Winjeetniya.

He became determined to find what Winjeetniya had ordered him to find—those dragons, and the women who controlled them, that led to the destruction of the Temple he had loved, the destruction that led to the disappearance of the High Priest he had loved.

Now that he was the High Priest, he had the power to act. He sent Emissaries in secret to all the Temples on the Island of Wallid, initiating high level dialogues with their High Priests about his assignment and asking for intelligence. In the end, it was not his people, the Windu people, but the few Wuzlim priests on the island who gave him the clue he was seeking: there were more strangers—white people who seemed to live on the island, rather than just visiting tourists—going to the compound of Chantana, the High Priestess.

Given the nature of the Invisible Lands, and where it hid in the skies above the planet, it had been necessary to attend the High Council in one's dream body. Angelica and Jasmine had fallen asleep in Regina's room on the top floor of the compound house. Regina was staying in Calley and Brighid's home in the Hidden Lands, watched over by Calley's children. Chantana had been summoned as well. She slept on the cushions in her audience pavilion, guarded by the Prophet and the King of Komodos under her floor.

Jasmine and Angelica took an herbal sleeping compound that would keep them out of their mortal bodies for twenty-four hours. They had fallen asleep spooning, Jasmine behind Angelica, holding her close.

While Guiles and Corey were waiting for the wen to return, they practiced their martial techniques with each other, the wen Onadaya coaching Tenara and Napat before she would demonstrate her superior skills on the men. Her skill with the long pole was something to behold—she could pole vault over an aggressor from a standstill, kick him in the head as she went over, and smack him in the head again with the pole from behind when she landed. Her pole was tipped with a steel cone at either end, coming to a potentially fatal point.

Onadaya was also deeply engaged in teaching the young wen the Mysteries of the Fleur de Vie, the name of the Order and its secret symbol. They were not yet allowed to have sex with the men, although Onadaya would take advantage of them, usually simultaneously, whenever she could. Jasmine and Angelica loved her so much that they were happy to share. Onadaya was so loud in her ecstasies with the men that the younger wen couldn't sleep and indulged themselves with their fingers whenever it happened, sometimes with each other's fingers.

At supper that afternoon, Onadaya was filled with a sense of foreboding. The ghost of a Madeleine appeared in her morning meditation and warned her, just a single word, "Danger". She told the others that they must stand watch that night, taking turns.

The High Priest had formed two teams of men, nine men to raid the compound of the foreigners, killing all of them, three to invade the compound of the High Priestess, to kidnap her and bring her to him for interrogation.

Tenara was on watch from the balcony tower alongside Regina's room, sitting on a pillow, looking between the supports, head below the railing. She saw the shadow of a man climb over the wall of the outer courtyard, followed by a second man. She did not hesitate to ring the bell beside her and scream.

The sound brought Onadaya leaping from her bed, disentangling herself from the men, and wearing only a linen nightshirt that fell to her thighs, grabbed her long pole and a kukri knife, and ran down the stairs. The men, Guiles and Corey, naked, ran after her. By the door to the inner courtyard were more poles and knives. Their guns, illegal as they were, were locked away in their rooms.

Napat opened the door to her room a crack and looked out to see what was going on. She closed the door and looked frantically around the room for a weapon. She found only the sheath knife she wore on a belt when she was in the kitchen. She drew the knife, cracked the door again, and watched and waited.

On the balcony Tenara had picked up a waiting bow, nocked an arrow, and shot at the first man over the wall. She missed. She nocked another and hit the third man over the wall. She heard him scream as he fell. In her shock she froze until the seventh man came over the wall. She loosed again, and in the moonlight she could see that she shot him in the thigh. She didn't see the eighth and ninth man as she grabbed the quiver and ran down the stairs.

Onadaya ran into the courtyard and, because she had a kukri in one hand, she had only one arm free to thrust the long pole into the throat of the first man she encountered. He went down making gargling noises. As she whirled, Guiles and Corey passed her. Guiles took on the next man, kukri to kukri and dagger. Corey missed a man in the dark, ran past him and took on the next man. The missed man stepped toward and swung, slicing through his back. As he went to his knees the man in front of Corey sliced through his throat, and he went down, bleeding out on the stones.

Clinging to shadows, the man Corey bypassed saw the door to Napat's room open. He pushed it open and rushed in, tripping over Napat, who stabbed upward with her sheath knife and felt it slide into his groin, hot blood gushing over her arm and face. As he fell she crawled up his body, stabbing as she went. Sobbing, she collapsed on his corpse.

Onadaya, hampered by her knife, threw it at the next man she encountered. He ducked and when he stood up she whacked him right between the eyes with the pole. He saw stars and went down, struggling to stay conscious. Onadaya leapt over him to take on the next man.

Guiles, not so trained in kukri fighting, managed to parry the smaller attacker's blows, and finally losing patience and caution he caught the man's wrist and stepped inside and under the arm, pulling the wrist hard over his shoulder and dislocated the arm at the elbow. The man screamed. Guiles flipped him over his shoulder, and, hanging onto the arm, threw him hard on the stones. He stomped down on the man's windpipe, crushing it, grinding his heel on the man's throat until he coughed blood.

Unseen behind him another man attacked with his belt dagger and stabbed it through Guiles's trapezius. Guiles roared. Kneeling close by, Tenara put an arrow through the man's gut.

Guiles pulled the dagger from his shoulder, and, turning, saw a man run from the shadow, bowling Tenara over, raising his kukri high to slash her face. Guiles rushed the man, knocking him off Tenara, and stabbed him first in the throat and then between his ribs, piercing his heart. He and Tenara locked eyes and nodded.

One attacker was left standing, facing Onadaya. He charged, Onadaya jabbed him in the chest with both hands on the pole. She could feel the cartilage of his ribs part over his heart, and she did not stop. She was stopped only by the man's rib bones in the back. As he slowly fell to his knees, she pushed him over backward and pinned him to the stones until she was sure he was dead.

The man Onadaya had hit between the eyes groaned. Tenara stood, walked over to him, and put an arrow through his heart.

The three of them walked over to the man Tenara had shot in the thigh. He was whimpering in the shadow of the courtyard wall. She asked him in Windu, "Who sent you?" When he refused to answer, Guiles reached for the shaft of the arrow and worked it back and forth. They could hear the arrowhead grinding against the bone. He screamed. Guiles quickly put his free hand over the man's mouth. The man sobbed. Guiles removed his hand and Onadaya asked him again. He whispered back, "Vicious."

Onadaya nudged Guiles with a knee. He looked at her. She made a slicing gesture across her throat. Guiles did as instructed, running the dagger sideways through the man's throat, point emerging opposite the haft, and pulled forward, slicing through it all. Blood spurted at the man's head lolled. They all stood and looked back at the carnage.

At the High Priestess's Audience Hall the Prophet had been taking care of her while she was in trance, attending the High Council. He kept a low charcoal fire in a short brazier near her and kept candles burning around her. The three men sent by Vicious had no idea he was there. He heard the bikes pull up and the engines turn off at her gate. He heard the rattling as they climbed over. He'd heard three bikes, but only two men landed on the ground inside the compound. He withdrew into the shadows and picked up the silenced 9mm pistol from under a pillow where he'd slid it.

One of the men went around the back of the platform and stepped forward to the edge, right at the opening to the lair of the Komodo King. The other walked up the steps to the platform on the other side. He stuck his head through the hanging curtains. The Prophet shot him in the face, then again in the heart as the man fell backward.

A moment later the other man screamed as the Komodo bit and severed his leg. The Prophet went to the edge, looked down, and shot the man before he could scream again. He told the King to take the body away to the ditch to eat, and promised another body if he did what he was told. The Komodo huffed, tasting the air with his tongue, bit into the torso and dragged the man off into the dark. As he turned the Priestess whimpered, and he knelt, putting an easing hand on her shoulder and gently shushed her. At the High Council she shuddered briefly. He heard the third motorbike start up and drive away.

At Regina's compound they quickly realized they could do nothing for Corey. They saw the open door to Napat's room and entered cautiously. They turned on a light and saw her body lying on the body of the attacker. Guiles stepped forward and knelt, checking her pulse. "She's alive," he said, with a sigh of relief. Gently he turned her over, rolling her off the man. She opened her eyes, and said, "OK. I OK.". He got her up, and they retreated to the main house to clean up, take stock, and plan.

"Nine enemy dead. One dead on our side. One too many," Onadaya said, looking down in sadness.

"What shall we do?" Guiles asked.

"Hide and then destroy the bodies. Clean up the blood."

"I doubt the High Priest will file missing persons reports with the police about this. They were a kill squad. But I think we should be prepared."

"I agree."

"Do we wake up Angelica and Jasmine?"

"Not yet. The emergency is over, and they are safe once again."

"There are problems with waking them. The ghost can sometimes not reseal itself to the body completely. It's a side effect of the drugs. Let them wake in their own time.

"This will be very hard on Angelica."

"Yes," they all agreed.

They had just finished rolling the bodies into plastic tarps and dragging the bodies into Regina's basement when the Prophet and Chantana showed up at the compound. Guiles met them at the gate and escorted them in. In the predawn darkness the Prophet couldn't see the blood on Guiles's clothes, but a last shaft of light from the setting moon illuminated Napat cleaning blood off the stones and Chantana gasped, drawing the Prophet's attention. "We came to warn you, we were attacked… oh, I see." Napat sobbed and Chantana went to her.

"She won't wash the blood off herself," Guiles told the Prophet in a low tone. "She wants Jasmine to see her when she wakes up at sundown. It's bad. The man bled out on her."

The Prophet uttered a horrified "Geez. What happened? And how can I help?"

"You can help Onadaya with the bodies. She'll tell you what happened. Chantana can help clean up. And how about you? Are you and she OK?"

"Yeah. We have our own disposal. Komodo brand."

The Prophet walked into the house. He saw that a door had been raised up in the floor, and the sound of power tools was emerging from it. He went down the stairs and saw the most fiercesome sight in his life. Onadaya was standing alongside a table with part of a man still lying on it. She was naked, covered in gore and blood, her hair swept up and tied on top, dripping blood on the floor when she turned to him, circular saw in hand. She grinned at him, and her fierceness lit up the room.

"Bad men," was what she had to say, and turned back to her work. She severed a forearm at the elbow and tossed it into another opening with an open door set in the floor. He could hear water rushing. He looked in the hole, using a flashlight. He saw the dark water rushing and watched an arm land in the water and disappear. He looked at Onadaya questioningly.

"River stay underground all the way to the sea. Water witch show us."

True, he knew, the Order trained the Priestesses in the skills of finding water. And oil and other minerals. Many of these wen went on to specialize in finding lost or stolen objects.

"You hold," she said. "I cut." And gave another of those fantastically fierce grins.

After a day when his hit squad and his kidnappers had not returned, he sent a messenger scout that evening. The scout went by the High Priestess's compound first. Nothing was happening there, no lights were on, none of the three bikes were there, and her van was not parked in the compound. He went next to the white lady's compound. There were two small lights on in the upper floors. The van was gone. He couldn't see anything, but when the breeze was just right, he thought he heard a woman's keening. But he couldn't be sure, and decided it was just a far-off night bird.

13

Angelica's Sorrow

Angelica and Jasmine woke near sunset. The slant of the light in the room was almost horizontal. Angelica stirred first and reached for the hand that had been holding her close, kissed it, and slipped away from Jasmine. As soon as she sat up into the miasma of blood and grief surrounding them, she burst into tears. Her heart began to hurt, and she crossed her arms over it. Without grabbing a shawl, she slowly moved to the door and through it, holding on to the banister down the steps, weeping so hard she could not see. Guiles and Napat were waiting for her at the bottom. Napat was solemn, not weeping, and covered in dark and drying blood. Angelica went to Guiles and Napat brushed past her, on her way to Jasmine.

Guiles took her to the door and preceded her down the stairs. The first thing she saw was Onadaya and Tenara sitting in meditation by candlelight. Then she saw the table, cleaned of blood and lying on it was Corey, wrapped in two sarongs, his face upward, eyes closed.

She stumbled, Guiles catching her. She went to Corey, moved aside two candles to get close to him, and stroked his face. "How?"

Guiles answered, "In combat. He died as a Warrior, and as a Consort protecting his Priestess."

At those words Angelica wailed. She wailed until she screamed, climbing up on the table, kicking candles aside, to lay upon his body.

Then she wailed again. Wailed and wailed.

In Regina's room, Jasmine was wrapping herself in a sarong when the door creaked open and she turned and saw Napat. Actually, what she saw was a specter of Napat. She was still covered in dry blood and when she moved chunks cracked and dropped from her. Her hair was still completely stiff with it, her face a dried blood covered mask.

She sat on a wicker trunk near the foot of the bed. Jasmine kneeled before her. The sound of Angelica's wailing reached their ears. Napat reached into the pockets of her robe and withdrew an item in each hand. In her right hand she held the knife. She opened it and offered it to Jasmine. "This is what I killed him with." She opened her other hand and revealed a tube of flesh, a little longer than her thumb. "This is what I took from him."

Jasmine's eyes hardened, not with disgust or loathing, but with pride. She took them both and said, "I will clean these and return them to you."

14

The Towers of Marini

On the back side of the Towers of Marini, the side away from the sea, there were no habitations as far as the eye could see. With binoculars someone could see a village way down the valley, the houses so small they looked like specks with the magnification.

Freya had told Matthews that he was to practice diving and landing suddenly on his feet. She told him that his assignment was to pick up a person and fly them away, so she had him practice picking up a 200-pound sack of grain and flying off with it.

When he started practicing, he couldn't pick it up, so he practiced with rocks from the hillside, increasing their weights, working up to the sack. Early in the morning he was out on the slope below the north castle's rampart, rolling a rock into place and he glanced over at the fourth castle, the one with the beam sticking out at the top on the seaward side. Some motion in the corner of his eye bid him look.

On the rampart, he saw a human form step to the edge, and wings appeared above and behind it, and the person jumped, diving straight for the ground, headfirst, turning upright at the last possible moment and landing on their feet. They flew back to the top of the tower, not holding anything that he could see.

When he recovered from his shock at seeing another like himself (What, She made two of us?) he had to see who this was. He decided discretion was in order and flew along the frontside (against Freya's orders), flew to the tower with the beam, and flew over the top of its rampart. While he'd been doing it, the person practiced another dive, and he was waiting there when they reascended.

He could barely keep his mouth closed when he recognized the person as feminine. He caught himself staring at a wen with wings, a little less speckled than his, a little more white. He stood completely still, wings tucked away, and waited for her to see him.

When she saw him, she went into a fighter's form, prepared for aggression, and, narrowing her eyes, asked, "Who the fuck are you?"

He decided the most appropriate answer was to show her his wings.

Her response was to take a step back. "What the fuck are you?" she almost whispered.

He regarded her closely, dark skin, blue eyes, long angular jaw with bright teeth, hair wild and curly and long. She was almost as tall as him and maybe 30 or 40 pounds lighter. A lightweight frame.

He asked, "Does Freya have you trying to pick up heavy weights yet?"

She relaxed but didn't lower her fists. "No. Automatic weapons fire though, down in the caverns. Even with protection it hurts my fucking ears."

"You cuss a lot."

"And with good fucking reason." She paused, and then said, "Fucking People." Before he could answer she said, "Which kind are you?"

"The easy-going kind," he said.

She dropped her fists. "The fuck you say."

He grinned at her, his dopey grin. "Yup."

"Fuck me," she said. When he didn't move, she said it again, "Fuck me. Right here, right now." Then, "No wings."

"Wait, what?"

"You heard me. You Consorts are all the same. Sex on demand."

"Not a Consort."

"What?" she exclaimed, more than a question. "Fuck me."

"You said that before."

"Same words, different meaning."

"Oh."
"Well?"
"Well?"
"Can you be even a little bit nice?"

"No," she said. And she leapt on him, landing feet first on his chest. Basically, she kicked him over the edge with both feet.

Matthews fell about ten feet and whompfed out his wings. They were bigger than hers.

She said, "Goddess damn it. Yours are bigger than mine."

He replied, hovering in the air, "That's how you, the Feminine, made me. How She made me." He paused. "Do you remember it?"

"Fuck yes, I remember it. It wasn't any fucking fun, I hated it then, I almost sometimes can find my way to not hating it now. It wasn't a free choice. It was a live or die choice."

"So you chose Life?" The statement evolved into a question.

"Maybe. I was pretty certain I couldn't hate unless I lived."

"And what do you want to do now?"

"Most deeply I want to kill. Most commonly, I want to fuck. Eating is an afterthought."

"Were they raping you?"

"Yes."

"Is that why you killed them?"

"Yes. How do you know?"

"I see it. I see it around you. We should get around back."

She said, "No. I want to stay here in the sunshine." He dropped to the ground, and she followed. They pulled their wings in, and sat up against the tower walls, backs warmed by the stones in the sun, watching the sea in the distance, watching the climbing sun.

Eventually she sighed. "She," she said, pointing upward, "She saved me. She smelled the blood. Smelled the terror and rage I had. I'd already killed one." She showed him the filed nails of her hands, looked at end-on, the edges looked like a ceramic knife. "She smelled the blood, and entered into me. We killed the other three. I bit through one's jugular, smashed another's windpipe, and tore the balls off of the man who'd already dropped his trousers." She paused. "It was good to be covered in the gush of hot blood." She rolled her eyes maniacally.

"Holy fuck," Matthews said.

"Yeah. One kind of a Holy Fuck, anyway." She looked away and spit. "I hate this shit."

"Life or Death," he reminded her.

"Fuck you."

"Better than fuck off."

'I am not crazy enough to say 'fuck off' to my only friend."

And, at that, they fell into silence.

After ten minutes, Matthews reached over and took hold of her hand. She sighed, and something relaxed in her shoulders. She drew a deep breath, exhaled, and said nothing.

Matthews stood up but didn't let go of her hand. "Let's go around back."

She resisted, but not actively pulling away. It was almost a passive resistance, a becoming of dead weight.

They stayed there for ten more minutes, he standing, she sitting. About a minute in, she started weeping. "Fuck. Fuck. Fuckety fuck. Fuck. Fuck me. Fuck you. Fuck Her." Her tears went from a single track to all down her cheeks. "Fuck, fuck, fuck," she sobbed into her free hand.

Matthews wouldn't let go. "I won't let go," he said.

This brought a new round of sobbing, just as he had hoped. He had learned a little bit about what support looked like.

It took a while. Matthews sat down again, holding her hand, feeling that she couldn't handle any further contact than that. After she stopped sobbing, she took a long time to get her breathing back from ragged to normal. Then she sighed. "We should practice. I'm pretty sure we'll be working together." She stood up and dropped his hand. "Let's walk around back."

They did, Matthews giving her side-eye all the way around the base of the tower. She told him, "Enough with the side-eye already. I'm alright." Turning the corner to the back of the tower she stopped, raised her arms, and her wings appeared. With a massive push with her wings she soared upwards and landed on the parapet. She looked back at him and smiled—her first since she'd met him. He summoned his wings into existence, pushed twice, and landed beside her. "Heavy," she said. "We'll have to take that into account."

"Yes. I'm training to pick up something heavy. I think it's going to be a person. She has me practicing toward two hundred pounds."

"Hmm," she thought. "If I'm armed, that gives me a free hand to help."

"Let's practice diving together here first, then we'll go over to the other tower."

She nodded, stood up on the parapet, and held out her hand to him. He took it, stepped up, and fell over the side. The first leap was a competition to see who would pull up first. He did, and when she looked over at him with a grin of triumph, he shrugged and said, "I'm taller."

"Then let's try stopping above the ground, say 6 feet up, at the same time."

Matthews nodded.

On this next dive she stopped immediately, he continued a little further and bounced twice. "Momentum and inertia," he said.

"You'll have to work on that," she said, with a small smile.

He grinned, "With your help, I will."

She grinned back, nodded, and leapt up for the parapet.

She had brought some lunch with her, unlike Matthews, who would have just gone looking for a kitchen. They sat down on the floor of the tower, leaning back against the parapet out of the breeze, and she offered to share it with him. They split an egg salad sandwich and she had just broken off half of the orange she'd peeled and handed it to him. "How did it happen to you? The wings, I mean."

"When I was young, I had an experience with a doppelganger. Actually, a triple-ganger but one of us was murdered by a dark cult. The other survivor was a man named Quinn. His search for the truth had led him to the cult. I had nothing to do with it. I met him by chance in a bar in Memphis after all that fighting and magic had happened, and he was in a bad way, weeping in public and all. He talked about being touched by entities hiding in golden whirlwinds, and the end of the world. I got away from him as fast as I could.

"Years later I met him in another bar, and I told him I wanted to write down his story. He let me, dictating it to me and a recorder, and I'd type it up and try to make sense of it. At the end of it, I asked him to show me what it felt like, contact with the golden whirlwind. Instead of doing that exactly, he connected me with the Light of the Earth. I fell off my chair, blinded, and stayed that way for a long time. When I came to, I was a stranger to myself.

"I met a girl, she took me on vacation to an island in the Med called Kerkyra. In a vision of a flood from a volcanic eruption, I visualized having wings to escape, and suddenly they were there. I know now that the girl was a Priestess from a place called Stonehaven. Have you heard of it?"

She nodded.

"She was a Priestess assigned by Her," he said, pointing up, "assigned to come watch over me." He paused. "Now I can call Her and talk to Her. Sometimes it's in vision and other times it's through a Priestess. I'm here because She assigned me to come here. There is some task, some assignment we are supposed to fulfill, but I don't know what it is.

"How'd you come by yours? By the way, my name is Matthews."

She'd paid close attention to him the whole time he talked, looking for exaggeration or hyperbole, but there'd been none. In a deadpan voice, a voice without tone, she said, "At that fight I told you about. The one where, together, we killed four men. It was only a few months ago. She had to get me out of there. For some reason, some energetics or metaphysics I don't understand, She couldn't carry my body out by Herself, so She gave me the wings. She said something about 'Molecules of Madness.'"

"Molecules of Malice."

"You know about them?" Matthews nodded. "You can tell me later."

She stopped talking. Matthews could see she was engulfed in reliving sensations and feelings. She stood up, scattering bits of orange peel, leapt for the parapet and jumped off, turning and hovering in the air. "My name is Venge," she said, with a wolfish teeth-baring grin, full of the ferocity she felt. Then her wings disappeared, and she dropped out of sight.

Matthews said aloud to himself, "Fuck. I wish they would stop doing that." And leapt after her.

15

De Murgos

De Murgos returned to the surface. His cave on the dark side of the moon had become oppressive. It smelled bad, even in the rarefied sodium gas atmosphere. He kept being drawn back to the Pavilion of The Dead on the mountainside above the Temples, the Temple of the Mountain King now firmly settled on top of the larger Temple to Skreeva, the Pavilion of the Queen Old Woman stones rising through the Mountain King's Temple Floor. He didn't know what it meant but the whole thing smelled of power, like ozone in the air after the snap of lightning.

The Pavilion of the Dead, undisturbed by the Temple's overflight, preserved one of the miniature thrones on pedestals dedicated to him. It was the only one on the island not toppled. He could sit there, look down on the newly combined Temples and continue to contemplate how this had come to pass.

He also smelled the presence of the Feminine and would get angry at himself when he couldn't track it to its source. It just vanished at the Temple of the Concubines. He sat there, stewing in his own juices, anger making a trail of smoke above his head. And around it all was the smell of dragons.

He felt a little rumble in the ground, the throne in which he sat perched on a pedestal rocked slightly. He meditated, in order to re-establish some self-control. While in that state of mind, he thought it would be a good idea to extend his control again over the priests below Vicious. He could feel that since the Temple destruction, their faith in him had wavered, and it seemed to have been replaced by something else.

He extended tendrils of the fruit of worship, as he called it, the material he generated within himself using the energy from those who worshipped him, and let these tendrils find men who still valued him. He knew the energy made them feel happy, warm, and loved, with an emphasis on their superiority to all others. They *knew* him, they *loved and worshipped him,* in order to to be fed and feel their sense of superiority restored, particularly their superiority over women.

Eyes closed, he grunted when he realized that much of his feeding was going to restore the priests' sense of their superiority over women. Somehow, they had lost that sense of him, and he couldn't read, couldn't tell, what had replaced it. All he could tell was that these priests had somehow cultivated a different sense of happiness. And some of the priests found that this new sense of happiness was superior to his own.

He suddenly felt threatened, and the threat entered into him, causing a frisson of fear. He jerked back from his meditation and pulled in all the tendrils of the fruit of worship. Shocked that he had felt fear—he never felt afraid, not of anything. He looked down at the courtyard and the air above the floor began to waver, like heat waves rising from a black roof. The waves collected and organized themselves into a semi-transparent mandorla, or vesica shape. It seemed to him that he could see the stone floor of the Temple courtyard through the shape, but he could discern nothing within it. He floated off his throne and down toward the group of men gathering in front of the shape.

Quinn/Skreeva felt the energy rise behind him, while he was talking to the men gathered in front of him and telling them to be "Good Men, men that take care of the women in their lives, providing for them with a good and loving heart." He was just about to tell them the reward for this change in behavior when he saw the outline of a humanoid form appear in the air over the men before him, men whose eyes and ears were entrained to his voice.

Those priests whose eyes and ears were tuned to Winjeetniya's frequencies saw him in the air over the group of dissident priests in all his eye-blinding whiteness. They knew the legends of his power over lightning, and they expected their god would strike the dissidents down.

Electricity buzzed around Winjeetniya/De Murgos, rising in crackling bundles from the fire that burned at all his joints. It coalesced into a lightning bolt that fired at Quinn/Skreeva's vesica. It spanged off the surface, showering sparks, to the wonderment of all the priests.

Quinn/Skreeva laughed, out loud, in a frequency heard by De Murgos, and all the priests of both sides. The laugh turned the frisson of fear in De Murgos into an internal wave of terror that caused him to surge upward into the sky and disappear.

Quinn addressed the priests after the disappearance of their god. He said, "You see?

"That god is not your god. He made nothing, and you all know that it is Salakta who made us. This has been a part of your inner teachings for centuries. This new god is an interloper, a foreigner, who has been feeding on people like you for millennia. Do not countenance him in any way, not just by not looking at his face. Turn away from him, do not feed him. Turn away from him and instead be fed by the boundless grace of your true Creator, my true Creator, the great Salakta. Be fed from my table, the table of Skreeva and Darvatiye, the Mother of Myriad Creatures. Your adoration will be returned to you as happiness and simple joy."

In his cave De Murgos struggled to breathe, even though he was behind the curtain that sealed in his atmosphere. His mind raced, seeking to understand, eyes flashing side to side. He had never known terror before, even fear was scarcely familiar. As it faded it was replaced by anger, his old friend. In the past he had used that anger to murder pagans, refining his techniques over the centuries, until the people he regarded as his children had become self-managing in their practices and in their repression of the Feminine. In some cases, he'd manipulated his believers into murdering their own, on their own, without his involvement.

He smiled at the memory of that suffering, recalling the stoning of a pregnant woman. The memory titillated him and it finally cleared his mind and suppressed his terror. Now he could contemplate the fact that no one had ever successfully repelled his lightning. It confirmed for him the long-considered intention to abandon this rock, leaving it to suffer as it was, feeding from a distance as he sought out a new world to ravage. But not yet. He had a few more ideas and practices to instill that would assure the ongoing suffering of the people.

Suddenly he coughed, something he never did. The cough expelled a black molecule, so small it only caught his eye as a tiny shadow in a place that had no shadows. He caught it in his hand, closing his fist around it. The power of malice thrummed in his palm, and he laughed at the feel of it. This was the weapon he needed to finish the entrapment of his believers, his children.

Quinn/Skreeva sat in meditation with Darvatiye. He opened his eyes and asked Her to call She Who Comes. In a moment She said, "She is here."

"Beloved," he began. "I encountered him today. De Murgos. He was at the Temple. It occurred to me that he has entirely too much freedom. As long as he remains Indeterminate, he will remain free. Which means that if he becomes Overdetermined, he will die. Or flee the Rock, which might be just as well. We must find ways to lock him down, constrict his life."

She smiled at him, not Darvatiye's smile. She leaned forward and kissed him, not with Darvatiye's lips. He heard Her voice in his head, saying, "Thank you."

16

Dentata

It took Regina four days to get back to the Order's compound on Wallid from the Hidden Lands. Onadaya greeted her, smiling sincerely, happy to see her, but there was a grimness and a tightness about her.

"Are you OK?" she asked.

She nodded her head yes, then shrugged her shoulders, and shook her head no. "Bad men," she said. "They stink. And their blackness lingers in the corners."

Regina nodded. "Show me. Now."

Onadaya led her to a corner near where the wounded man had died. "Napat scrubbed it. No blood, but look there," pointing into the shadow. There were three, no four deeper spots of inky darkness.

Regina said, "Stay away from those. I will show you how to capture them without taking them on yourself. Then we will burn them. Show me where else."

Onadaya walked her around the compound, showing her the corners where the shadow molecules had gathered.

Along the way, they encountered the others staying there. Napat was barely responsive still, sitting on the edge of her bed. Jasmine was beside her holding her hand, providing silent companionship. Regina got on one knee before the girl, raised her face by the chin and looked in her eyes, then she nodded. Looking at Jasmine she said, "I will be back to help her."

Next, they went to Tenara. Onadaya said, "She killed three." Regina, in Nahasi, asked her, "Are you alright?"

Tenara's eyes shown with pride. "All my life, bad men all around me. Here, I am free. Bad men not allowed," she replied, grinning. Regina hugged her hard.

Guiles stood up and hugged her. Onadaya said, "Three also." She looked at him questioningly. "I'm fine. Not my first kills. I feel bad about Corey, though. Angelica needs your help."

Angelica was sitting on the edge of Corey's bed when Regina and Onadaya entered the room. She had been weeping, eyes and nose red. She held a cloth in one hand, her other closed in a fist. Regina sat beside her, put an arm around her, and opened that hand with her other one. Angelica drew a ragged breath and let it out. "I cannot stay here," she said.

Regina replied, "We know. The Order knows. When your new Consort gets here, you will travel."

"New Consort? Are you serious?"

"Yes. You cannot be allowed to travel by yourself. The world has shifted since you have been here. It is filled with malice, and no wen is safe anywhere."

Angelica looked surprised. "Malice? What are you talking about?"

"A profoundly evil cloak entered the world, and then it decayed, leaving molecules of itself to spread around the world before we could retrieve what was left. Men, raised in misogyny, are particularly vulnerable and they take their hatred out on wen randomly. No one of the Order goes anywhere by herself anymore. And you should remember, we are at war. The Council has declared it."

"I remember. Is what happened here a part of it?"

"Yes. The malice is here, even in the corners of this compound. It will need to be cleaned up."

"Can I help?"

"Yes. You and Jasmine and Onadaya will do it. I will show you how. You all need to know. And come with me now, I want you to see something."

They all, Regina, Onadaya, Tenara, Angelica, and Guiles, went to Napat's room. Jasmine remained sitting next to her, holding her hand.

Regina stood before Napat and raised her arms in invocation. Then she lowered her arms, her hands in profile over the top of Napat's head. She uttered words in a language none of them knew. After a moment, a cloud of golden light appeared between her hands. She said a few more words and the light began to spin. It formed a small golden whirlwind between her hands. In the top of the whirlwind a form appeared, a miniature form of She Who Comes. People gasped, it was beautiful. A sound, a single note, was heard by all, high and pure. The form of the Goddess, the True Creator, descended through the whirlwind into the top of her head, the light disappearing with the Goddess. When it was finished, Napat looked up, her eyes gone completely black.

Napat whispered, "I see. I see now the light, the cloud of golden light, and I am going there to rest." And she fell backward across the bed, asleep.

Regina said, "When she wakes, she will be healed. She will not be as she was, because she has killed. You who have killed know this. But she will be good, and free of her malaise."

Regina sighed. "I am tired now and going to my room." She turned to Onadaya, "Come with me friend."

After dinner, the Prophet and Chantana joined them after an expedition to her compound to verify that everything was in order, everyone sat together. They were all tired but curious to see how Regina dealt with the molecules of malice. She put her hand into the shadows where the molecules floated. They were drawn to her hand, some circling it before they joined, looking for a host. Slowly her hand lit up and with little flashes of brightness, the molecules were consumed in the fire of her life force, her chi.

"This is a power I am allowed to share with you all, given the nature of the times. It will not harm you, and it goes away unless it is in the presence of the molecules. If you want it, stand up and hold out your hand, palm up."

Everyone did as Regina suggested. She brought the light to her forefinger and touched it to the sacred energetic wheel in each person's palm. "Now go to every corner of the place, light it up, and see what comes."

Not every corner held the molecules. Tenara encountered a cluster in a corner near the stairs, hesitated and timidly put her hand into the cloud. Chantana, watching across the room grinned at her, chiding her for her hesitancy. Tenara growled back at her, and Chantana laughed. Then her hand lit up and the little black dots were consumed in the flashes of light. Tenara laughed in turn, commenting, "It tickles!" Chantana responded, "See? You can trust Regina." Tenara, still growly, said, "When I know her better."

Chantana stopped and stared at Tenara. "What else is it that you need to know?"

"When I figure that out you will be the first one I come to."

When they were sure all of the molecules in the compound had been destroyed, they reassembled in the dining room.

"I have something to show you all," Regina said. She pulled a piece of golden cloth from her bag and spread it out on the table.

From a few there were gasps of recognition. It was the inverse of the icon of the Fleur de Vie, the inverse of the icon of the Order. The design occupied the middle of the cloth. It was circular, with what could only be described as teeth pointing inward, overlapping in places, creating a closure.

"We are at war," she said softly. "This is the Fleur Dentata. This is our battle flag, and tomorrow it will fly over this house, below the nation and island flags. No one will understand it, or notice it even, with all the tall staff flags they fly here. But it will serve as a standing prayer, just like theirs do. But for now, tonight, we shall work together to cast a Spell of Forgetting on the Priests who knew of the attack on this house. We want them to forget that they ever thought of attacking us. We will focus first on the high priest, the one known as Vicious."

17

The Prophet

"Mom, you're gonna be a Grandmother."

"Chantana?"

"Yes,"

"Excellent choice. How will you manage?"

"Not sure how much of a choice it was. We don't know yet. We have an idea, but it is difficult. She has her obligations to her people, but she does not believe they will accept me as her partner. I am a foreigner, and a white man. The plan seems to be that she will spend half her time over on Wiley with me. She thinks that she will not be recognized there. But I have my doubts."

"What does your Conscience tell you?"

"My Conscience tells me to do the right thing in the moment and not be attached to plans right now. We can have them but be prepared to let them go and change them on a moment's notice. Adaptability, resiliency, buzzword stuff. There's a lot of uncertainty out there, even though it looks calm at the moment."

"And more uncertainty is certain."

"Say more, mother."

"We have our plan. And you have a place in it. We are uncertain of its outcome, of course. And we are also uncertain of what De Murgos is planning."

"Tell me my place in it."

"It will be as it was before, with the Queen Old Woman stones. Except this time, we will use a global network."

"What? There are Queen Old Woman stones networked globally?"

"Not at the moment. But the Order has been secretly distributing the stones for decades. As it is here, they are distributed in the foundations of sacred buildings. They are buried at the intersections of ley lines. Every place the Order has acquired a motel, which is in most countries in the world, there is at least one stone. The stones will serve as nodes and relays when we go active. There are Priestesses near most of the stones to add their power to the grid. Your job will be to use the grid to distribute the desire to develop a Conscience. And to develop one at all costs and as quickly as possible. We will all be adding the sense of urgency. We believe a Conscience is the only thing that will free the people from De Murgos's hypnotic hold over their lives. Even now war is breaking out between his oldest child and his youngest. The middle child hates both of them and is praying that they destroy each other. Of course, this will never happen, and all of it, all of the suffering, feeds De Murgos. This time it is vicious enough that he will, we hope, overeat, as it were. We hope he will eat himself stupid, and stop searching for us, so that he does not interfere with us while we are laying the trap."

"Trap?"

"Yes, he does not have a Conscience himself. If it works, we will starve him of worship as well as the vibrations of the suffering he has caused until he has to leave."

The Prophet of Conscience thought for a moment, letting it all sink in. Then he said, "He is a monster."

"He is a parasite." They sat in silence for a moment. Then Regina said, "We should tell your sister she's going to be an aunt."

18

Nazeem

Nazeem straightened up, pulling the wooden forms from around the short row of mud bricks in his father's brickyard. His back ached. And he saw no point in building up a stockpile, in the event that someone would stop by and need any of the several hundred bricks he'd already made in the past few weeks. He didn't believe anyone would come around and buy them. His father's business was dying, replaced by cinder block and poured concrete.

But he was mindful to obey his father's wishes. His father no longer beat him, he having turned into a strapping young man, muscle built by the years of hard labor, but he was still living in his father's house, and wished to keep the peace with him for the sake of his mother and sister.

He wanted to leave Wekka, deeply wanted to leave and go to Europe. In Europe, he believed that he would have a chance to make something of himself, and more importantly, to be himself. It had been four years now since he had realized he was gay, his affections and longing going to other men.

In the years that he had been staying after the religious school day was over, ostensibly to help his Memon with cleaning, his Memon had seduced him, and took him as a plaything, commanding him to do what he could only feel was naturally the Memon's due. He had no problem with servicing the Memon in all the ways that he was commanded. It felt natural to him, and that it was a part of his devotion that he owed to his superior. After the Memon was transferred to another school, it took him a few more years to realize the reason why it had felt so natural. He loved men and he always had.

And it was despairingly disallowed by his faith. Forbidden. Faith by fiat. If he was found out it would mean prison, at best. And he might be stoned in the streets before he ever got there. He understood why the Memon had sworn him to silence, a silence he had never broken.

His mother suspected, of course. When she cornered him one day in the yard he lied about it, as if she couldn't tell. When she asked him why he showed no interest in girls he told her it was because they were too poor, the family had nothing to offer as a bride price. This was the opening he needed to tell her about his dream of emigrating. She was surprised, but she smiled. She said she was planning on sending his sister abroad also, and for the same reason. She said she was in the process of setting up a situation for his sister where she would work for a wealthy couple as a maidservant. And she had promised him that she would inquire about whether or not they would take a manservant, as well. She thought it likely, given what she knew of the couple. And it would be better for his sister if he went along and acted as her protector. She told him that it would take a few more weeks for the arrangements to be made, and that she was making them through the old woman known as the Market Queen, who ran a shoe stall.

In the meantime, she told him that the couple would be coming to the market, and that a meeting would be set up. She implied that there was something they would ask him to do, and that he should regard it as a test for his worthiness to accompany his sister.

Fantasizing about this opportunity for escape made it hard for him to pay attention to making mud bricks. His father shouted at him to hurry up, and threatened a beating if he didn't speed up—a beating he knew would never come. He was stronger than his father, and he knew his father knew it. He took hope in his mother's words, "Al-lat made you. She did not make a mistake."

19

SHAMBHALA

Quinn was drifting again when he felt someone take his hand. He thought for a moment it might be Darvatiye, to whom he was now the High Consort. Although, in this current incarnation as Skreeva, God of Destruction, it was held by the people to be more powerful than Darvatiye, the Mother of all Life, but he knew for a fact it wasn't true. The Truth was that Death would not exist without Life, and hence Life was antecedent. He knew the Truth of this, because She Who Comes was allowing the face of Darvatiye, one of Her incarnations, to carry the child that She and Quinn had conceived—the child that would replace him. Every moment of his life was tinged with Gratitude.

But the hand did not belong to either She Who Comes or Darvatiye. It belonged to Lee, Regina's daughter by a Djinn.

He looked at her and remembered that he knew who she was. She smiled at him and said, "Come with me."

He found he could follow her without walking. All he had to do was lean in the direction he wanted to go. He realized they were in a kind of tunnel. The walls seemed semi-transparent, and he could see nothing through the walls. He assumed it was because it was still night out, because the tunnel was faintly lit with the color of moonlight. "Where are we?" he asked.

"We are in the Eternal World," she replied, looking at him. "It is a part of the Noosphere.

His eyebrow raised in question.

"It is the world where no Time passes. It is the Time of no Time. It is the world of the Mind of the Planet."

"But there is still before and after. Is there still cause and effect?"

"Yes. That is because these are also properties of Space. They are not just temporal features—they are not only constituent elements of Time.

"Time is very relative," she continued. "Without space everything would collapse. Everything cannot happen all at once, because then Nothing would happen, and it would all return to the First One. She wanted a manifest Universe, and still does. The Universe shall remain manifest."

They traveled for what seemed to him to be a while. The light in the tunnel changed, and became the color of sunlight, which meant they'd crossed into dawn. Time was still passing outside the tunnel.

The tunnel ended, opening onto a landscape. They stepped out onto a small flat space and paused, looking around. A bird flew past them, landed in a tree, and sang to them. "Is there time here?"

"Yes, but it passes very slowly compared to the everyday world. You won't feel it as any different, because the Time of you is passing at the same rate as the rest of this place."

The bird flew off. "It is the Crier Bird. He will let the others know we are here."

"And here is?"

"Shambhala."

He looked around. They were in a large bowl, as round as a volcanic crater. Just beyond the walls rose four mountains, one in each direction, with a column of light rising from each peak, fading as it rose into the sky. Below them was a city, with eight spokes radiating from the center with houses, mostly white with red tiled roofs along either side of what he now saw were roads. In the center there was an enormously broad building, he could not estimate its height.

She said, "Time, for the most part, only appears to pass here. You can stay here for six days. When you return to the sphere of the mundane, it will be the morning after the night you came with me. Don't worry, nothing in the everyday world will require your attention."

"Umm humm," he said. "How is it that this place is not seen from above, like from a satellite?"

"It, like the Hidden Lands, is phase shifted from the rest of the world. The light that shines here is reflected differently, at a different angle than what everyday people see. They can't see us, therefore we appear to be invisible."

They took the path down the side of the mountain, heading for the road beneath them.

Walking the street, they saw many people of all races, masculine and feminine, and many children of different ages. As if she was reading his mind, she spoke to him. "My father brought me and my mother here when I was young. He was a refugee from the outside world, and the Rulers here had allowed him to stay. He seldom ventures out."

"He's still alive?"

"Yes. As a Djinn the son of an Embla, those favored creations and helpers of De Murgos, and a mortal wen, he can be very long-lived. He is not immortal, he can be killed in different ways, and indeed, De Murgos hunted them down and killed many of them, and gave a few of his regents, kings and magicians, the skills necessary to entrap them and use them. It was a form of torture."

"You mean like the bottles and the seals of Solomon?"

"Yes. My father has some other skills, and he was able to avoid detection. As far as we know he is the last of his kind."

Quinn-Skreeva felt a deep bowl of sadness form within him. "How sad, the whole story."

She nodded.

"Can I meet him?"

"Would you like to?"

"Well, yes, of course."

"I shall arrange it."

They arrived at the threshold of the central building, which he recognized as the hallowed Library of Shambhala, said to hold a copy of all the books that were ever written. He figured it might be a mile across in both directions, but he was surprised at it not being taller.

"Only six stories?"

She said, "The archive stacks go more than twenty stories below ground."

They entered and paused just inside the massive doors. There was an attendant sitting behind a curved wooden counter, who smiled and nodded at Lee and then gazed fiercely at Quinn, who was looking very much like Skreeva. "Greetings, your Majesty." The title startled Quinn.

After a moment's hesitation he nodded and said "Greetings, friend." The attendant smiled.

The interior was arranged in spokes of hallways radiating out from two central circular staircases, paired with suspended cross walks, reminiscent of the DNA molecule. The beauty was incredible and brought a tear to each eye. Lee glanced at him sideways and said, "Yes, it is very beautiful." She led him down four floors to a hall where there were stacked scrolls and leather-bound books. Though none showed their age, he could intuit some were very old. She told him, "Here, I think you shall find your answers as to the nature of the Golden Whirlwind. You have only to call me, and someone, if not I, will come to you.

On the fourth day he realized that he had read everything that he needed. The Golden Whirlwind was composed of light, the light of the mind. It was drawn down from the Noosphere, the planetary 'sphere of reason', by the suffering of a person who had already achieved their own Mind, independent and individual. The suffering could be a paradox or an extreme contradiction, but not just a suffering of the mind and the Spirit, but also a suffering of the Body and the Soul, it required a greater suffering of the whole Being, a suffering nigh unto death.

He recalled his two encounters with the Whirlwind. The first when he was working on the Mississippi River, after the energetic thread had been cut and the vortex of it slammed into his solar plexus. The first encounter with the Golden Whirlwind happened a week later, all these events being in the realm of which he hadn't yet known anything. After surviving the cut thread he developed a second sight, a sight that allowed him to see into the minds of those who were searching for him, looking to kill him. Then he saw the fragmented souls of angry martyrs, long dead, trapped by their anger over having died for an untruth, too crystallized by their belief, their erroneous belief, to be eaten by De Murgos.

It occurred to him now, that not even De Murgos could eat certain kinds of shit.

Even his dreams had bent to searching out the understanding he needed of what had happened to him, what was happening. His pain was constant, his suffering extreme. Everything hurt—the clothes on his skin, the movement of work, the food in his mouth. If he couldn't figure out what had happened and what to do about it, he believed, no, knew he would die. In his dreams one evening he was speaking with a famous spiritual teacher, when he was pulled back into his room by a presence. It was the presence of a Dangla. The room smelled of shit, with the Dangla having smeared feces around the walls, and there was a huge pile under him, where he had soiled himself. He knew he couldn't clean the mess before his off-watch time ended, and he knew, more importantly, that he had no idea about how to drive off the Dangla standing in shadow in the corner of the room.

In his despair, he allowed himself to die. And that was when the Golden Whirlwind descended, and disappeared into the top of his head, just as the door opened by the man whose job it was to wake the next watch. He had seen the look of surprise and horror on the man's face and saw instantly what he saw—Quinn's hair flying in the twist of the disappearing Whirlwind. The man slammed the door shut.

The blast of the Whirlwind's passing wiped the filth off the walls, drove away the Dangla, and only the stench remained. And when he rolled out of bed he was panting in ecstasy, standing in a cloud of golden light, struggling to breathe and stay present. And the Whirlwind had taken away all his pain.

What he read here in the Library of Shambhala confirmed for him what he had read elsewhere but not yet understood: What happened to him was the Enlightenment of legend. Not some smaller scale Illumination of the Mind, but the installation and infusion of every cell with the power of the Light of Mind. The Light imbued him with another pulse, the pulse of another heart, a Higher Heart within him, along with his own pulse as well, and it pounded in every limb and organ, swirling from different places on his body, places he would come to learn of as chakras, wheels of energy and force. It was a long time before he would figure out that a Higher Body would require a Higher Heart. And what the feelings were, the Higher Feelings that went with it, the depth of the Grief, the height of the Ecstasy, the intensity of the Pain and the easing of Pain, that he could command.

It was a few days after this encounter that he felt a disturbance in his low back, a pain that traveled up his spine in the form of a whirlwind, releasing into him even more energy and expanding his range of perception. In time, he had come to understand this as Overcoming the Kundalini Buffer or the Release of the Kundalini Serpent. He heard voices all round him, like a chorus, singing to him what they thought about any action he contemplated. It was all he could do to get them to all stand on the same side of his awareness. It was then that he understood that even though he had attained an independent mind and individuality before, he had still been living essentially for himself, and now he knew that he had to live for others instead.

This was when, standing on the levy, he made the deal that had come to define his life: Mankind's freedom for theirs, speaking to the angry dead. And then he confirmed the deal with words, "Yes, your freedom for Mankind's."

And the chorus answered back, "And your freedom for Mankind's." He had accepted the terms, not knowing what it meant, nor how he was to sacrifice his freedom, or fulfill the deal.

As it had turned out, some outside force, one he never perceived clearly, brokered the deal. He was compelled to lie down and endure the sensations of being born, but in reverse, feet first. When it was done, he sat up and gave the power back, knowing that he didn't deserve to keep it, he had not worked hard enough for it, and that many had given their lives striving for what had been given to him. The power flowed from him, from his eyes and mouth and ears, from his hands and feet, from the wheels of force.

When it was over he sat there, a pale shadow in the darkness, and the voice of the chorus said, "She is dead, she is dead, she is dead." It was the birthing that killed her. He had only the vaguest idea who she was, then he knew it was the dark queen riding the beast whose appearance would have, according to the Book of Revealings, triggered the end of the world as he knew it.

He had no idea who "she" was, even though he had seen a woman of power manipulating others with her hands in his dreams.

"May she rest in peace," he said three times in response. He remembered the hollowness and emptiness he felt when he went outside, climbed to an upper deck, and watched the rising light of dawn chase away a night sky filled with ranks of large black birds. Then he thought, "What if I have to continue to sacrifice my freedom so that they all stay gone, and the people can go free?" and he felt fear at the thought. He chose, in that moment, to behave as if it was true until he could know that it wasn't.

He found the source book for a quote he'd encountered when reading the mostly-exoteric material that was available to him: that when a student was getting close to Enlightenment his Master would stand guard to make sure that no entity was hiding in the Whirlwind, looking to enter and take over the student. There was even an illustration, one that he spent a long time looking at. The master's face was filled with fear, the student was sobbing, and even through the swirling gold light a smile on the face of the interloper could be seen.

And remembering the second encounter with the Golden Whirlwind, lying on the bench in jail, freezing, head pounding from the beating the police had given him, he had given up in despair and was sliding toward death, he was sure that it was De Murgos hiding in it. And he realized that, weeks later when he felt De Murgos sliding sideways out of him, then turning to face him, face him without his mask, to put his hands on him, and fighting with him, Quinn succeeded at looking upon De Murgos's face even as the entity's hand came down upon his forehead and ended his vision, his capacity to see into that world. He realized that De Murgos had left him because he was too rough, too crude, too uneducated to be of any use to him. And he laughed out loud, causing heads to turn and stare at him.

He'd never had a master, let alone a "god" to master him. Yet nevertheless, when De Murgos appeared to him a few weeks later when he was contemplating leaving and told him to "Wait" he had waited for decades, in vain he now knew, because De Murgos never came back. In that time, Quinn had made himself small, cutting off his budding psychic powers by not developing them, letting them wither on the vine, because development was not Waiting. He had made himself as insignificant as he could, until he could do it no longer. And he knew now, also, that De Murgos had forgotten him.

He also discovered a section in the Library on De Murgos. Great minds in ancient times had discerned that, functioning as a god, he had been responsible for more death than life. He was seen as an interloper, interfering in the affairs of humans, leading them to believe in him, promising them immortality as he led them to slaughter. They called him the Demiurge and blamed him for most of the suffering of everyday people.

Even though it had cost Quinn most of his life, he was suddenly happy that he had been forgotten. Near the end of his time in the Library he found a dialogue between philosophers that was almost two thousand years old. It concerned the question why, in the case of the appearance of De Murgos to mortal humans, he would most often command the person to not look upon his face. The speculation was that if he were to show his face it would have to be a mask, and that the mask would interfere with his power to command the people telepathically into doing his will. And this would explain why he had a different appearance for different peoples—he wore a different mask. Near the end of the dialogue, one of the philosophers speculated that De Murgos was faceless, that he had no face. "Imagine the horror, and the terror."

The partner in the dialogue said, "No, he has a thousand faces, all the masks of god." The dialogue concluded. Quinn's smile was grim.

Grief and grim victory. With further victory yet to come.

He got up from the table and left the building, heading for the mountain opposite the one from which he'd entered. He walked past the end of the road, following the path upwards. About halfway up, he stopped and sat down heavily on an old log that gave a little under his weight. He sighed. And then he heard a voice, startling him, in a language he understood but had not heard before, "Get off me."

He jumped up and looked toward where the mouth should have been. He saw only two all blue eyes looking at him. The log stood up, revealing arms and legs, and an enormous phallus, swinging as he stood.

And Quinn knew, mind still plugged in somehow to the library, that this was a Djinn. And moreover, it was Lee's father. He bowed deeply and said, "Elder, please forgive me."

"What you don't know is likelier to kill you than what you do know."

"Who you know and who you don't know doesn't follow the same rule."

"True enough," the being before him hummed, and a mouth began to show in the textured bark of his face. "Since we don't know each other, I am unlikely to kill you. Very good. Come let us sit over there on that stone. It too is alive, but slow enough that it won't wake before we move again."

As they sat, side by side, looking out over the ancient caldera, Quinn said, "I am a friend of Regina's."

The Djinn's eyes lit up. "Tell me about her. How is she?"

"You don't know?"

"I don't look." Then he said, his face grim again, "Out there, even my gaze can be tracked."

"Lee?"

"When she comes, we talk of other things, mostly her life. The most she would say is that her mother is fine."

"We are close. You should know we have been intimate."

An arm settled down across his back, heavy as a tree limb. The Djinn laughed. "You and a thousand others."

The realization surprised Quinn. The Djinn spoke the truth.

"I always speak the Truth. Except when I don't," and the humming sound became a guffaw as his mouth came fully open. The branch slapped Quinn on the back. So Quinn told him what he knew, and that there was much about her that she kept hidden from him.

"As she did me. She even kept my paternity hidden from me until the girl matured. And her ability to travel through Eternity. Lee told me she got that from me," he said, and his voice contained more than a little bit of natural pride.

Quinn quietly said, "I have one coming, too."

But before he could say "With whom?" he looked at Quinn and saw layers of fear and complexity and decided it was wiser to say only "Congratulations. My name is Micah. And you are not what you seem to be."

"Unlike you?"

"Less so than you, certainly."

On the morning of the sixth day Lee came looking for them. They'd moved several times as sitting on the rocks had woken them up. The rocks expressed their displeasure by blowing air up their asses, causing them to fart both injudiciously and stupendously. She knew where they were by the sound of their laughter rolling down the hills.

His last night in Shambhala, Quinn dreamed. In his dream he was with a Priestess, sitting in congress in the first position. Her head was down so he couldn't see her face. Then her crown lit up, a circlet of silver flames with a purple flame at the center. Suddenly he felt the presence of the Higher heart beating at the top of his head, and shortly he had a sensation of the top of his head coming off. He felt a single large flame, bright enough to illuminate the ground around them both. He looked up and the flame was feeding a golden disk in the sky only a few feet above his head. He looked at it in amazement and looked down again toward the face of the Priestess. She too was looking up, amazed, and in that light he knew that his partner was She Who Comes.

Quinn woke up to Darvatiye settled beside him, feeling the swell of her belly against his back. "The Time between Times," he thought, and smiled.

Then he felt She Who Comes slide into Darvatiye, felt the shift in the shape of her arms, and he smiled again.

"Rest, beloved." Two voices as one.

20

The Men's Rebellion

The violence against women by men continued to grow globally. Assault, rape, and gang rape increased in almost every country. The Order organized small squads in cities and towns, especially near military bases. The squads would appear to be small groups of friends out for an afternoon or evening and intervene, either verbally or physically, if needed, to draw violence to themselves, so that it would expend the accumulated malice in men.

Madeleines and their assistants, called the Crows, would be assigned to each group, helping them target which men had accumulated in themselves dangerous levels of the Molecules of Malice. In western countries this was easier—there was greater freedom of movement. In other places, the squads would take advantage of the Order's controlling interest in various hotel chains. They would show up as tourists and take advantage of local contacts as tour guides to gain access to places where the Molecules had spread. They often waited in airports, with trained Crows watching for the accumulations of Molecules around people's feet, dragging the dark dust with them from wherever they had come. In these situations, the squads mostly engaged in clean up, sometimes using themselves as attractant forces, because becoming involved physically would have led to interactions with local law enforcement, which was to be avoided. As always, the

Order was to remain as hidden as possible.

The men in the squads, trained Consorts all, had learned to take the malice into themselves, containing and controlling it until they could safely expend it, either in exercise or meditation, or most importantly under the ministrations of the hands of the Priestesses.

Yet despite these efforts, the accumulated effects of millennia of misogyny continued to enrage men and target women. Any press coverage of a violent incident spawned copycat incidents.

De Murgos, in his cave on the dark side of the moon, felt the hatred and the terror and grew strong feeding on it. He loved the wars between his three children—the dying, no matter in which version they believed, would die commending their souls into his hands. He would receive them in bliss and lick his fingers afterwards. But he particularly loved violence against women, especially those women who believed in his beneficence. The irony was sweet on his tongue.

Whenever men would gather in small groups, the topic of women, their rights and their freedoms, and their utter disregard of men's feelings, wants, needs, and opinions, would come up, men reinforcing each other's anger, and leading to vows to each other to reaffirm the old way of doing things.

The impact of the Molecules of Malice was particularly strong in Central and South America. In cultures where the women were already oppressed by the attitudes of Machismo, the women were victimized more strongly than ever by domestic violence. Beatings for infractions of the Code of Machismo became common. Every village seemed to have a family that was particularly dysfunctional and the men, angered by too many people and not enough work, were quick to use their fists in their frustration.

Calley had been relieved of Her duties as High Priestess of Stonehaven, by the Madeleine and Diana, when She was summoned to help in Wallid. When her work on Wallid concluded, She was assigned by She Who Comes to keep Her promise to go to Brazil and visit the Thunder God Dchango, and, once there, help Inmanzha and Oshune organize the resistance and support the women.

21

The Mechanic

Mecklenburg Knowlton arrived at the Wallid International Airport exhausted and achy. He wished he'd had enough foresight to upgrade his ticket to business class, even if the Order wouldn't. He swore to himself that the next trip he took, he would do it himself.

Although the lines were long, he got through customs quickly. The customs agents were efficient, and the island was a popular tourist destination. He had nothing to declare and only a carry-on suitcase and backpack. He knew he could obtain whatever else he needed.

Stopping at the currency exchange, he looked around carefully for the spotter for the thieves he'd been warned about. There was no one near, especially no one pretending to not be watching. He exchanged $1,000, thinking that he wouldn't need that much money, but he could always leave it behind.

The taxi ride to Boodun, the city Regina Moon Halter's compound was near, was almost two hours away. He opened the file on Angelica Jones on his tablet. He remembered her clearly, having been ordered by the Madeleine to project his ghost to her bedroom two nights before she left home for Stonehaven. He remembered playing piano for her in a different dream. He remembered watching her, as he leaned up against the wall in back on her first day of class. He remembered how impressed he'd been with her presence of mind.

What he did not know, and would take a little while longer for him to figure out, was that the night in her bedroom was the night she conceived the Dragon, and when he did figure it out, and considered what it meant, he would not be happy.

The High Priestess didn't tell him that was why he was being assigned to her, his first assignment off the Stonehaven grounds in nearly a decade. She led him to believe he simply needed a change of scenery. Already, he missed the simplicity of his work assignment. Caring for the tractors and mowers at Stonehaven had given him a deeply satisfying handful of years.

He remembered his initiation as a Consort. It had been so long ago, and he was so settled in that role, that it was hard to remember. He had been led to understand that if he handled this assignment well, he would be put on the list for initiation as a High Consort. He thought to himself, sarcastically, that he could hardly wait.

He returned his attention to the file. The photo of Angelica was taken unawares. She was scowling at something that irritated her. It made him think of her as a fierce beauty—not that she showed it in any behavior, but that in time, the fierceness would wake up in her, and he hoped that he would be able to facilitate that. He loved being around wen who were able to step into their Warrior Shadow and bring it present. They triggered his own Warrior to emerge, which made him feel his strongest, and he loved strength.

The taxi dropped him off at the gate to the compound. He was impressed, it was like a little walled village. He could feel the magical wards around the place and touched nothing. He called the number he'd been given. A middle-aged dark-skinned wen with a long braid, accompanied by a much older wen, hair still black except for the shockingly well-defined white stripes. He recognized her, Regina, from her many stays at Stonehaven. She smiled at him, and he smiled back, even as he saw a big man with one hand hidden behind his back, as if he was gripping a pistol. He didn't smile back when smiled at, so Meck nodded at him. The man nodded back. Meck flashed the OV sign at him. The man didn't nod this time, in keeping with the rules.

The wen saw the sign and smiled at him. He bowed to Regina, happy and serious, and spoke her name, "Moon Halter. It is a blessing to be in your presence again."

She, happy and serious also, inclined her head to him. Palm up, gesturing to her side, she said, "This is the High Priestess Onadaya. She is the manager here. Onadaya, this is an old acquaintance of mine from Stonehaven. They called him the Mechanic, because he is good with machines. Also, his real name," she said, leaning toward Onadaya and whispering theatrically, "is Mecklenburg."

He bowed to her as well. She smiled broadly, leaned forward and took his face in his hands and kissed him on the forehead. She pulled back, still smiling, this time at the consternation on his face.

She said, "Happy to have your mind here." Then she said, "Mech Meck. Same name twice. Very special." Her lower face went tight, her lips somewhere between indifference and distaste. But she kept her eyes sparkling, to show him she was joking, and to see if he would look her in the eye. He searched her absence of a smile briefly before he looked up. Once he did, he smiled back at her. She nodded, he had passed a test.

They each took an arm and walked him up the short flight of stone steps to the courtyard level. They stopped at the second gate and introduced him to Guiles, standing sentry. Onadaya said, "This is Mech Meck."

Meck groaned, Regina grinned, Guiles raised an eyebrow. "Same name twice?"

"No, no. She's just joking. Meck short for Mecklenburg. Also, I was the Mechanic at Stonehaven for many years."

"Well, then, Meck, welcome to Wallid," and Guiles shook his hand. He stepped aside, and bowed, arm extended. "Welcome home."

Stepping into the second courtyard he sensed a second very strong circle of wards, strong enough to invisibly stop a man in his tracks when fully charged. "Why so much protection?" he asked.

"When we were attacked by the priests, we had not been using them," Onadaya answered.

"There was no need yet. You have read about the attack in the file on Angelica, yes?" Regina asked.

"Yes," he replied. "I am sad for it. How is she?"

"She lives," Onadaya shrugged.

"She progresses," Regina added.

Guiles said, "She'll recover. He was not her Consort very long.

Long enough to feel her crush on him to have potential, but not long enough to realize it into something deeper."

Regina said, "We'll introduce you to everybody else first." She reached behind them, pushing Meck forward, and said, "Mech, this is Guiles, High Consort, and assigned to the High Priestess Jasmine. We'll go find her first."

The group passed several one room cabins built up against the walls on either side on their way to the main house. They entered the main house and Jasmine was sitting at the feasting table working on her laptop, topless in the heat, wearing a sarong wrapped around her waist, in the old way of the native wen on the island, before the restriction of outside religious imposition. She stood up for the introduction, breasts swaying, smiling as she shook his hand. Then she kissed Guiles, in a way that made it clear who belonged to her. She smiled at him again and went back to her work.

The group made their way to the kitchen, sans Guiles, who sat down next to Jasmine. There, as she knew they would be, Regina introduced Tenara and Napat, both also topless, and clarified that they were Novitiates of the Order. Tenara gazed at him frankly, comparing him, Regina suspected, to the deceased Wade. Napat retreated into her shyness, blushed and looked down even as she shook his hand. They were both surprised and pleased when he greeted them in traditional Nahasi, the banned language.

Onadaya remained in the kitchen with the young wen. Regina slowly escorted him back out of the house into the inner courtyard. "She is not healed," Regina began.

"How could she be?" Meck responded. Regina put a restraining hand on his shoulder.

"She is not healed. But she knows you were sent, and she has agreed to meet you. She knows she must leave here, and she knows she cannot travel alone. There is to be no expectation as to the nature of your relationship. And no time limit placed on how long it will take you two to become intimate. But the Madeleines have looked, and they say all bodes well."

They stopped by one of the cabin doors hung with black cloth. Regina knocked. There was silence, so she knocked again. They heard a muffled "Enter."

Angelica was sitting in a shaft of sunlight by the mirror brushing her hair, which had grown much longer since she'd graduated college. Her face was weary at first, but when she looked up towards the others, the light shown on it and she glowed. She didn't smile, but she glowed. Meck's breath caught slightly. What he saw he could only describe as resiliency radiating. She stood as Regina said, "Angelica, this is Mecklenburg Knowlton. The High Council assigned him to you."

He nodded his head slightly then solidly returned her gaze as she searched his face. "He'll stay in the cabin next to yours," Regina said. Angelica's breath caught a little. Corey's cabin, she thought. Except for gifts he had given her, the rest of his belongings had been dropped into the river beneath the house, with Angelica taking the lead in the Ceremony of Letting Go. The Ceremony had been effective, in that she felt unpulled in any direction and centered in herself.

Regina left, leaving the door open. Meck sat on his heels, resting his hands on his thighs and regarded her with half open eyes as she turned back to the mirror, finishing her hair. She regarded him from the mirror. "You look familiar. Have we met?"

"Yes, at Stonehaven. I was the Chief Mechanic there. We met briefly the morning of your first class there."

"Yes, I recall now. You were standing behind me at the back of the classroom, leaning against the wall. I passed you on the way out at the beginning of the break. We locked eyes, I looked away, and when I looked back at you, you were still looking at me."

"Yes. But we actually met before that."

"Really?" she asked. "Where? When?"

"I will show you."

The air next to him started to oscillate. The oscillations coalesced into a form, identical in image to his soma. Angelica knew it was his ghost body. She turned in her chair to face him. Suddenly there were two identical forms in front of her. Then, still in the same sitting position, the ghost body rose up in the air, as did the hair on the back of her neck. Then the ghost body spoke. "I came to you in the night, before you left home for Stonehaven. I was assigned to you even then."

Angelica gasped as the memory flooded in, remembering the sex they'd had as the most spectacular of her life. Her belly tightened and the outline of the dragon's egg she carried secretly, still in her womb, thrummed.

"I know you, Consort."

"I know you, Priestess."

They sat a long time, not moving. He contemplating her, she contemplating both of him.

She watched as he brought himself back together. He sighed and remained seated on his heels. There was nothing else to say. He rose to his feet and left the room, going back to the main house to get something to eat and hang out with Guiles and Jasmine. Angelica appeared briefly, bringing dishes from her cabin, and returned carrying a covered tray. She nodded at him as she passed and smiled faintly as she looked away.

That night Meck slept on the ground outside her doorway. He had waited until her light went out to lay down. A light sleeper, he rolled out of the way and sat up when she opened the door. She came out, took a few steps and stared up at the night sky. When she turned to go back in, she did not look directly at him. Her smile, as she passed him, was shadowed in the moonlight. She left the door open. He was unsure what it meant, so he reached up and closed it gently, resuming his post. The thought crossed his mind that it was hardly a 'post' if he was lying down, was it?

He wondered what to call it and settled on 'station' because he was stationary. He smiled and slipped back into sleep.

22

Emmalia in Town

Emmalia loved her time with the Elder and her Consort. She loved listening to their stories of their assignments before they'd been assigned to each other. They found that they both no longer wanted a different assignment, and the Order had never asked one of them. In their late seventies, their ease together, and their good humor, were enhanced by the adoration for each other in their eyes. The adoration was fed by decades of worshiping that which was the most prominent manifestation of the creative forces of their somas. They rested on the mountains of their souls. Their spirits lifted with joy whenever they glanced at each other. And all this was palpable to Emmalia.

And besides, it gave her the opportunity to speak French.

After one such visit, Emmalia had to ride further into town to check for mail at the Post Office. There were two men loitering across the street and when they saw her they started smirking, hitting each other's biceps with the backs of their hands as they each made a comment, and they laughed. The laugh felt tinged with a little bit of malice to Emmalia. She put her helmet on without buckling it, stuffed the mail in her jacket, started the engine and kicked off, quickly but without haste, just as they were halfway across the street headed for her. She repressed the urge to flip them the bird.

Left standing in the middle of the street, jaws clenched in anger at the rejection, the meaner of the two men, Dominic, said to the other, Evrard, "We should follow her." They both had moto-cross bikes at home. Evrard said, "We'll meet at the bottom of the trail in an hour. Bring some lunch."

Emmalia's extended senses told her that the incident was not yet over.

Early in the afternoon she thought she heard a couple bikes far down the valley, engines at low rev, but the sound stopped.

She knew that most people in the town knew of the cabin, and probably knew that an American girl was staying there for several months. She thought that she had better be prepared for visitors, welcome or unwelcome, and set about making it so.

The first thing she did was to set her wards. She made them strong enough so that a man would pause before crossing them. She left a space big enough to park two bikes on either side of the one-track where it came up onto the flat where the cabin was built. Then she went into the house and made a stew large enough to feed her guests. She used her knowledge of herbs to doctor the stew and gave herself an infusion of another herb that would counter the herbs in the stew. She sponge-bathed from water heated on the stove, changed into comfortable and easily shed clothes, and, thinking briefly, smiled about putting her riding boots back on, she opted to tie on an older pair of lace up hiking boots. She tied them on loosely. She applied a little eyeliner and scented herself. She loosely piled her hair up on top of her head.

She left her keys in the bike and threw a tarp over it. She set her splitting ax up outside behind the woodshed, thankful that the Order had firewood delivered from further up the mountain twice a year. Finally, she set up her wards inside the house, empowering herself by disempowering anyone else who crossed them.

Then she went outside and sat down in a chair, leaned back and watched the westering sun. The sun was still two hands high when she heard the low rev engines again.

23

THE BLUE HAG

In the Initiation Cistern at Stonehaven, The Mind of All Life on the Planet sat in bemused meditative silence. A faint golden light emanated from Her. She leaned back against a boulder that had been included in the stonework walls and sighed. Opposite her, against another boulder, a spark of blue light grew into a cloud of light that resolved itself into a feminine form, wearing a skirt and shawl, barefoot, long hair carefully braided.

When the blue image finished coalescing, She Who Comes spoke out into the chamber, "Stonewen, I need someone with whom to speak. I get tired of talking to myself, sometimes even when the image is different enough for me to imagine that it is not just a part of myself. But you and I are different, and it is because we had a distance happen between us. No contact or connection for hundreds of years. I have not even looked into your past to see what you have learned, and what wisdom you possess. But my intuition tells me you are wise, and I note that you are returning to me of your own accord."

"The Terror of my Burning kept me hiding in the darkness for a long time. The initiation of the wen, here underground, made me curious, and drew me out."

"And you have been wonderful. You are a wonder."

"So, Beloved, what worry furrows your brow?"

"I think it is time to add a vector in our counterattack on De Murgos. And I am troubled by how to apply the strategy," the Goddess said.

"Tell me."

"You know that I am trying to create a Neomythic world. A world where the Truth, with its science and Reason, Ecstasy in all its power, and the development of a Conscience, with its capacity to discern The Good, these three principles resting on the foundation of the Mysterious. I believe that a lie believed in the Soul inevitably corrupts the Soul. It seems to me that if I were a member of one of the religions of De Murgos, and that I believed in the lies that were taught there, it wouldn't matter how Good someone was otherwise, the lie would be entangled with the Truth. I have had enough of the Lie, and people confusing the metaphorical with the literal. I am tired of the fundamentalism. I am tired of the ignorance.

She Who Comes confessed, "So my question becomes: is believing in the lie enough to warrant destruction, no matter how Good a person is otherwise?"

Stonewen paused, trying to discern how to respond. "The destruction of a house is not the same as the destruction of a person."

"Ah, I knew you would help me see what I had conflated." She Who Comes smiled.

"Oh, I see. Would you like me to take down the houses where the lies are told, but spare the people?"

"I do not want you to spare the people, that is a part of my problem. I have been hurt too much to not want their destruction. But how can I destroy them if they are good people, despite believing in the lie? Shouldn't their basic goodness protect them from the malice of the lies?"

"If we destroy the malicious and their houses, will we not be rid of them?" Stonewen asked.

"Perhaps. But De Murgos counts on that suffering as a part of his food. He eats dark food as well as bright food. He will notice."

"Will he not notice no matter what you do?" asked Stonewen.

"Yes. He will notice, but we want to control what it is that he sees. We want him to see the consternation of his peoples, not so much their grief. Otherwise, he will feed on it. And I will need that grief during the reconstruction, after the establishment of the Neomythic Age, to help heal the planet. All their grief when they realize what they have done, and had done to them, belongs to me, not to him."

"Then I think you are right. Their religious houses, not their religiousness. For now. But be warned: when he sees their consternation, he may come to investigate."

"Yes," She Who Comes smiled and looked away, as if into the future. "And so. How good are you at creating controlled earthquakes? And can you make sinkholes?"

"I don't know. Shall we practice?

She Who Comes appeared in the meadow with Stonewen, holding hands. She pointed to the old clapboard building with a steeple.

"Do you recognize this place?"

"Yes. It is where my burning occurred. The pyre was just over there. The building is not the same one as then. It is rebuilt on the same spot though."

"Are there people in it?"

"Not often. It is too remote because the people moved away. They only return on special occasions."

"Do the people who come here believe in the lie?"

"Yes, most assuredly. I suspect even the dead in the graveyard alongside it still believe in the lie."

"So, let me see you take it down. Smash it down!"

Stonewen sank into the earth, leaving a hint of blue haze behind. The Goddess could follow her trail to the church by the ripple her passing made under the grass. The ripple ended at the corner of the church. The near corner began to vibrate slightly. The vibration spread, rippling at the four corners of the building. The steeple, with a small bell at the top, began to sway, bell clanging. Then, with a groaning sound that only stones can make, the entire structure collapsed in on itself, timbers snapping, puffs of dust rising up over the ruin.

The groaning stopped. Suddenly the Stonewen appeared standing next to She Who Comes. A lock of her hair had come loose. She blew it away from her face, turning to smile at the Mind of All Life. She grinned in triumph. When She grinned back, Stonewen's smile turned a little wicked.

"So, you used the vibration in the rocks," She Who Comes said.

"Yes," Stonewen replied. "I called it to me by Resonance. It wasn't even hard work to amplify it. It just came through the ground, I collected it, and touched it to the foundation. The building shook itself down."

She Who Comes smiled generously at Stonewen. "Are you busy? Got anything going on in the next few weeks?"

24

Machismo

Calley was freed from Her temporary commitment as High Priestess of Stonehaven when She Who Comes summoned Her to Wallid with another mission: to help with the replacement of the Temple to Skreeva with the Temple of the Mountain King. Calley recalled Her promise to go to Brazil and offer Her services to the god of Thunder there, the Orisha known as Dchango.

Before going to Brazil, Calley, Storm Goddess and daughter of She Who Comes, returned to the Invisible Lands for a brief time to visit Her children, Her sister Bree, and to spend some time with her lover Alam—now visibly aged, despite their best efforts, by their time together in the Visible Lands. The passage of Time had slowed for him again, but there was no reversing it. He looked at least ten years older than Her, perhaps fifteen years, and when She saw him, She felt that pang of loss and sadness, knowing that his mortality would arrive even there, eventually. It made their time in each other's arms more sweet, and unbeknownst to him, made Her commitment to him and his welfare more strong within Her.

Bree agreed to continue to take care of Alam, and his needs. Now that Matthews was off 'fucking that other bird,' she said mockingly, She had the urge to take Alam to Herself again. But She confided to Calley, as sisters sometimes do, that as a Face of She Who Comes, She would sometimes enter into that 'other bird' when she and Matthews were coupling, sometimes while they were flying together. She said She hadn't been able to imagine what that felt like for humans, and She was surprised and grateful for the experience.

Calley gathered Her children together and they had a long day listening to each other's stories, feasting, and spending the night under one roof. At dinner time, Grandmother She Who Comes made an appearance, and thereby made everybody happy. Very happy indeed.

The children had some idea of what She was up to, and She shared with them as much as She thought useful. The essence of Her plan was to use Mountains, and their feminine spirits where they still existed, along with a network of Queen Old Woman stones, to attack De Murgos from the high points, the points closest to his home on the Moon. It would be too easy for him to trap Her people in the Feminine Spirit of the Valley. It had been while She was communing with the Spirit of the Valley, the one that never dies, when De Murgos had taken Her, and imposed himself on Her for the first time, not knowing Who She Was.

The children, young adults now all, retired first, intending to be up and away to their respective realms early in the predawn darkness. Alam fell asleep sitting up, hands with fingers crossed over his belly, head hanging down. It was then that She Who Comes spoke with Her daughters about the Molecules of Malice, and the problem they presented.

As She spoke, it became clear to Calley that She would be given an assignment. She Who Comes spoke of the state of Misogyny in the world, and where it was worse. North America and Europe were the safest places for wen and were also the places where the Order was strongest, so there was less to do. She talked about sending teams, and possibly squads of Priestesses and Consorts, to different parts of the world, knowing that their presence, their meditations, and their sexuality would interact with the Spirits of the Land wherever they were, serving to ameliorate just a little of the hatred, still strong—not only in places where the religions of De Murgos were the dominant force in people's minds, but in other places, where the patriarchality of the lie against the Antecedence of the Feminine ruled the culture.

As anticipated, the assignment came. Calley was to keep Her

promise to visit the Thunder deity of the Orishas in Brazil, Dchango. While She was there, Her assignment was to assist in the removal of patriarchally abusive priests, and to find ways to help the Orishas undercut the rising current of machismo that was threatening the lives and safety of women and children.

The Molecules of Malice were in the dust of the streets, swirling in the wake of passing feet.

Calley took on Her mortal form to travel to Brazil. She could have simply willed Herself there from the Hidden Lands, but She wouldn't have remained solid enough for long enough. And She no longer wished to leave Her mortal form at Stonehaven, now that Alam had returned to the Hidden Lands himself. There would be no one to watch over Her, to guard and protect Her. Alam's mortal form was aging quickly in that continuum, and She had wished him to return home and into the preserving pace of time in the Hidden Lands.

So She found Herself at the start of the trail over the mountains to the village and Little Sack Cove. She dimmed the color of Her hair to that of silver clouds and added lines to Her face. In the last village before the start of the trail, She had to walk past an outdoor bar, men leaning on it, drinking beer in the middle of the day, many back from their morning net casting. Her frostiness kept the men's lechery cool without them knowing it. Only when She had passed did one man mutter under his breath, "I could melt that ice with my heat for her." And the image of it, her writhing beneath him, dissipated in a flash of light that he thought hit him just above his eyes. His eyes rolled backward for a moment looking for internal damage. Finding none but forgetfulness, they returned his focus to the bottle in his hand, staring at his cracked and dirty fingernails.

She was following little flashes of Quinn's ghost chi. She had practiced attuning Herself to a frequency resonant with his (a frequency She had known intimately with him several times), and as She drew near, the light would flash so She could see it. And if She were still, when that happened, She could sometimes see what he had been seeing. So She perched on the sitting stone at the top of the first ridge, having walked out to it on the headland through the short thick brush. She saw the line of Cracked Teeth Rocks that served as breakwaters for the bay, and beyond that the Ocean, gray and swelling, she knew and could feel it, all the way to the ice-shrouded South. She knew that Quinn had rested there, too. A man led a donkey carrying empty wooden crates tied to its back and sides, coming up from the direction She was headed. He didn't see Her, didn't even look Her way to see the view of the ocean hidden when one walked the jungle-sided trail.

She got up and walked the steep trail down into a narrow valley and up the other side, paved with moss covered bricks so slippery that the donkeys walked beside the path. She emerged into a meadow and passed a house, painted cheerily with portraits of the old couple who had once lived there. Continuing down the slope toward Little Sack Cove, She encountered a standing stone. It looked natural in its setting, as if it had fallen from high above, end over end, and landed where it stood, completely vertical. She saw more flashes of Quinn's ghost chi. He had stood there and put his hand on the rock. She heard him say the word "Sentry," which he must have spoken aloud standing there. She paused, put Her hand on it, and said aloud, "Hello. I am here." Which was enough, she thought to Herself.

She continued down the trail, smiling even when she encountered another brick lined hairpin turn at an angle of almost 80 degrees. At the bottom, the trail ended in a boardwalk that led her to cross a fast-moving stream. She came to the gate and stepped into a yard raked like a Zen Garden with religious symbols from all faiths made of little rocks that were enclosed in small rock circles. She looked toward the one room house, but the shutters were all closed. She could see that Quinn had entered the house and spent time inside. Through the closed shutter, She could see the image of the Shaman writing at his table. She knew She would pass this way again, and could meet him then.

She went back to the stream, loud in its rushing, past the rocks, sweet water hastening to join with its elder sister the salt water. She pushed aside the foliage and saw a path leading uphill along the stream. She saw the flashes of ghost chi lighting her way. The footpath was clear, though the way was steep. Sweating, she pushed a slip of hair away from her face and paused. She looked up and could see a thin trail of smoke rising. "Not too far," She thought to Herself.

She drew a breath and resumed the climb. Another 50 meters and She emerged into the clearing. She saw the three wen in the clearing, topless in grass skirts. The Crone was sitting in front of a door to a thatched roof house, working on finishing a reed mat. The Mature and the Maiden were at the fire, stirring something in an iron pot suspended from a tripod. The Mature was adding a crushed leaf of an herb to the pot when Calley stopped at the edge of the clearing and looked around. She said, in flawless Portuguese, "I come seeking sanctuary."

All three wen smiled at Her and gestured for Her to come forward. She removed Her shirt and bra, unlaced Her boots and stepped out of them, picking them up and carrying them, as She walked barefoot into the clearing.

At the back of the clearing was a long house that seemed to be made of living vines and covered in blooming flowers. From the opening stepped a dark-skinned wen with black eyes, topless also, wearing a grass skirt that came to mid-thigh.

"Oshune," Calley said, bowing Her head.

"Calley," Oshune replied. Then, smiling warmly and in perfect English, said, "We have been waiting for you. Mother told us you were coming. Come inside and sit. Turning to the Maiden She said, "Leti, go bring some cold juice from the stream, and give it to our Friend." Smiling, Leti did as she was bidden.

25

SHOPPING ACROSS NORTH AFRICA

In the month since they had left Marseille, Jennifer and Julius had stopped in bazaars and markets in all the safe capitals across North Africa. They made small purchases of well-made antiques, haggling appropriately, and arranged for these to be shipped to a warehouse in Marseille, tipping the merchants well so that they could be reasonably certain the purchases would be shipped. From Rabat to Algiers, skipping Libya, to Tunis then to Alexandria. From there, they rented a car and stopped in Cairo. They drove to Redahd then on to Wekka.

In Alexandria they procured papers, passports, and travel documents from a forger deeply indebted to the Order. It was a mystery to them how he had obtained passport photos from the family without the father knowing. When they met the old woman in the market, they knew. Neither of them had met anyone with her particular shade of gravitas. Her manner of speech was such that her suggestions, sometimes mere utterances, were obeyed as direct commands. When they met her behind her shop selling cell phones and modern shoes, she told them to sit down, and they both felt the weight of her words pressing down on their shoulders, forcing them to bend their knees.

"I see you are wondering," she said. "I feel it, and I hear it, too." They nodded politely while she called for tea. "I am Madeleine," she said. "Trained in the old way, as the first Madeleine was. Do you know what I mean?"

They both nodded. She spoke in impeccable English when they were alone, happy to have the chance to practice. "It is very old, thousands of years, and very secret. The Meemons have no idea, nor should they. Preserve the Secret. Protect the Secret. The Secret is very old as well, older even. Nobody knows how old," she said as she perused the documents. "These are very good," she said. "They will do."

She went silent as a young wen entered with a tea service on a tray. "This is my granddaughter."

When she was gone, after curtseying and bowing to the guests, the old woman said, "They will be traveling to you in Egypt. The daughter has been seeking employment as an au pair, so the cover story will remain intact. After your introduction to her this afternoon, you will return to Egypt and wait for her there. She will be traveling with her mother and her brother. We must observe propriety if this is going to work. Traditional propriety. That is why she cannot travel with you."

Then she paused. "I am told that her brother has been given an assignment. One that he will have to carry out soon. He will be a refugee, a hunted man if his identity is discovered. I am told that he will not become known, that the cameras that could identify him will be disabled. I hope so. A mission like this one is fraught with peril," she said, removing from a voluminous pocket a vial wrapped in wet-formed rawhide, stoppered with a cork. "Do you know what this is?"

They both shook their heads 'No'.

"It was delivered to me just yesterday, by members of the Order. Do you know anything about it?"

Again, the same head shake.

"Just as well. Compartmentalization. Only for those who need to know. I am old. They will not torture me. They'll just shoot me in the head. Gladly, for it has been a good life. But what you do need to know is that you will have to take the brother with you, along with your new 'au pair'. Will this be a problem?"

Jennifer answered, "I think not. There is room."

"Good."

Julius, who knew nothing of any of this, kept his impulse to raise an eyebrow under control. He intuited the old wen's powers of observation, especially when she made it appear that she wasn't looking. He knew that his role was to appear solid and stolid. But informed, not stupid.

26

Matthews and Venge

Matthews and Venge were practicing their diving from the back side of the tower. In their weeks of practice, Matthews had bulked up and was able to lift one hundred pounds easily and fly with it. He had just successfully picked up one hundred seventy-five pounds and flown to the tower with it for the first time. Venge was looking at him strangely, one eye focused and one not, looking at him but seeing something different than the other eye. She quietly reached behind her and unslung an AR-15. "I saw Freya today. She gave me this to practice with."

Matthews whistled and said, "Of course there is a gun." Then. "How much ammo?"

"A 20-round clip. And a spare."

Matthews whistled again. "That's a lot of bodies."

"She wants you to learn how to use it, too. There's a firing range in a cave under the castle. No one but the Order knows about it."

"Are you in the Order?"

"I have sworn a vow of secrecy that somehow holds me to silence, even if I wanted to talk about it. I can talk about it to you, which means you're in the Order, too."

"Are you on the path to becoming a Priestess?"

"Not yet. Maybe never. How about you, as a Consort?"

"Not yet. And maybe never. But I did take that vow of secrecy. I don't know anybody that I would tell anyway. But then, I've been to the Invisible Lands. I'm going back there when this is done."

"I wish I had someplace to go back to."

"You do. You can come here."

She looked at him again with that strange gaze. "We're going to die tomorrow. Or in a week. I think we should fuck. Maybe spend the week fucking."

He hesitated, thinking of Bree, and in that moment he flashed on an image of Her, smiling and nodding her head "Yes!"

He said, "I think you're right." He tossed the rock over the edge of the parapet. "I think we should get started now. Then lunch. Then target practice. Then we should probably fuck again."

She laughed and showed her teeth.

"And then a third time," he said. "Before we sleep."

"Hah!" she scoffed. "We start here and now." She laid the rifle aside, leaning it against the parapet. She unzipped her jacket and dropped it. She kicked off her boots and dropped her jeans around her ankles. Her wings appeared and she flew to hover in front of him, bouncing between two and three feet off the ground. "Come on, slowpoke. Get a move on, pokey."

He smiled and took his time, enjoying her agitation. When he dropped his pants, kicked them off, and stood up, he was fully erect. Her eyes widened at that, and then her breath caught on the inhale when she realized how beautiful he was.

Then his wings appeared, and he rose into the air so that his phallus was at the level of her mouth. She reached for him, pulled him toward herself, and put her mouth over him.

Freya had instructed her in the basic techniques of phallus worship. She held the head of him against the roof of her mouth, sliding slowly back and forth with each beat of her wings. She touched herself between her legs and came immediately, dripping on the stone floor. The feedback from the orgasm washed up her spine and over the top of her head, focusing on the roof of her mouth. Her mouth flooded with the sweet nectar of her hidden gland, her eyes rolled up in her head and her vision filled with the golden light of the Palace. Her head rolled back as she swallowed, and she settled slowly to the ground, eyes closed, hand still wrapped around his phallus. She smiled as he settled to the floor in front of her. "I begin to understand," she whispered.

"Let me help your understanding," Matthews whispered back, stroking her hair, taking her face in his hands. He kissed her, tasting the remains of the sweetness in her mouth.

She responded, pressing her body to his, feeling suddenly and for the first time in her life, voluptuous.

Still gripping him, she felt his hardness pressed against her belly, and suddenly she wanted him inside her as much as she had ever wanted anything in her life. She pushed herself upward with her wings, putting him against her opening, then she slowly settled herself around him, sliding him into her in fractions of an inch at a time. When he was fully sheathed, she was on her toes. She wrapped her legs around his hips, draped her arms over his shoulders and whispered in his ear, "Fly. Fly with me."

They rose up in the air, holding the first position. They thrusted each other in syncopation, wings moving in alternate beats. Then he shifted, matching her beat. She came again, rocking on him rocking her. Her head went back and she flew to the Palace again, the Palace of a Thousand Lights. She saw the Goddess there, the True Creator, She Who Comes, as a being of golden light, sitting on a throne radiating the light. She began to tremble all over, the tremble of ecstasy. The tremble became a thrashing of her limbs and a twisting jerk of her torso.

She was gone, lost in the ecstasy and he held her as she journeyed, certain that she would return to him if he just held on, held her still ensheathed upon him, held her still, and let the long whole spasm of her ecstasy pass through and settle out. He landed softly, still holding her to him, and waited. In a moment she sighed and lifted her head from his shoulder. He set her on her feet, sliding her off him, holding her steady. She put her hands on his chest, leaned in and kissed his heart. She turned toward her clothes, and realized that she'd left him standing there, still erect.

She pointed at it. "Are you OK?" she asked.

He grinned hugely and nodded. "I'm good. Good until next time. Let's go eat,"

Putting her boots on she couldn't help watching how he struggled to pack his erection away inside his pants. She laughed when he muttered a whispered "Ow" as he zipped up his pants. He looked at her and grinned. "It ain't made to be this way. I had to promise it I'd let it out later."

After they ate in the kitchen of the old nightclub, food kept ready by the Order to accommodate a large number of visitors, they descended a set of hidden steps into the caves below.

After target practice she looked at him, left eye pupil swollen large, like some predator's prey, hiding in the darkness, frozen in the dark. Her right eye pupil contracted to a pin prick, focused on killing, shrunken with blood lust.

Then she told him that is how he will know when she is crazy… when her eyes go wildly different. He is not to trust her then, no matter what she says, and she, for her part, will try not to speak.

They fucked like hawks mating in the sky, clasping hands instead of clawed feet. Their hands become like their claws, their legs like tails. Her legs stretched along his hips like feathers, she grasped him with her phulva as sure and sharp and strong as clawed feet, locked on to him, never to let go, so tight he could not detumesce even if he came.

They fucked like hawks mating in the sky, in free fall, pulling up at the last moment, taking turns at it, and laughing into the wind. And the wind stole their laughter away.

They alternated between who withdraws from whom. They laughed when they screwed up the order of taking turns withdrawing, when she withdrew first twice in a row. She looked at him; she was lying, she apologized but she did it on purpose, to see if he'd catch her in the lie.

And he did! He knew it! She saw it in his face, the repressed scowl, the suppressed cry of foul, and he adapted without speaking a word. For this, this adaptation, this refusal to blast her with his expectations, this exception to the rule, she turned around and offered him herself from behind.

Flying. He gave up on that idea quickly and took her. Took what she offered. But he pushed her down, belly on the sun-warmed stones. She could have resisted, and she knew he would back off, but in that moment, she wanted him.

She wanted him enough to surrender.

He snorted with lust, snorted an animal sound that made her tremble. He growled at her, she growled back, her voice trailing away into a sound that might have been a prelude to a sob.

He stopped.

She said, "I weep for Beauty."

And she started to tremble with orgasm before he was even halfway in.

Overhead the hawks called to each other, circling.

Resting on the parapet, he said, "My mother told me, "Never marry crazy or stupid. I've done both."

"Who did? You did, or she did?"

"She did. I've fucked both, but never married."

"I'm not stupid you know."

"Yes."

"But you know I'm crazy."

"Yes."

"A man would have to be stupid not to know I'm crazy."

"Yes."

"Your affirmations are boring."

"I am being simple on purpose. Neither crazy nor stupid. If you want me to talk, say something conversational."

She laughed and shook her head.

He smiled. "It's OK. We're good."

"So, we're partnered?"

"For the mission."

"She told you?"

"Yes."

"Tell me."

"She told me not to tell you."

"Why, do you think?"

"It's a test. A test to see how crazy you really are. Like, can She trust you with a loaded gun."

"Can She?"

"I'm certain of it."

"Why am I crazy?"

"I don't know. Do you want me to guess?"

"Yes."

"I think you were born this way. I don't think anything happened to you in your life that made you crazy."

"My mother put me in a harness with a leash attached to go with her to the grocery store. So I pretended to be a dog." Then she smiled and glanced at him sideways. "It's how I learned to fuck like a dog. I locked you in. You couldn't have gotten out if you wanted to."

"Unless I came and could detumesce. I didn't want to. I wanted to be inside you."

And then the tears came. "You would have stayed with me until I let you go."

"Yes."

"Why?"

"You are the manifestation of what I worship. You are the manifestation of what I adore."

"You adore crazy women."

"No. I adore you."

"What? Are you crazy, too?"

"Yes. I just have better self-regulation."

"What?"

"Yes."

"Show me."

"All along I have been showing you. She showed me, and I am following Her indications."

"You see Her?"

He went silent and looked away. Then he looked down at the stone floor. Then he looked up. He gazed upward for a long moment then looked away again. He spread his wings and took off straight up. "We talk too much. Especially when we could be fucking."

He flew high enough that his wings caught the light of the setting sun. She saw him cross his arms over his chest. She saw his wings disappear. He plummeted out of the sky, dropping past her with his eyes closed and his face serene.

In shock she sat frozen for a moment. Then she leapt for the parapet, hands braced on the top for what she might see, and leaned over.

And there was nothing to be seen. He was gone. He had disappeared.

In an internal shock wave, the loss hit her. It hit her in the gut so hard she heaved, almost vomiting lunch.

Then she heard a voice behind her. "Partners for this mission."

She nodded, turning to him. "Partners for this mission." She gazed at his face. When he looked up She Who Comes looked back at him through her. She said, "It was not just her test."

He bowed his head, then thought better of it. He got on his knees, put his head on the stone floor, and stayed there until he felt the gentle whoosh of Her departure.

Venge sobbed again, and said, "I weep for Beauty."

27

STONEHAVEN

Madeleine and Diana rose early to perform their Devotions, Prayers, Blessings, Meditations, and Illuminations. They alternated taking the lead in the Morning Exercises for those living on the land. Sometimes they would divide the group into one at the Mansion and the other down at the converted Barn. Diana would coordinate the ritual sacred dance performances. Evening lectures were focused on the Four Principles of The Order.

> 1) The Truth: science, corresponding to the Spirit, and Mind.
>
> 2) Ecstasy: The Tantras, corresponding to the Soma, Sensation
>
> 3) Development of Conscience: Feelings, especially Higher Feelings, corresponding to the Soul, and The Objective Need to seek the Proper Way of Being, and hence knowing right from wrong for ourselves and each other.
>
> 4) The Mysterious: the Whole, because science cannot know everything. Humans in Pursuit of the Proper Way of Being use this principle to find their way when faced with not knowing.

With Calley gone and Alam returned to the Hidden Lands, the position of High Priestess had been assigned to Diana. Since she needed to spend more time at home with her children and husband, she was gone for either one or two weeks in any given month. She assigned all the management to other Priestesses and Consorts, but held the position, and took Craft to be the High Consort. In order to keep balance a Priestess had been assigned to her family as an au pair, taking her husband as a Consort in her absence. Of course, the sex when she was home was spectacular.

Wade's half-Naiad child, a boy, turned into a blessing for the folks at Stonehaven. He was a happy child, always drawing a smile from those whose duty it was to make sure his human half had enough food to eat. The mother was given permission to roam further in the watershed, understanding that her primary focus was to serve as a scout for any interlopers and trespassers. She could not leave the water for very long, only minutes, so she was grateful to have something to do. Wade's son, also named Wade for obvious reasons, could spend several hours a day away from water, and it was hoped that he could eventually spend an entire day, only making sure that he bathed at night.

Reports began to appear in the news that temples, churches, and mosques were collapsing all over the country, their foundations giving way, and no one could understand it other than calling each event a highly localized earthquake. Sometimes the shaking would appear on seismometers but only as a low amplitude high frequency signal. Diana, who knew that this was the work of the Stonewen, was delighted with each report.

It wasn't long before the press realized that the only houses of worship being targeted were the house of worship of De Murgos. Speculation was rife that it was the work of demons, but Diana knew that there were no Dangla involved. There were also reports of Embla sightings near the destruction. For Diana, that meant that De Murgos was being kept informed, and she was glad that there was no known connection between Stonehaven and the Stonewen.

De Murgos sat on a tree branch of an old chestnut tree, neither knowing nor caring what he sat upon. His gaze was securely fixed upon the verandas of the Mansion, and the people sitting out on them. Fed by the wailing of his worshippers at the destruction of their houses of worship his fever had broken. His last dream was of a great queen, a dark queen, riding a beast. It was she he was intent on finding. He knew that the team he'd formed of the Dangla and Embla had been here in their preliminary searches for what De Murgos now realized was the same being as the dark queen in his dream. He recalled what he believed was a visit from her when he was lost in fever. She had proven impossible for him to catch, which he blamed on his weakened state. The Dangla and the Embla had disappeared, and he could imagine no one having the power to destroy them or hold them against their will. But, then again, he couldn't have imagined anyone being able to cut off the Slayer's arm. He closed his eyes and dreamed again of the harlot on the beast. She turned to him and smiled. She spoke and said, "It will not be the way you think it will be. Get off the rock. Get off me."

He was so astonished he fell out of the tree, landing hard, not laughing at himself, his mind filled with one word, and one word only: "Beauty". His next thought was, "Someone pushed me," but looking around—there was no one there.

But one of the men sitting on the veranda had seen His Whiteness falling. He called Security immediately. Armed men and wen rushed quickly toward the grove of trees. De Murgos was so lost in his enchantment he did not hear them coming. They saw that he was naked and appeared unarmed. He came to a crouch, putting his hands over his face. "Do not look upon my face," he muttered, and leaped straight up. He shot up like an arrow, flames bursting from his joints, until he disappeared into the blue.

"What was that?" someone asked.

"That was De Murgos," Craft replied.

On his way up De Murgos remembered something he'd long forgotten. Decades earlier a mortal had tricked him into having his face looked upon. He remembered his embarrassment at being tricked and saw how his not wanting to look at it had made him forget. He resolved to enact the second part of the Prophecy. "Those who look upon the face of god must die."

But before he could kill the trickerous and deceptionary human, he had to find him.

28

Regina's Assignment

Regina found Ketrak meditating in a large almost empty room in the middle of his castle, hidden like the Hidden Lands, high in the Himalayas. The room was spare in its furnishings, a few pillows with his weapons hanging on the wall and standing in a corner. The heat he generated was enough to keep the room warm. He sat nude and Regina dressed traditionally, except in the way she pulled her hair up. She was excited by the assignment, and loved being in her ghost body, while her physical body was safe on Wallid. Her ghost body was full and luscious, and appeared as she had when she was 20, but her mind retained the wisdom of her 80 plus years.

She stood before him, smiling voluptuously, in the spot where the gaze of his almost closed eyes was focused. As she watched, his enormous phallus came erect. He himself was enormous, almost 30 meters tall. Regina resisted the urge to climb up into his lap and embrace his mighty tool, wrap her arms and legs around it. The image made her smile more broadly, more hungrily. She thought to herself, "Is that a pickle in your pocket or are you happy to see me?" She laughed out loud with joy.

He exhaled through his nose, sounding almost like a sigh. The smell of this one alone had given him the erection. He opened his eyes halfway. "What brings you here?"

"I am a Servant of the Mother behind your Mother. She told me to go find you in the palace of your Mother, before She became your Mother. This is Umanna's house."

"Are you dreaming?"

"I am not in my dream body. I am awake and in my ghost body."

"Why are you assigned to me?"

"Because the Mind of All Life on the Planet is in need of a God of War. You are the last one left, the rest are ghosts themselves.

"So, this is my time, then, yes?"

"Yes."

"Who am I at war with?"

"The interloper known as De Murgos."

He grinned hugely. "An honor then."

"Yes." She paused. "You know you may die?"

"I have fought his people before. Two of his peoples, in fact. I am still alive. My people and my land are still alive. Still alive with those She put here, our kind and mortals."

"Songs will be sung about you."

"You want me? Even my terror?"

"Show me your terror."

He stood up. Massive, giant, bloody, hung with entrails, bodies clutched in his hands, gore dripping from his lips, laughing the berserker laugh. He stomped on Regina's ghost. It had no effect. She appeared there, her body above his foot. She shot up to him, to look him in the eye.

"I remain unterrified."

Instantly sane, he laughed, and smiled at her, flashing his teeth. He diminished in size, till only a head taller than her. "So how good are you?"

"You are a god. You tell me," she said, reaching for his phallus.

Electricity leaped into her hand. The shock of it drove her momentarily back into her body, sitting in her meditation room on Wallid.

She returned to Him and he asked her, "Where did you go?"

"Things are very different for me, as I am in Time and you are not. You cannot die, well, actually you can, but time alone cannot kill you as it does us mortals. Being in time gives me the opportunity to confront my death, time to struggle with my fear of death, and doing that makes me fearless. I am fearless to be here with you.

"I look as I do because both my dream body and my ghost body are malleable. I can choose to look how I want. I chose my form from when I was 20."

As he watched she changed her skin tone to a darker hue, matching his. She looked up at him from under her eyebrows, and he uttered a short, gasping inhale. "You are the most beautiful woman I have ever seen."

"Love me" she said. "I shall become more beautiful yet." And she moved closer, put her arms over his shoulders and turned her face up toward his. "More beautiful than this," she breathed up into his face, breath laden with frankincense and cinnamon.

"I must have you, mortal or not."

"I know. And so you shall." She snapped her fingers and said "Kneel. Kneel and worship."

And he did.

Hours later, nuzzling her neck, Ketrak asked Moon Halter, "Why cannot things stay like this?"

She sighed and answered. "Change is present always, not so True for Life and Death. But when these are present, they, too, are subject to Change. Change happens quickly for us, not so much for you. So, when the Mortal and the Immortal are together Change happens at the Immortal pace, but only for a while."

29

THE ANTECEDENCE OF THE FEMININE

She Who Comes loved the union-mind state with Darvatiye. Resting within Her, feeling the growth of the child She had conceived of Quinn-Skreeva, happy with Her choice to let the babe be fostered in Mother Darvatiye, She Who Comes felt as happy as She had ever felt. There She could find Her way easily to that place within, where all the words stopped.

So She was surprised one night when She heard the voice of Her Mother, Sola, calling lightly to Her. She opened Her mind to the golden light of Her Mother, and bathed in the Love that came with that light. "I come with good news. When the enemy first imposed himself on you, you came to me for help. As you know, I sent the plea along to The First One, The One Who Made Us All, asking Her to help you. I know you to be long-suffering, and Her reply has taken millennia of your time to reach me, but your help has arrived. It is a weapon. The final battle will be soon, and I will be with you. I will deploy the weapon when the moment is right and you shall be its channel. You need only protect your eyes. I love you, child. I will be with you. Now rest."

She Who Comes rested. She rested in the hope for the future, even the far future, when Her Fate, as yet Indeterminate, might take Her into the realm of becoming a star Herself.

Darvatiye hummed to Herself. She felt good. She felt good being pregnant with the new god-child. She was looking forward to returning home to the mountain, where she was known to the Land as Umanna.

She felt good about Her assignment to the new Skreeva, the mortal who had been known as Quinn. He knew how to carry himself as a god, and had the requisite humility around Her. His ability to know when to defer to Her wishes was more highly developed than any assignment She had taken on before. The voice of Salakta, whom she knew as She Who Comes, spoke to Her, saying "His knowledge of his own mortality bids him to know how to behave."

She loved She Who Comes all the more for allowing Her to be the Creator's surrogate, even knowing that the pregnancy would take a few months longer than a human one.

Darvatiye smiled and the song in Her head rose to a crescendo that moved Her to journey to Her mate. She found him holding an audience simultaneously at several of the dozens of temples dedicated to him. He had decided that the best way to change men was to appear to them, an uncommon behavior. The old Skreeva had mostly turned up in the temples to feed upon worship and desperate prayers. She stood behind him, Her hands on his shoulders. He smiled at Her presence and began to speak.

After repeating the biological evidence that the Creator is Feminine, focusing particularly on the parthenogenic capabilities of sharks, snakes, and condors, and pointing out that nothing Masculine was capable of that kind of manifestation, he said, "Put the feminine first in your life, first in both principle and practice. If you put the feminine first, your life will get much better. Do not walk in front of her, unless there is danger ahead. Do not walk behind her unless there is danger behind. Walk beside her and put her first in life. Equals you are, but for this one thing. The Feminine came first. This is the Truth, and if you act in accordance with the Truth your life will become both Good, and Beautiful."

Darvatiye was so pleased She dropped Her invisibility. When the men let Skreeva's Truth into their hearts they could suddenly see Her. They could suddenly see Her, standing behind Quinn, putting him in front of Her, putting him before Her. Their hearts melted with understanding of what they could foresee happening in their own lives.

So they began to put the Feminine before themselves, put the

Feminine antecedent to the Masculine in their consideration and in their daily lives, living into what Quinn promised them would happen. Skreeva smiled upon them and told them to tell the people.

As Darvatiye's belly swelled, so did Her need for sex. The child within her was too young to pay attention to what was going on in the outside world, but She had a plan to bring his awareness into the fields of Ecstasy when he was ready. She knew it was the surest way to bring him into the world as a happy child.

Before and after an appearance at a Temple, they would embrace and engage in feeding each other. They would sit in the first position, gently rocking, taking turns leading the motion. They took turns journeying to the Pool of Awareness, the Pool of Undifferentiated Sentience, bringing back that Sentience into themselves, increasing their awareness of the world, and of each other.

When She was ready, She would stand up and feed Quinn-Skreeva directly, raining into his mouth, all over his face, down his chest, soaking his phallus, growling and shouting, then She'd settle herself on him again. He would use his tongue against the roof of his mouth to trigger the gland to express itself, mixing the sweetness of the Ambrosia with the salt of the rain, and swallow, drenched in Sentience and Ecstasy.

And when She was ready, he would stand up and feed Her, the head of his phallus planted on the roof of Her mouth, Her tongue stroking it from below and he would release when he felt Her mouth flooding with the Ambrosia, eyes rolled back in Her head. Sometimes She would hold him there, refusing to allow him to back away, or to detumesce, and he would sit, and they would return to the first position, She sighing with pleasure.

After one such extended session, a four-for as Quinn-Skreeva called it, he lay back and asked Her, "How big did you have to become to give birth to a full-grown elephant?" referring to Her son Ganshee. Her answer was to grow to that size standing over him, towering into the sky. He laughed joyfully at her and said, "I could just walk right in."

30

Emmalia's Defense

The bikes pulled up over the rim and stopped, the wards working just as she'd hoped. She emerged from behind the cabin carrying an armload of kindling, smiled and waved at them with her free hand. She set down the kindling by the door and walked over to them, still smiling. She raised her voice a little and told them, in French, to turn off the ignition. She watched the surprise in their faces. The men took off their helmets and gloves and looked at each other.

She stepped forward, introduced herself, and shook their hands, one at a time, pausing, holding their hands until they told her their names.

She asked them, "What brings you all this way?"

Dominic replied, coolly, "We wanted to see where you lived."

"True enough," she thought to herself.

Evrard added, "We've never been up here before."

Emmalia smiled, reached out and touched both their hands gently, planting energetic seeds of protection and cooperation, and said, "Would you like to come in? I have some coffee, and some wine, if you'd like."

Both men nodded. She turned and walked toward the door. The men looked at each other. Dominic stuck his tongue out and waggled it around. Evrard put two fingers up to his face and stuck his tongue out between them.

Emmalia could feel the surge in machismo energy behind her. Stopping at the door she looked back over her shoulder at the men. "Could you guys bring that kindling in with you?"

She smiled when they each picked up half of the arm load and brought it in. She smiled at them again, happy that she now knew she could expect compliance from both of them. She said, "I'm just about to have some supper. Would you like some?"

Both men's stomachs rumbled. "It smells very good," said one. "Delicious," said the other. "Yes, please."

She'd laid out three bowls, knowing they'd eat. She'd eaten barely half of hers before they asked for seconds. Smiling, she got up and served them another bowl. She could feel them relax into their machismo, being gratified by being served. Emmalia thought to herself, "Who is serving whom?"

She thought of She Who Comes, and a shiver ran through her. Her vision seemed to darken a shade. She moved around the kitchen, turning on the lanterns on the wall. Then she offered them wine again, and they started drinking. In not too long a time she brought out a bottle of brandy and she passed it around, everyone taking a turn pulling on the bottle.

She built a fire in the fireplace and began the seduction by offering to massage Dominic's shoulders. He shrugged off his jacket, and as she worked his shoulders she sighed, and turned on her own inner heater. She kissed him on top of his head, and commented on how warm it was. Evrard was looking at her pathetically, so she laughed, went over to him, lifted his face and kissed him on the mouth. She looked back at Dominic, he was leering at her backside, so near his face he could smell her when she leaned over to kiss Evrard. She said, "It's warm in here, and I think I have too many clothes on. Her shirt had a snap front, and she ripped it open and dropped it off her shoulders. She stood there, lifting and massaging her breasts, sighing, and she said, "There. Now that's better." Then she looked at the men and said, "One for each of you. Come here.

Both men came up to her, leaned down, and licked her. She held their heads to her, and they sighed. She knew in that moment she had them. Holding their faces to her breasts she kicked off her boots. She said, "You both have too many clothes on." When they stopped after taking off their shirts she said, "Keep going." She dropped her jeans and stepped out of them naked. When they stopped, leaving their underwear on she said, "All the way. I want to see." They did as they were told. She reached for their phalli and they stepped forward. She dropped to her knees and fellated them both, first alternating then both at once. She rubbed their phalli together, looking for the one that resisted. Evrard tightened up and suppressed an urge to pull away. "Fine," she thought. "I'll use Dominic."

She stood up and pulled them along by their phalli over to the edge of the bed. She sat Evrard down, pushed him back and climbed up on his lap, facing away, putting her feet on his thighs, inserting him in her. She pulled Dominic close and put the head of him up against her opening, sliding it along Evrard's phallus below. She felt herself begin to stretch as she tilted her hips up to Dominic, forcing him inside her with her hand. She got him all the way in and growled. "Move," she told them.

They did, and in only a few strokes she rained, laughing as the contraction forced Dominic out of her with a plop, soaking his belly, making him laugh with her. She reached for him, and put him back in, barely working at it this time, he taking over the insertion. "Move," she commanded them again. This time they kept moving until she felt the wave pressure build up inside and the orgasm descended from deep within, the contractions releasing an energetic wavefront that squeezed the men within her so tightly they couldn't move and they groaned with pleasure as the wave rolled over them both.

She squeezed Dominic out and rotated on Evrard, got on her knees and lifted her back side to Dominic, spreading herself with her hands. She felt him blundering against her perineum until he found the right place, and she opened herself to allow him in. He entered her with a slow steady stroke. She came, she ass-gasmed, almost immediately, raining all around Evrard, soaking him. "Hold still," she told them and she rocked back and forth, sliding on both at the same time, until she orgasmed again. She collapsed forward on Evrard, and told them both, "Move again now. Stroke me." She ass-gasmed again, raining again, and she pushed Dominic out, slid off Evrard and got on her knees between his legs.

She looked at both of them. Their eyes were half closed, their breathing slow and steady, and she knew the drugs were coursing through them, leaving them totally at her mercy and suggestion. She pulled Dominic down on his knees beside her and grabbed a handful of hair and drew his face in close as she fellated Evrard, who closed his eyes and trembled in ecstasy. She took the phallus out of her mouth and pulled Dominic's face toward her, toward it. She held it up for him with her other hand and brought his face to the other man's phallus. She thrilled when he took it in his mouth. With that hand full of hair she moved his head up and down on it. The thrill of watching it brought her to orgasm again, raining on the floor between her knees. She passed it back and forth between them until she was sure that his enthusiasm for a phallus in his mouth approached her own enthusiasm for the same thing. She grinned triumphantly. Evrard groaned with his eyes closed, but she was sure that she'd seen him looking at them with barely open eyes. Her grin broadened. Dominic kept working it on his own.

She decided she'd stop short of hypnotizing them into one of them being penetrated. She used her mastery of oral technique to induce an orgasm first in Evrard, finishing him, using the alchemy to change the substance of him into a substance useful to her, her mouth flooding with secretions from the hidden gland at the back of her throat. Evrard fell into a deep sleep. She kept a hand on Dominic, inducing a shivering orgasm in him when his buddy came, feeling his friend's ecstasy through Emmalia's hand. She stood Dominic up and finished him quickly in the same way. The drugs kicked in fully then, and he sank to his knees, fell to his side up against the bed and he, too, fell asleep.

Emmalia stood up, finished the alchemical processing and swallowed, feeding herself with their essences. She raised her face to the sky and raised her arms in triumph.

She had bested the enemy and diverted what she was certain would have been an attack upon her.

She sat at the table for an hour, sipping brandy, watching them sleep. When they stirred, she knew it was time to move them outside. She got a blanket for each of them from under the bed. She hung one over Dominic's shoulders, used her hypnotic voice to get him to stand up with her help, and led him outside, helping him to lay down. She went back inside and did the same thing with Evrard, laying him down in a heap beside his friend. She went back in and threw their clothes outside near their feet.

Finally, done with her night, filled with triumph, she padded on naked feet through the rising moonlight, deadbolted the door and fell asleep in her own bed, grinning and sighing, and trembling with one last orgasm.

In the morning, in an undeserved act of mercy, she took coffee out to them and set it on the ground. She imbued the liquid with the Spell of Forgetting.

She stood there, wrapped in a sarong and shawl, and called to them by name. They both sat up groggily, holding their heads. She stood there, magnificent, sipping her coffee while they fumbled for theirs. When she was sure they were both awake enough to hear her, she used the Voice of Command and said, "You guys can come back up here anytime, but you have to come here together." She went back in the house and closed the door.

In ten minutes, she heard their bikes start up and slowly motor down the hill. She went outside, picked up the coffee cups and stood there, for a long time—listening, she, and She Who Comes, listening, remembering, for She Who Comes had been with her the entire time, watching, guarding, suggesting, guiding, and enjoying the ecstasy with every breath, the entire time since she'd first thought of Her earlier in the day.

The men had never noticed that Emmalia's eyes were not her own.

31

KERKYRA

Angelica entered Regina's meditation room on bare feet, scarcely making a whisper of sound. She sat on her heels beside Regina and looked over at her. Regina's eyes were gone completely to white, her breathing slow and even. Angelica heard a sweet voice in her inner ears, saying, "Her ghost is away on assignment. I will summon her back for you."

Regina sighed suddenly and turned to Angelica. Her eyes had gone completely black with the presence of the Goddess in her. She blinked once, slowly, and her eyes returned to normal.

"Child," she said, "Is it time for you to leave?"

"Yes, Teacher. We are both packed, and soon the taxi will be here to take us to the airport. Onadaya called it for us."

Regina nodded slowly, her ghost re-integrating. Suddenly she leapt toward Angelica, her face changing to someone unrecognizable. She pushed Angelica over on her back, pinning her down with her hands and knees. She laughed then, and said, "No, you cannot follow me here. I will return to you when I am able." She sat back and let Angelica up. "Sorry about that. I was busy with someone. He was very interesting and very skilled. But sometimes impetuous and aggressive," she said, tilting her head to the side as if listening to someone. Or something.

"I can see that," Angelica said. "I hope, at least, that you were having some fun."

Regina smiled broadly and nodded.

"I was hoping that you could tell me more about where Meck and I are going."

"Well, as you know, it is an island in the central Mediterranean called Kerkyra, and it's a part of Greece. It's not too small, nor too large, but it has some features that make it ideal for us, for the Order. There's an airport that can handle commercial jet planes, but there are no gates, per se, just roll up staircases. As usual, various members of the Order own property there, and our usual array of real estate holding companies put us into the rental business for tourists. One of our outfits on the island is a nonprofit oceanography research company. There is a cave with an underwater entrance, and we have a small submarine, big enough for about eighteen people, that we use to study the bottom and the marine life. There is also a dragon."

"Whaat?" Angelica asked, raising her eyebrows.

"Yes. Almost three thousand years ago, when these dragons here were turned to stone in order to protect them, there was a dragon there that was also turned to stone for the same reason. And it lays there now, a small island just off the coast in shallow water, waiting for its resurrection. The High Council of the Order is curious to see if you can establish contact with it, maybe even wake it up. We could use it in the next battle. Our belief is that this next fight will be directly with De Murgos and his forces. We believe that he has slowly woken up to us and he will seek to rub us out."

"And the High Priestess?"

"Yes, her name is Byuteo. She is old, and wise, and cynical. I am told she has acquired enough life force that she can fly, like the legendary masters of old."

"How old is she?"

"Older than me by at least a decade. I am also told that she spends most of her time in her ghost body these days, so she can look any age she wants. If you can, you should ask for her blessing immediately upon first meeting her. Go to one knee, hold your hands out in the beseeching mudra and bow your head. Her very touch is an initiation into her world. Do not be impatient, hold the pose for as long as it takes. If she grants it, you will become as a flame in the twilight of the ghost world."

Regina closed her eyes and hummed softly. "She sees you. Already she is smiling."

Meck called from the courtyard, "The taxi is here, Angelica. Time to go."

When Angelica came out followed by Regina, everyone was there, lined up and smiling, giving her hugs. Onadaya whispered in her ear, "Come back. I will be here."

Kerkyra was on the other side of the planet from Wallid. The trip would take more than thirty hours, factoring in the waits for connecting flights. For the overnight stretch they had reserved business class seats, so they could lay down. But for the first and last legs, they booked 'plus' seats with extra leg room. Shortly after take-off on the last leg, Angelica napped. She leaned her head on Meck's shoulder. It was the first time she'd touched him since the assignment began. He smiled at the thought of the possibility that he might no longer be sleeping on the floor, across her threshold. He inhaled the air over her head deeply, drinking her in, untangling the notes of her scent until he found the scent from her center. He found it delicious, dream-worthy, and with that he also fell asleep.

They arrived on Kerkyra and made it easily through customs. Luggage in tow, they stepped out on the sidewalk and saw a man holding a sign that read 'Angelica Mecklenburg' smiling broadly at them. "What do you think?" Mech nudged her. "Is the sign a sign?" She smiled at him, also a first. She went up on her tiptoes and kissed him on the cheek.

"Could be," she whispered, and kissed him on the cheek again.

That evening Angelica relented the rigidity of her grief. She and Meck sat in the first position for over an hour, belly to belly, Angelica rocking on his phallus. When they leaned in toward each other and they sat heart to heart, Angelica began weeping. When her heart hurt as much as she could stand, she leaned back away from Meck and wept hard. When the moment passed, she leaned in again, and reconnected their hearts. When the grief rose up again, she leaned back again, titrating her grief, but staying connected at their roots. When she could breathe without sobbing, she settled into him completely, arms draped over his shoulders, sighing into his neck.

Slowly she started rocking on him again, and he rocked too in complementary rhythm. With her grief cleared a little bit, she felt a pulse of anger arise within and she suddenly bared her teeth and growled. In her fierceness their bellies slapped together. She came, also fiercely, raining around his sheathed phallus. She sobbed against him again, but this time, instead of grief, it was a sob of laughter. "I broke it," she said, fiercely whispering. "I broke the spell."

Then she stood up, bucking her hips against his face, feeding him the sacred rain heavy with salts. Then she slid down on him again, smashing herself against his wet chest, and whispered again, whispered fiercely, "Feed me." She rode him like he was a cantering horse. "Gallop for me." He raised his hips up for her, held steady, his small motions like a horse's hooves hitting the ground, waves of impact feeding into her with just the slightest motion. She came one more time, her entire body shaking, then she went limp in his arms. He stood up and turned around, lowering her slowly to the bed. She rolled to her side, pulling her legs up as he covered her with the sheet. He reached under and held her hand as she traveled, as she journeyed.

He put himself in the correct state of mind to track her. As he expected, she had found Corey. They were holding hands, facing the ocean on a moonlit beach. They were talking, and he stayed far enough back so that he couldn't hear their words. Then they were smiling, then they kissed. He could feel Corey's hunger to be alive again, and his resignation to the reality that he couldn't come back. Angelica turned away from the ocean, dropping his hand and making for the trail. Corey turned to watch her and he saw Meck standing there. His eyes widened with a little surprise then something shifted in him. He smiled at Meck, nodding his head. Then he disappeared, simply vanished.

Angelica stirred and withdrew her hand. Sighing she sat up and said, simply, "Water." He passed her a bottle from the nightstand.

Later, spooning with him as they slid toward sleep, he asked her, "What changed?"

She spoke slowly. "When I fell asleep with my head on your

shoulder, I had a dream. In it we were standing somewhere naked, I think the edge of a cliff. I could hear waves far below. You held your hands over my head and summoned my crown, green flames circling a red central flame. You said, 'Remember the Red." I woke up aroused, seeing everything through a red filter. I realized that you were reminding me of my sexuality. You were summoning me back to what I am, a sexual being. I realized that if you could summon my crown, if you could summon me back to myself, that I should let you. That's what changed.

"I'm sorry that it took so long. And I want you to know that I appreciate all those nights you slept across my threshold. I tried to sneak over you a couple times, but I couldn't do it. You must be a really light sleeper."

"I wasn't asleep. I was resting, but I was practicing extended awareness exercises. It's why you couldn't get past me. I could sense you moving well before you got close. When you're close I can smell you, hear you breathe. I can see shadows of you in the darkness made by the stars. I wasn't asleep, I have a duty to you. I believe it can be fulfilled impeccably. I intend to do so."

She reached around behind herself and patted his shoulder. She sighed and relaxed more deeply into him. Her last words before she let go into sleep: "I am a sexual being. And I am over and against death."

In the morning they had coffee on the small balcony outside their hotel room in sarongs and shawls. Angelica felt shy, and Meck couldn't stop smiling at her. Finally, she said, "Knock it off."

He could only grin more broadly. "We're supposed to meet Byuteo today. They'll send a taxi. It will pick us up at 11 and take us to her. The idea is to have lunch together. Do you want to get dressed and go out to get some breakfast? Or do you want to fuck?"

"Let's do both. Fuck and feed. Then feed and fuck."

Dressed, finally, they got in the back seat of the car sent for them, without breakfast. They arrived at the Institute for Mediterranean Marine Ecology and were ushered into an office. A very old wen, very much not in her ghost body, sat back in an armchair, dressed in a floor length silk robe, waved at them briefly, and went back to staring at her laptop screen, sitting on a high end table near her hand.

Angelica took a few steps toward her then went to her knee as Regina had instructed. Meck followed suit. Angelica, in a steady voice, said, "Bless me High Priestess, I beseech you."

Byuteo looked long at her, gazing at her. She felt her crown activate under the gaze, and heard an old dry voice say, "Dragon Wen." She uttered no sound as she stood, but Angelica could later swear she heard the elder's joints creak as she stood. With a steady, firm step she went first to Angelica, laid her hands on Angelica's upraised palms, and Angelica shivered, first at the cold, then at the heat. Then the pulse of the Higher Heart manifested in their hands. The Elder hmphed, the Priestess gasped. The Elder removed her hands, stepped over to Meck and did the same thing. The Elder leaned in and whispered something in his ear that made him smile. She turned, walked back to her chair, and said "Sit," over her shoulder. They both sat on their heels on the stone floor at her feet.

She said, "Everyone from the Order who comes here must go to the Temple of Her on their first day here. The driver will take you. Prepare yourselves and open to the vision that awaits you there. Return by supper time and we will dine together."

Angelica's almost empty stomach groaned in response. The Elder laughed out loud at that and dismissed them with a wave of her hand.

The driver pulled over at the side of the road at a bent and open gate, strung with bent hog wire fencing which Angelica could only assume was meant to keep the goats in. The goats were long gone, judging by the age of the dried goat manure they stepped into out of the car. The driver indicated a series of steps made of old pediments and capstones from marble columns. They walked up, feet raising puffs of dust. They found themselves standing on a stone platform, about eighty by fifty, covered in a handspan of dirt, with tall dry grasses weaving in the sudden light breeze. They knew it was the floor of the ancient Temple.

They immediately felt the weight of almost three thousand years of age, but the weight was rising up under their feet, not pressing them down. They knew the world they saw was about to be inverted. As they walked to the eastern edge of the platform, the old floor of the

Temple, they came to understand that it was not space that would shift, but time.

Suddenly it was sunrise, and the Temple was tall and whole around them. The edge turned out to be a series of broad steps going down to an old road, and on the steps, they saw a vision of Priestesses dancing to a quiet drum and cymbal rattles, all wearing flowing white, turning, summoning, beseeching, the morning sun to rise. They were stilled and stunned by the beauty of the Vision.

They stood still, breathing quietly after an initial gasp, waiting until the breeze dried the dripping sweat running down their spines.

They heard the voice of their driver shout the word "Time!" Mech looked at his watch.

"Three hours have passed," he said.

"How can that be?" Angelica asked. "They've only just finished the sunrise?"

"I think time moves slower here."

"Oh."

"What did you see?"

"I saw the Priestesses of Her dancing on the steps, summoning the sunrise."

"As did I. Exactly that."

Later, near the end of the drive back to the other side of the island, she reached over and took his hand. She leaned in toward him and said in a low voice, "What did she say to you that made you smile?"

"She said, 'You smell like her, and not like yourself. This is a good thing.'"

Angelica grinned, leaned into him, and sniffed. She sneezed at the snootful of dust.

32

Stonehaven Talk on the Truth

"What we begin with, where we begin, is with the importance of the Truth. And what is True is what is Knowable, and when you Know something, rather than simply believe it, that Truth becomes a part of you, you become more True, and you become more of a Truth.

"Knowing a lie for what it is, not being seduced into believing a lie, is a critical skill that we develop. It is called Discernment. Discernment is the ability to tell Truth from falsehood, and to tell falsehood from Truth.

"Discernment is also the ability to know when to tell the Truth and when to Lie. Many people lie all the time, to themselves and others, about all kinds of things. We only Lie when it is necessary to protect the Good. In this way, if we are Good, we may lie without hesitancy, and without fear of guilt. No one is owed the Truth simply because they demand it, not even if they expect it.

"The Truth belongs only to those who are capable of Discernment and Understanding. But even if you are not capable of Understanding, believing in the Truth is better than believing in a Lie, particularly in the Big Lie.

"What do I mean by 'better'? I mean more Good, more Beautiful, and more True.

"What is the Big Lie? That the Masculine came first.

"That is one of the reasons the Truth is so important to the Order. The Order represents the Truth that the Feminine came first. The Masculine is a derivative experiment being conducted by Nature and Life, authored by the True Creator, as She is known to us, She Who Comes. In my opinion, the experiment is at risk of failing, primarily because of the Big Lie.

"Even if a Truth is easy to Understand, it may be difficult for everyday people to understand because they already believe they understand something, something untrue. Stubborn creatures that we are, many would rather cling to the Lie they believe, than risk the discomfort caused by letting go of the Lie and believing in the Truth. And this is particularly true for the Antecedence of the Feminine. This Truth makes many people very uncomfortable because it threatens their world view, the basic tenets of how they order their lives, whom and what they serve, and whom they don't.

"And then we come to the problem of myth, the stories that everyday people believe in that they use to organize their lives.

"We are born open to imprint, more open and vulnerable than any other species, and we imprint on what our parents and our culture believes, and our conformity is guaranteed by our fear of ostracism, exclusion, and banishment. This is fear of rejection, and to a child especially, this invokes the fear of abandonment and death.

"We are born so open to imprint because of our big brains, which are a part of the experiment of human life on this planet. We can't stay in the womb any longer, or our heads won't fit through the birth canal. Elephants, in whom gestation can take two years, have lots of time to develop their brains. They arrive able to walk, with their instincts—their original instructions—intact and ready to go. We are born helpless, unable to walk, with only the most minimum set of instructions.

"And onto that blank slate, onto the open-to-imprint brain, the parents and the culture write the most incredible falsehoods, all based on their false beliefs. The myths of the culture gets written in, instead of the Truth. And the child is threatened with all kinds of terrifying and horrible punishments if they dare to question the Belief, dare to challenge the falsehoods of their myths.

"Here, we are allowed both to believe what we want, and to Know the Truth. Out there, we have to be careful not to trigger those with the emotional disease known as Fundamentalism. If provoked, they might kill you; even unprovoked they can pose a threat to the freedoms of others.

"And understand this: it is not because they are afraid of you, it is not aggression against you. It is self-defense. For many humans, questioning their core mythology feels threatening to them at the level of their mortality, your questioning is a mortal threat and they feel it is their right to rub you out.

"And here is the Truth you must understand. Science and the fossil record shows us that Life existed for hundreds of millions of years without sexual reproduction. It is called in the vernacular of biology 'mother-daughter' reproduction. Sexual reproduction evolved later with the appearance of the Masculine as distinct from the Feminine. But there are species as highly evolved as sharks, and snakes and condors that can reproduce parthenogenetically, usually giving birth to genetically identical daughters. No Masculine can do that. The Feminine is Antecedent and the Masculine Consequent."

The audience responded, "The Feminine is Antecedent and the Masculine is Consequent"

Diana continued, "Moreover, embryologically speaking, in the womb we all develop Feminine genitalia first, the Masculine only develop later.

"The Feminine is Antecedent and the Masculine is Derivative."

They responded again, "The Feminine is Antecedent and the Masculine is Derivative."

"Finally, the Feminine is antecedent in Time. Every wen is born with all the eggs she will ever have. The egg that became you was made by your grandmother when your mother's body developed in your grandmother's womb. The sperm that became you was perhaps 24 hours old.

She paused, taking a sip of water.

Then she continued: "Understand the purpose of The Truth within you. The Truth is food for your third brain, the brain of your mind, the brain of your Spirit. You cannot spend your life eating lies and remain uncorrupted. Only the Truth is fit food for you, especially if you are working on the Alchemy in the Tantra. Any belief you may hold will corrupt you, if it is false. And you don't want to include a corruption in your crystallization. It will destroy you, and all your efforts. It is better to abandon all your beliefs, 'o ye who enter here'. Seek only knowledge, not validation, not security, not comfort. The moment you abandon your beliefs, you will begin to find True Validation, True Security and True Comfort.

"This is what I have to say. May She Who Comes bless you all."

Diana fell into a meditation. Nobody moved. After some moments she opened her eyes and said, "Are there any questions?"

"Yes," asked a young man, a Consort in Training, scheduled for his Initiation. "What is the Truth about the Kundalini Buffer?"

Diana smiled broadly. "Why do you ask, Jackson?"

"Because I'm afraid of it. I'm afraid of the Release. I'm afraid I will lose my mind."

Diana nodded her head, still smiling. "You speak the Truth. Thank you!"

She paused and looked up thoughtfully, waiting for the words of her answer to form, seeking guidance as to the answer. Then she started, smiling, "The Truth is, that we don't know for sure. We have a lot of experience helping people overcome the Buffer, the so-called Release, but we remain uncertain about how it forms, and why it forms.

"But we have a working hypothesis that seems close enough to the Truth to be useful. We believe it forms in childhood, as parents and the culture imprint their beliefs on the young brain. We believe it is part of a defense mechanism for the child. If the child should come to see the Truth, that might be counter to its familiar, tribal, or cultural mythology, it would put their life at risk, so the buffer is set up in the Psyche to keep them from seeing or feeling the Truth. It happens automatically as a part of our instinctual survival mechanisms. It operates similarly to the repression mechanism for trauma.

"And, of course, there is a pernicious consequence for us, as humans, that this buffer be established. The energy of the central falsehood around which a child's life is organized creates a corruption that has very negative consequences. The Buffer makes the child live for itself, rather than for others as an adult. It creates what is called egocentricity. It creates sociopaths and psychopaths. It creates pathological narcissism. And it is the most pernicious of all the buffers we set up in ourselves, of which there are many. Any Truth that we encounter that we refuse to see is the result of a buffer.

"You remember the three steps of evolution in the Soul? Sympathy, Empathy, Telepathy?

It inhibits Sympathy to the point that it is easy to ignore the Suffering of others. Sympathy means that you come to experience an emotion that is similar to the emotion another is feeling. If you can relate to another's suffering by finding a similar suffering in oneself, then that is Sympathy. For the child it may be mostly imitation and imaginary. Momma is crying, so I have to cry, too.

"The Buffer almost completely precludes the experience of Empathy, that is, actually feeling what another person is feeling. Telepathy depends on the existence of an empathetic foundation, especially accurate, word for word, image to image telepathy.

"But most people under the influence of the Buffer, as I said, can barely feel sympathy for another.

"This topic is explored more deeply in the Talk on Ecstasy and the Soul."

"Is there another question?"

"How do we know that the crystallization of Higher Bodies is real?"

"The True answer is we don't know. We don't know. It's a hypothesis. A working hypothesis. We do not get a lot of feedback from the departed, as we had hoped. Rachel Adams has shown up since she left us, but not in repeatable and reproducible ways. Hence no scientific method. No scientific method, no objective proof.

"However, the Order has had some repeatable success with our ghost bodies. Some of the Madeleines, and some of our Attained Elders have had success with projecting their ghost bodies, not just to so-called Higher Realms, but here on this plane of existence. These ghost bodies are palpable and can be engaged with. What we don't know is the extent to which these can survive death, nor for how long. This is true also for dream bodies.

"So we practice, not so much crystallization as we practice alchemy, according to the tantra of the old ones, the old masters. The Eight

Orgasms, and the Seven Orgasms, are repeatable, hence knowable in the sense of Truth.

"There are other forms of Knowing, to be sure, but these kinds of Knowing tend to confine themselves to individuals and are not directly shareable.

"One thing that is directly shareable, repeatable, and reproducible is the Resonance of the Higher Heart. We will say more about this in a different talk."

"How do we confront the Lies within ourselves?"

"Disidentification. Separate yourself from yourself, the part of you that wants to know and the part of you that wants to believe. When you are disidentified, you can see it and study it at arm's length.

"However, you must be sincere in your desire to see the Truth. Remember, we can lie not only to each other, but also to ourselves."

33

Maithuna

Calley kept Her promise to Dchango. Their coupling brought monsoon rains to the land around Them. It rained so hard the fisherman stayed on land until it stopped, knowing that the force of the rain beating on the water would drive the fish deeper than their nets would drag.

His laughter became the thunder and Her squeals of delight the sound of the lightning ripping from the clouds.

When it was over, Calley snorted softly and sat up from the pallet set up for Her in the bower. Oshune was there smiling, Her dark skin tinged with silver edging, and with Her was someone who looked so much like Oshune, but with a golden tinge to Her skin, that Calley knew immediately who She was: Inmanzha, Goddess of Salt Water.

They both smiled, and said simultaneously, "Thank you for the replenishment."

Calley smiled back. "You're welcome. And while I was out there, She Who Comes came to me, touched my forehead, and an idea appeared. It seems it is a way to combat the Molecules of Malice energetically, to strike a blow against the machismo ethos. Would you like to hear it?

"It is called in another language 'Maithuna'".

"Yes, please do tell," Oshune nodded.

Inmanzha added, "Our people are being harassed here by the forces of De Murgos. And even within our circles, our men are infected with this terrible Malice. Attacks have occurred on our Priestesses, sometimes even by their own men, or their Consorts. The Malice overrides their Conscience."

"And so, I need to know," Calley continued. "Are you able to call your adherents? Send them a message to show up at a particular location, at a certain date and time?"

"Some of them," Oshune answered. "Some attain enough clarity in their meditations and prayers that either of us can appear to them. They will know us and respond. And we will have help," She said, gesturing through the door out into the yard. Two male figures were standing close to the fire, drinking soup from bowls. One was raven-headed, the other looked like a small bear. "These are Ogun and Oshossie, our brothers. The Orisha of Warriors, and the Orisha of Hunters."

"My thanks," Calley called out in Portuguese. Both nodded at Her and then began talking excitedly. Calley knew what They were talking about—the recent sex She had had with their elder brother. She could feel in Their gaze that They were wondering if They would get so lucky.

She grinned and looked back at the Sisters. "What do you think?"

They grinned back at Her. Inmanzha spoke, "Do what you want. But I am certain they will have sex with some of the Priestesses they are sent to call."

"Or maybe a couple of the Consorts," Oshune added.

Calley asked, "You call them Consorts now? Rather than Priests?"

"Oh yes," Oshune continued. "We realized that to call them Priests gave them a false sense of equality. That equality fed an even more false sense of superiority. For decades this had caused no end of troubles, especially when it mixed with the falsehood of machismo. We changed it, and the worst troublemakers are gone. Those that stay are working on appropriate humility. We, and the Priestesses, love it."

"Well, I think we can borrow a famous statement from the Wristians. "The Truth Shall set you Free."

"I like that."

"Me too."

"I grow tired of dealing with machismo. Inmanzha, shall we call Yours or Her's first?"

"Oh, please call mine first. To what?"

"To sex on the beach. Look, your sister Wali used to, a long time ago, induce her followers to have sex in public. With onlookers. I propose to you a variation. Couples on the beaches having sexual embrace, first position to begin with, in the presence of each other. We can make a line on the firm sand at the water's edge. If you want, you two can walk among your devotees, making sure the Feminine attains the ecstatic states of consciousness a Priestess deserves. The only problem, and it's a big one, is that the male gods must be kept out of the Consorts. The reason for this is that the men won't remember the Feminine from the ecstatic state. Their displacement of their awareness by a male god leads to memory loss. And that memory loss will enable them to still behave from the place of machismo. But if the Masculine psyche remains intact, it will remember the transformative power of the Feminine ecstasy. And the Masculine psyche will, if exposed to Feminine ecstasy and remembering it, turn from dominance to entrancement. It will bring out the impulse to serve the Feminine, rather than demand that the Feminine serve the Masculine. For the Masculine, to serve the Feminine is to serve Love."

Ogun squawked at his sisters, and Oshossie shook his head slowly side to side. "Ogun wants to know what they can do if they are not allowed to merge with the men."

"They can show up for the wen by themselves. The Priestesses can be trained to have sex with the gods. Can your brothers show up in a more solid form? It can be harder for the men to be trained to couple with the Goddesses, especially She Who Comes. Often there is too much power in Her Presence for them to remain erect, but there are exceptional men who can be easily trained. All you need do is find them among your ranks. And if you cannot find enough Consorts for all your Priestesses, bring two Priestesses without Consorts, so they might meet your brothers, so to speak."

Both Ogun and Oshossie nodded their heads affirmatively. As Calley watched, Oshossie grew taller, lost his fur, and transformed into a very handsome light brown skinned man. Ogun transformed his raven's head into a good-looking black-haired man with a well-trimmed goatee. They moved close to Calley, holding out their hands. Oshune said, "They want you to touch them."

Calley did, and they both felt solid to Her. She grinned at them and they grinned back. Oshossie's response took the grin as permission to jump on Her. Calley slapped him away, lightning in Her hand.

"Oww, ow ow," Oshossie howled. Calley just shook her head, grinning, as Oshune and Inmanzha giggled.

"Learn to speak my language first, cad," Calley growled.

"Very well," Inmanzha started. "Why should we do this thing?"

"Food," Calley answered immediately. "The energy released by the Priestesses when they are in their ecstasy has special properties. It can be directed to feed the people, including the Consorts, and to feed the world. It provides both psychic and spiritual food. It feeds the Soma of the Priestess and feeds the Souls and Spirits of those around them. It can even feed the Goddesses, and the gods."

Calley watched the impact of the ideas settle in with them. The sisters looked at each other, then at their brothers. The brothers nodded back, and the sisters nodded at them. They turned to Calley. "We'll do it," Oshune said. In English. "We'll call the Priestesses tonight as they sleep. We will tell them to dress loosely, and beautifully. There are enough men who have let go of the idea of being Priests and adopted the thinking of a Consort. We will tell them to bring a Consort and meet us at the beach down below in four nights."

"Very good," Calley smiled. "We'll all have some fun."

Up the mountain thunder rumbled.

"Yes, you too!" Calley shouted.

Four afternoons later, the first boat threaded its way through the rocks that had rolled down over the ages from the mountains and into the bay. They were experienced pilots that knew the waters and the Goddesses hired them to ferry the Priestesses and their Consorts over to the beach. It saved them from walking over two mountains on that tortuous path in their ceremonial clothes. Each boat, four boats ferrying ten couples each, were met on the beach by the three women in service to Oshune: the Maiden, the Mature, and the Crone. The pilots were taken over to the shaman's shack on the rocks set back from the beach and plied with hypnotic herb infused alcohol and induced to sleep, unallowed to witness what was going to happen on the beach.

The Priestesses had all been told that Inmanzha would come,

and they were to follow Her instructions. The couples sat on sarongs spread on the hard sand, just where it was dry, wen in front of the men, looking out over the water as the sun set over the mountain behind, and from the sunlight's shadow racing away from them, the moon rose from the sea before them. As the moonlight flooded over the cove, the water calmed. Candles were lit.

Inmanzha rose from the water before them in Her golden waterfall form and walked to the edge of the beach. Oshune appeared at the mouth of the stream that ran down through the beach in Her silver waterfall form, stopping at the edge of the sea. Calley stood at the back of the beach, holding hands with Oshossie. Dchango appeared behind Inmanzha, naked from the waist down, fully erect. He stepped in front of Her, and turned to face Her. Ogun appeared in his handsome man-form behind Oshune, also naked except for a broad shawl, and erect. Both males sat down. And then the Goddesses sat down on them.

In their minds, everyone could see the phalli sliding in. Or rather the Goddesses sliding the phalli into Themselves. Everyone heard the voice of Inmanzha in their mind, telling them to do what She did. The power of Arousal was in Her voice. When someone embodies the energy of an archetype, they move from personal time and space to transpersonal time and space. When the men stepped into the energy of the Archetype of the Consort, they responded. When the wen stepped into the energy of the Archetype of the Priestess, they responded. They did as they were bid—Consorts and Priestesses.

All along the beach, the Consorts sat down cross-legged. The Priestesses leaned down, took the Consorts in hand, and lowered themselves. Forty penetrations happened simultaneously. There was settling. There was breathing. There was rocking. There was holding and caressing. And then there was Ecstasy. Heads thrown back, hair hanging Ecstasy. Cries, moans, a scream and then another, and then all of the Priestesses raised their arms, palms out, palms up, energy pouring out, they fed the world. They fed the people. The Souls and Spirits near the beach laughed when the thunder rolled.

The color of golden light in the Temple of Undifferentiated Sentience, the Palace of Golden Light, brightened, filling the minds of those who fed it with brilliance and light.

Brilliance and light.

This is how and when and where the last battle began.

De Murgos in his cave felt the slightest of trembles in his feet. The feeding of the World had reached even the moon. He turned, swiftly, back and forth, expecting the True Creator to emerge from the walls around him. He felt the frisson of fear again, and did not know what it was, he knew only that change was upon him, and that he would have to fight to stay here, to keep his peasants aligned with his need to feed. The light in his cave brightened barely perceptibly. And he didn't understand what it was. He only knew it was indigestible.

34

WEKKA

The old wen in the marketplace, Nataji, leaned on the counter in her kitchenette and put down the spoon. She was tired. When she accepted the training to be a Madeleine she did not understand the impact of the nature of assignments. The Order chose her husbands for her, all three of them, and unpredictable for her, her fecundity left her with a couple squads of children and grandchildren, only one of whom was open to hearing about the Order, and Natanji knew that because of the kind of questions she asked.

She had been Nadeen's teacher, Nadahlia's mother, teaching her about how to summon and read the Oracle. Painting the palm with henna, symbols that were sometimes Arabic derivatives, sometimes Hindi derivatives, other times what she was sure were ancient Egyptian hieroglyphs. This was how she came to understand how old the Madeleine line was, the first Madeleine being the Consort of the Prophet known as Wehuda and a fully trained Psychic and Priestess in their mysteries—mysteries all but gone from the world, except for the little bit that she, and others like her carried. The power of it all made her wonder whose consort was whom's.

But she remembered that she saw what she was involved in as a manifestation of the three faces of the Goddess—Maiden, Mother, Crone—Nadahlia, Nadeen, and herself, Nataji.

This manifestation of that eternal truth made her smile and reassured her that she was in the right place, doing the right thing, no matter what the men, engrossed in their Wuzlim hierarchy of worship, might say.

She knew that if she kept to herself, and kept her mouth shut at their blasphemous behavior, she'd survive. And the Order had made sure that she prospered, always in secret, and always just enough to be justified by her station. She was without a husband now, and grateful for it, but it still made her nervous, concealing the car in the courtyard of her house under a sand- colored tarp. In time, soon now she hoped, the Order would invite her to leave this assignment. And perhaps offer to move her away. She hoped to train her one curious daughter as a replacement.

She took the vial of the mysterious fluid out of her pocket, set it on the counter, and stared at it, wondering what it was. And what Nazeem was supposed to do with it. She was told she would be given instructions when the time came, and that she was to summon him to her, and give them to him herself.

She hoped she wouldn't have to wait too long.

She didn't. Two weeks after she had introduced Nadahlia to Julius and Jennifer the word came from Nadeen. Nadahlia was late. Nadahlia had come to her mother the day before, saying, "Momma, I'm late."

Nadeen replied, "What do you mean? Late for what?"

"You know, late late. That late."

Nadeen thought a moment. "Oh, that late." Her heart rate spiked, and then she thought she felt her heart drop through her feet into the ground. She stepped back and put one hand against the wall to support herself, and her other hand, the Oracle hand, to her heart, imploring the Oracle to tell her what to do.

After a moment she heard the calm voice say, "Wait two weeks to be sure." She breathed with relief that they would not have to flee tomorrow. And then the voice said, "Tell Nadahlia tomorrow. Tell Nataji, she you will tell you what to do."

When she told Nataji, Nataji confirmed,, "Wait two weeks. If still no moon, you'll go. Send Nazeem to me. We must prepare him." She picked up the spoon again and stirred the lamb stew. Children and grandchildren must eat, after all. Since her neighbors, the people in her world, saw her as a justifiably relatively wealthy widow, she made sure they had lamb.

Nataji had a fleeting moment of longing. When the Secret was gone, perhaps the assignment would be over. Perhaps the Order would release her. She wondered, with a smile on her face, as she often had, where she might go, what she might see, and what she might do.

Nazeem came to her the next day, discomfited by having to talk to the Crone. Of course, Nataji knew he was gay, the Oracle had told her. More precisely, the Oracle had shown her how the Meemons had used him when he was a child. For him, it seemed perfectly natural that he would do what the Meemons asked him to do. His pain, and suffering came when they would turn away from him, or worse, go away from him. It was only as a young teenager, at the onset of puberty, that he came to understand how different he was from most men in his faith. And how dangerous it was for him to be what he was, as an adult. Indeed, it was impossible to be what he was in that culture. His secret longing, concealed even from his mother, and of course his sister and certainly from his father, was to find a way out.

To find a way to someplace where he could be what he was and love whom he chose.

And now Nataji promised him that chance, if only he would do this one thing.

He had a lot of questions. He knew his face would be covered, but they had cameras. What if his hood and veil slipped? The cameras would be turned off.

How? By people who wanted to help him.

What if he was caught? He would be saved by people who would help him.

What if he was stopped at the border? He was to tell the border guards the truth—he was the man escorting his sister to a new job in Egypt, and his mother was going along to make sure everything was above board. They had all the papers, passports, visas, and contracts to validate what he would say if questioned.

But the success of everything depended on what he was being assigned to do.

In order to deal with being a gay man in a homophobic society, he had had to cultivate a lot of indifference to the beliefs of those around him. He knew he was a human being, and worthy of being treated with that much dignity.

He took the vial the old woman gave him, about a pint in size, wrapped in wicker to protect it.

She told him, "Make sure you can get the cork out before you enter the circular procession. You go in, and get out. And if there is a problem, help will be there to get you out. This is what I have been told to say." And she made a cutting motion with her free hand. He hid the flask in an inner pocket of his robe, bowed his head, and stepped back.

"Remember," she said. "The day you are to do it is the day your mother says to you at dawn, 'Do it'." Come to me for your final instructions. Be here at first light. I will have told her, and I will have told her because everything else, everything necessary for your safety and your family's safety will be in place."

"What about my father?" he asked.

"Does he know who you are?" she asked.

"No."

"Does he really need to know?"

After a thoughtful silence, "No. I wish he could know, but it is not possible. He would, of course, think that somehow it was about him, and not about me. He might even beat me to death."

"Then you shall say nothing. And leave it to me to handle any problems that arise."

Nazeem nodded again and backed out the door.

35

STONEHAVEN TALK ON ECSTASY

"Tonight, this talk is about Beauty, and the Beautiful. We will talk about the second pillar of the Order," Madeleine began. "Ecstasy. The simple Truth is that Ecstasy is your birthright. By which I mean it is a state of consciousness that you are born with the capacity to attain. And, like everything else in this Life, work is required to attain it.

"In this case, the work required is internal as well as external. The internal work is principally the development of the ability to experience, or at least tolerate, powerful sensation. Sensation greater than average. This can be a hard task for people. Sensing something intense is scary. But just as handling spiders and snakes can help overcome the fear of these, so too, the willingness to endure sensation can be increased and expanded.

"The external work amounts to appropriate behavior. And not just private behaviors, such as how you touch yourself when you are alone..."

There was some laughter in the room.

The Madeleine smiled.

"The external work applies to your behavior toward each other, your behavior toward the Sacred, and eventually your behavior toward the Divine. And you must work to develop your relationship to what we teach. You were born not knowing how to read and write, and you had to work to learn how to do these. Your brains are already wired to allow you to access this state of mind, you need only to learn the Way.

"Learning to access ecstasy, and you Consorts learning to assist with the induction of ecstasy in a Priestess, should be your primary focus here. And you Priestesses must work even harder. You have to learn how to endure the sensation so you can ride it to the Palace of a Thousand Lights and return from there. You may do this fearlessly because your Consort will be trained to track you there and bring you back home.

"And you Priestesses must also do something very special. You must, in your Spirit, and then in your Soul, and finally in your Soma, create a place where She Who Comes can abide. Not forever, but just for a while. She Who Comes is the current manifestation of the True Creator. It was She who made you. She established the Natural Laws that created you and the Laws that gave you the potential to access Ecstasy, your birthright. And you must learn to do this because She feeds on Ecstasy. This is why She looks to enter into you. And your Ecstasy will feed Her when She does, making Her stronger, as well as more available to you.

"You Consorts will learn to hold space for this manifestation in your Priestesses. And for this, She Who Comes will let you see Her, know Her, and love Her. And She will love you in return and bless you.

"And one last thing you Priestesses must learn. You must learn how to rain, you must learn how to ejaculate. And you must do this for a specific reason. You must feed your Consort, just as your Consort feeds you. More than the Tantra, this is the Alchemy. And you all must follow the procedures to process these substances.

"Now, you are all released to go practice. And I want to hear you!" she said, smiling broadly.

"Wait, I see there is a question. Yes?"

"What about the men? When do we get to access Ecstasy?"

"Ah. In the original model of this tantra, which Rachel Adams, bless her, brought back to this country, the men entered the same altered state, the state of displacement—displacement of awareness, what the word Ecstasy means. When the awareness was displaced in men, a god would enter into them. It would possess them, as the Goddess possesses the wen. But the Goddess was and is willing to share the place of awareness of this plane of existence. You experienced Consorts know this, because you can see it in your Priestess's eyes. Sometimes it is the Goddess looking back at you, sometimes it is your Priestess. And the Goddess is willing to leave if the Priestess, aware of the occupation—not a possession—simply asks Her to leave. Also, She is willing to leave if the Consort asks Her to leave.

"In the original practice Skreeva would enter the men, Salakta would enter the wen. It was not good. Skreeva would not let go, not return to his realm. Not even when Salakta would implore him to let go. And Skreeva, when not engaged in congress, can be a very disturbing and angry god. In his cult these days he calls himself the god of Transformation, but the transformation almost always results in Death.

"So we, or rather, our predecessors, decided it was too dangerous to allow him to enter. Even several experiments with lesser deities, such as the Green Man, were failures in this regard. The males are too angry, too eager to possess, too reluctant to let go. It was too dangerous. There are bodies buried here, so say those who Know.

"And this is why the men are trained to not allow themselves to be possessed. This is why the men are trained to end the possession by the Goddess if it becomes too intense. The gods are not welcome in the men of the Order. The reward is that the men get to see, and feel, and experience the presence of the Goddess themselves, not through the veil of an angry and disappointing god. When you see your Priestess through your own eyes you will see the Beauty of both the Goddess and the Priestess, and the presence of the Goddess will change your Priestess into the manifestation of Beauty.

"Does this answer your question?"

"Yes, quite thoroughly, and honestly, frighteningly. My thanks to you Madeleine, and blessings upon the Elders of this Order."

"I will add one thing to your understanding. The true key to masculine access to Ecstasy is learning to separate orgasm from ejaculation. While the Feminine can have eight different orgasms the Masculine can have only seven. Most men only ever have one."

36

WASHING THE STONE

Venge and Matthews appeared in the shadows at the back of Nataji's shop. Bree had given Matthews a talisman from the Hidden Lands that would make them invisible so long as they were in physical contact, skin to skin worked best, like holding hands. Through cloth, sometimes a partial image would appear, wavering at the edge of perception.

They had taken a commercial flight from Italy to Cairo, then picked up a car that had been reserved for them and driven to the seaside villa west of Alexandria, rented by Julius and Jennifer. Venge was immensely pleased by the opportunities for intimacy offered by being with another couple in the Order. Julius, at over two hundred pounds of muscle, was too heavy to fly with, but Jennifer's squeals of delight, echoing back over the water in the dark, had been intensely amusing to all. It turned out that Venge, no surprise, knew more about pleasing a wen than Julius. Matthews, not being a Consort, and hence unable to take their training, was often in 'watch and learn' mode, which suited him just fine. Julius was magnificent to watch.

Julius had driven Venge and Matthews to the border, where a rooftop room had been reserved for them overlooking the ferry dock. From there it was a two-hour flight, as angels fly, to Nataji's shop with her home and walled courtyard behind. They had taken off about

01:00, flying low, just over the rooftops, avoiding both radar and power lines. Their passage was as silent as an owl's. They had stopped to rest on an empty rooftop, leaning against a parapet. When they recognized Nataji's house from a satellite image, they landed in the courtyard. The door from there to the back of her shop was open. They found a back corner, lay down, and slept until Nataji entered at 05:00.

She spoke in Italian to the darkness in the corner. "You know, old people don't sleep as deeply as the young. The sound of wings, big wings, woke me last night. Quietly, so as not to wake the children in the house, tell me your names. And I shall make us all some tea."

So they sat together in the predawn darkness, introducing themselves to each other. Nataji spoke a little bit about how difficult it was being isolated there with only short duration visits from the Order. She believed the Order had long ago promised to extract her when she was ready, but she had chosen to endure based on her perceptions of the wishes of She Who Comes. She knew that she was cared for, and would be cared for until the end, when she chose to leave this assignment. She was happy now that she had stayed. The normal parts of her life—husbands, children, grandchildren—had all been good, and when the time came, she was ready to leave them behind. She was ready to see the world beyond this city, and spend her last days among people like her, people who understood what it was like to have the 'Second Sight'. She was happy now that she had waited, for She Who Comes had come to her in a dream-vision a few weeks ago and told her that she was to have a role in something important. And to trust that she would escape interactions with the authorities.

She inquired as to their histories. She was surprised at both Venge's short time in the Order, and by Matthews not being in the Order at all. When their purpose was explained to her—that they were there to protect Nazeem in his sacred task, and how, she asked them to show her their wings. She drew in her breath sharply as these unfurled in the cramped space, not completely but enough for her to see. She asked Matthews if she could touch his, then Venge. "I feel the force of them, they are not like bird wings," she said.

"They are not," Mathews said.

"But they work," Venge added.

Nataji sighed. "So today is the day, then. My long wait will be over soon. Here, put these on and I will go and wake Nazeem." She gave them both long robes, in the style that men wore, which would conceal their western-style clothes. She gave them both the wrapped cloth headdresses with a veil attached that would obscure their features, leaving only their eyes exposed. Returning to her house she noted the unusual fog that had rolled in from the nearby sea, obscuring everything to the roof tops. She went into the house and woke Nazeem, who had spent the night, told him to get dressed and come to the shop for tea. She had people she wanted him to meet.

Nazeem had been concerned about his father, and Nataji had said he'd been called to the next city to bid on a mud-brick house and compound wall for a home on its outskirts. It was a long distance and he would not be returning until the next day. Plenty of time for Nazeem to complete his mission and escape with his mother and sister.

Dressed identically to Venge and Matthews, Nazeem entered the shop through the backdoor and Nataji beckoned him to sit with the guests. She bid him sit down and put a plate of dates in front of him and poured him some tea.

She began, "These people are here to help you, should you get into any difficulties. They do not speak our language, but we share enough knowledge of Italian to communicate. If you get in trouble, all you have to do is follow what they indicate. You will be safe. Now listen. These are your instructions.

"In ancient times, centuries before the Reformer came, the structure that houses the black stone was a Temple to the Goddess Al-lat, yes, which is where your mother's family name comes from. The black stone was once whole but in the wars that followed the Reformer's actions the town was taken by others, the rock removed, and it was smashed before it was returned to the temple. Now the pieces are kissed or touched by putting one's head, or hand, through the hole in the silver collar. You are to avoid this stone.

"Instead, when you arrive at the entrance to the Temple grounds, you are to mix with the other pilgrims, and join them in their circling the Temple. You will be brought close to the black stone by the crowds, but you are to bypass it and go around to the other side of the temple, to the opposite corner, because there is another stone there, a red stone, a large stone embedded in the foundation, held to be the Stone of Happiness, which fell to earth and was discovered near the same region as the black stone.

"The old foundation is concealed behind a curtain that covers a veneer of stone. When you get to that corner you are to drop to your knees in prayer. You may touch the curtain and bow your head against it. You will find that there is a small ledge where the foundation veneer extends beyond the veneer covering the walls of the Temple. And then will come the hardest part of your task. You are to take the contents of this vial," she paused to remove the stoppered bottle from an inner pocket of her dress, "and pour the contents across the back of the ledge, so that the liquid in this bottle has the chance to pour down behind the seam in the veneer. Do your best not to be seen. If you are seen, and a cry comes out about you, these two," she said, nodding toward the strangers sitting in the dark, "will provide you with an escape."

She looked at the bottle and its wax sealed cork and decided, "We will open the bottle here, then re-cork it. That way you will not have to struggle to open it there, in the moment."

She picked up a knife from the table and scraped the wax away from the lip of the bottle. She uncorked it and a smell wafted through the room. A fecund smell, which both the strangers recognized with indrawn gasps. Matthews said to Nataji in Italian, "It is rain."

Nataji, aware of the double entendre, asked him, "Whose?"

He replied, "It reminds me of a Storm Goddess I have encountered."

Nataji smiled and pressed the cork back into the opening.

"Time to go," she said.

Over the arena that housed the ancient Temple, Calley drifted, as diffuse as the fog She had summoned from the nearby sea. She could sense the long gone, long dead Goddess Al-lat as the faintest of presences, happy to be reached out to by Calley, smiling at the prospect of liberation. At about 10:00, She reassembled Herself and examined the electronic security system in the arena with its surveillance equipment aimed at the crowd below from all angles and views. She smiled, no cameras focused above the roof-line.

Nazeem had joined the line of worshippers entering the arena to pay their respects. He had never understood the required pilgrimage, and he was thinking that no one understood its requirement of participation.

Calley knew who Nazeem was, and what his role was. She knew She had to protect him, as he was the emissary fulfilling a promise She had made to restore the voice of a fallen star. Her mother, She Who Comes, had long since given Her permission to travel where She willed, and She was happy to discharge this debt. It was Her rain in the bottle Nazeem carried. For some reason She thought of a question Her Mother had put to Her once: 'Why do one thing at a time when you can do ten?' She smiled again, assembled Herself into a lightning strike, and, with a peal of thunder, struck all ten of the satellite uplink dishes from the security system, rails of lightning spreading out like spider legs.

The electricity traveled through the cable and into the computers destroying their hard drives and rendering the cameras blind. The security forces were on their radios immediately, confused and uncertain. There were a thousand worshippers on the floor of the arena, packed shoulder to shoulder, all of whom had ducked at the lightning flash, and were now milling in confusion. The commanding officer ordered the ingress gates closed but allowed those already within to continue with their devotions. Calley, Her coalesced form unseen in the fog, returned to Her diffuse state smiling with the thought "Lets see De Murgos top that," and then, "Get off the rock. Get off me."

Venge and Matthews assumed their position on the roof of the building closest to the Temple, which was positioned in the center of the arena. Venge was holding Matthews' hand so she could come under the spell of the talisman from the Invisible Lands. She found herself liking it, remembering their airborne couplings, and found her palm sweating into his. He turned and smiled at her. Despite herself, she smiled back.

Two hours later Nazeem had worked his way around the arena and was nearing the east corner of the Temple where the black stone was embedded in the walls. He suddenly had an image appear in his brain that he did not understand, but he knew he would understand it someday. It was the image of a giant red vertical slash, topped and surrounded by hair, with a hole at the bottom, and it was into this that the pilgrims were sticking their heads, in order to kiss the stones within. He felt the presence of an irony he could not understand, yet it made him smile.

He made his way around to the other side of the Temple to the opposite corner on the western side. He drew close to the building and fell to his knees, placing his forehead on the wall. He sensed nothing but the stone under the cloth. Head bowed, he fished in his clothing for the bottle. The woman to his right glanced briefly at him, the man on his left was lost in a religious trance.

He held the bottle in his left hand, hidden in his robes, raised his head and looked at the narrow shelf the fingers of his right hand had found. There was a small hole in the veneer mortar at the corner, the result of the mason's sloppiness. He uncorked the bottle and poured a line of fluid on the crack in the mortar seam. He paused and poured most of it down the hole. He continued on around the corner to his right and the woman noticed his strange behavior, catching a glimpse of the bottle. She looked down along the corner and saw where the draped cloth had become damp in places. She set up a cry, pointing at him. He stood up and walked away into the crowd.

Guards started to look at him, move toward him. Matthews and Venge looked at each other, nodding. They stood up, dropped hands, becoming fully visible to the people below, and manifested their wings. A cry went up from the crowd, some voices calling "Embla, Embla!" and then The Voice was heard.

It started low and rose inexorably to a scream that forced everyone to put their hands over their ears and look down. Into the crowd, Venge and Matthews dropped. Matthews tapped the talisman, going invisible, landed and wrapped his arms around Nazeem and flew back to the rooftop. For an instant Venge, rifle over her shoulder, fully costumed, wings out, stood there alone. Then she flew up to the rooftop. Matthews touched her and they all disappeared.

The Voice decrescendoed to a soft "Ahhh". Everyone looked to the Temple in awe. Matthews swung Nazeem around to his back, telling him to hang on.

Venge, unable to restrain herself, released a burst of rifle fire from her gun. Everyone ducked. Then she took Matthews outstretched hand

and disappeared again from view.

The pieces of the black rock began to sing in chorus with the red stone.

They took Nazeem to Nataji's. Nataji put him in the car and sent him to go get his mother and his sister. They were waiting, bags packed, papers in order.

Venge and Matthews lay low at Nataji's until darkness, when it was safe to fly across the sea to their room above the ferry dock.

Everyone was in good spirits, happy even. The happiness spread from the stone into the city. The constancy of its song induced a kind of audio amnesia in the people. They knew only that they were smiling for a reason they didn't understand. Even as the rumor of the Emblas at the arena spread, the tellers were smiling and happy.

Later that night, having finished, Venge whispered into Matthews ear, "So that's what happy fucking is like."

37

STONEHAVEN TALK ON CONSCIENCE

"Tonight's talk," Diana began, "Is on the third pillar of the Order. It is about Conscience. It is about The Good. I want you to get this analogy: Conscience is to Morality as Knowledge is to Belief. Conscience is a faculty reserved for Human Beings on this planet. And it is scarcely used. Morality is simpler. And more rigid, whereas Conscience tends to be fluid and has fewer dictates.

"Conscience is an experiment, an evolutionary experiment. You are aware that in our teaching we speak of the human as having three brains: one for the Soma, the sensory brain; one for the Soul, the feeling brain; and one for the Spirit, the thinking brain. And you all know what parts of the brain inside your skull correspond to this distinction and what parts of the nervous system, the various neural plexuses, correspond to those parts of your brain.

"And the Conscience represents, if you will, a fourth brain. This is the leading edge of evolution for us. Its place in the brain is in the Prefrontal Lobes. This is the part of the brain that develops interneuronal connections last, beginning in the late teenage years and continuing into the early twenties. It's lack of development until that point is why military conscription begins at 18 years old. The teenager is easier to train to kill. When a thirty-year-old has a developed Conscience, or even a strong moral conviction against killing, it may be impossible to get that one to kill, even in self-defense.

"And the fact of this lack of development is, perhaps, one of the reasons that teenagers are generally believed to be lacking in judgment, especially good judgment, and hence, do things that are risky to their lives and health.

"For, in most people, this part of the brain, with all its connections, remains dark and inactive.

"What this part of the brain is supposed to do is integrate the other three brains—thought integrated with feeling and sensation—as well as integrate the two halves of the brain, the hemispheres, because the hemispheres are not identical in their functioning. And, in mediating these internal conflicts a new function arises: the ability to choose right from wrong, and eventually, Good from Evil. And with practice, you all can learn to do this Objectively, not just relative to yourselves. In fact, as far as your egoic desires go, the Conscience is the antidote to ego. If 'I' is in the place of ego, Conscience is the place of 'Not-I', if you will.

"We know this because your Conscience can lead you to make sacrifices that your ego is absolutely unwilling to make."

Diana paused, smiling mysteriously, looking up. Then she resumed.

"If you need proof that what I am saying is True, everyone of you is here because your Conscience, not your ego, led you to be here."

There was the sound of people shifting in their seats, and some clearing of throats.

"Yes?" Diana queried. "Is there a question?"

"How do you know that?"

"Because you wouldn't be here if it weren't True."

"But you don't know me. I'm new here."

"But you're not new to us. Here, let me prove it. Stand up and walk towards me," she said, standing up herself and walking toward him. "I have something I want to say to you that I want only you to hear." She walked to the bottom step of the round dais. When he was in front of her she put her hands on his shoulders, stood on her tiptoes, and whispered something in his ear. He blushed. She kept talking and then he laughed, nodding his head. He stepped back and she said,

"And I will not tell you how I know that. Yet."

When they had both resumed their seats, she said, "Mind if I ask you a question? Do not feel compelled to answer it." He shook his head, 'No'.

"Thank you," Diana began with a gracious smile. "Why did you blush just now?" She watched him think through it, watched him decide that she didn't ask him to tell the story of it, just answer the question 'Why?'.

"Because I made a mistake," he said finally.

He was rewarded with a huge smile and "Thank you. Thank you for answering the question. Would you entertain another one?" She watched him look through his inventory of verbal traps, some place where he was afraid she might catch him. None seemed likely so he said, "Yes, please do."

"You do not blush at all your mistakes, do you?"

"No."

"Another question?"

"Yes."

"Why did you blush at this mistake?"

"Because I was mean when I should have had sympathy."

"And there's that word, 'should'. Each of you: What 'shoulds' do you have in your life? There are only three kinds of questions: What?, How?, and Why? 'Why' is where your shoulds go. But the Why question has different answers at different levels of the brain. At the level of his brain where the 'should' is that he should have been more sympathetic, and not mean, this is the level of his Conscience working. And the blush is an organic response to making a mistake. Not caused by some implanted morality. No morality says, 'never be mean', although to be fair, many advise that you be more sympathetic.

"And I want to emphasize that this is the beginning of Conscience. You must use your skills of Discernment and Discrimination to separate what you "should", raising her fingers to make quotation marks in the air, from what you Should, without quotation marks, and learn to identify which shoulds are implanted in you and form the basis of your moral world, and which ones rise organically in yourselves.

"And, mind you, this is very, very, dangerous work. Do not destroy your moral constructs before you are self-aware enough, and strong-willed enough, to use your nascent Consciences in their uneducated and undeveloped states. Wait until you can count on your Conscience to be your Guide. If you leap too soon you will die. Because you will not yet have learned to fly and you will fall.

"As the song goes, 'Let your Conscience be your Guide'.

"And, in my experience, two people at the same level of development will always agree in matters of Conscience. Not so, with morality.

"Any further questions at this time?" She looked around the room. Seeing none, she continued.

"As you will recall, our studies of sacred and esoteric anatomy have pointed out the connection between certain areas of the brain, and neural structures called plexes throughout the body. As you might expect, there is one such plexus directly connected to the prefrontal lobes, and to which it is connected via the glands, the endocrine system, as well. And this plexus has as its focus the human heart. Your human heart. And it should come as no surprise to you that your heart is just as undeveloped, just as uneducated, as this part of your brain. The heart can become infused with all kinds of feelings that, properly speaking, should remain confined to other parts of the brain. For example, the heart can be afraid. The heart can become angry, or even filled with hatred. Those parts of ourselves, those already have homes within us, and they all covet the heart. They all see it as new territory to be occupied.

"So, this is why so much of our program is about the development of Conscience, and about the development of the Heart. When both parts are operating the way they should, the Heart serves as an additional sensory organ for the Conscience, both perceiving and confirming that a choice or a decision or a realization represents a path forward in the Proper Way of Being.

"Exercises in developing discernment and discrimination, and exercises in Ethics and Values, will continue daily. I believe tomorrow's Exercise is how to tell the difference between Principle and Meta-Principle.

"And remember what Socrates said, 'The Good is the most Beautiful'."

38

Escape from Egypt

The Al-lat family drove to the town near the beach on the Mediterranean coast in western Egypt, where Jennifer and Julius had rented a small chalet owned by the Order. The drive was uneventful, the ferry crossing slow and easy, customs was a glance at their paperwork.

Nazeem had trouble driving at first. He was nervous that he'd been identified while washing the stone, but not even the woman next to him had gotten a clear look at his face. Everyone was talking about the manifestation of the Emblas, and the newly singing voice, and not about him.

They arrived at the address their mother had carried, clutched in her hand since they left their house. Nazeem, watching her in the rear-view mirror, thought she must be praying over it, willing them to arrive safely. She was.

The chalet had six bedrooms and a small house at the back of the lot for the house manager, who was also cook and housekeeper. And she was an initiate of the Order, responsible for communications with the Market Queen, the old Madeleine on the outskirts of Wekka.

Each of them, Nadahlia, Nazeem, and their mother Nadeen, had their own bedrooms, for the first time in their lives. Nadeen sat on the edge of the bed and wept with relief. She thought of the note she had left for her husband, describing in no detail, where they were going and why, with a promise at the end that she would reach out to him when they got settled in. She wept anew at the thought that she had no idea if she would ever be able to keep her promise.

That night at supper, Jennifer and Julius both had wine, which they offered to share. Nazeem took a glass, just to try it out. Nadahlia, now eight weeks into her pregnancy, declined, as did Nadeen. He didn't get what all the fuss was about.

They all slept well that night. The next morning Julius and the house manager went out to confirm arrangements for a boat rental made earlier. They inspected the boat, an 8 passenger cruiser used for sport fishing. Julius took it out for a spin with the owner, proving that he was a capable pilot. Julius dropped the owner off and took the boat with him to dock it at the short pier behind the chalet. Nazeem was waiting for him on the dock when he arrived. Julius threw him a rope and told him how to tie it off. Then Julius climbed out and tied off the stern.

Nazeem looked at him, the question obvious on his face. "We are going by boat?"

Julius considered. "Yes. We will be going to a larger boat. On the way I will show you how to drive this one, if you like."

Nazeem's fear was dampened by his excitement. Enthusiastically, he accepted the offer.

The afternoon was spent packing up. Jennifer and Julius had spread themselves out around the house waiting for their guests. While Nadeen talked with the house manager, Nadahlia and Nazeem watched television, something they had not had at home. After supper, Julius and Nazeem carried the luggage to the boat and safely stowed it underneath in the forward cabin. Everyone boarded and put on life vests. Jennifer cast off and was the last to join them on the deck.

Julius kept his promise and stood behind Nazeem, directing his hands to reverse the propeller and back them away from the dock. Turning, they directed the boat to the channel that headed to the sea. Slowly they moved down the channel, lights off in the darkness, leaving almost no wake.

The sea was rougher than the channel and Julius goosed the throttle a little. When they were far enough from town to see by starlight,

Julius turned on the dash light and explained the compass to Nazeem, and how to follow it. Then he pushed the throttle farther forward, putting the boat on a good pace, heading due north, and let Nazeem take over the helm.

He went to the back of the boat and sat down next to Jennifer. He looked at her, beautiful in the faint light, and spoke to her in English. "So, I don't get it. These seem to me to be everyday people. What's so special? What's the big Secret?"

She considered, before she spoke. "Haploid, not diploid."

"What?"

"Haploid, not diploid."

"What?"

"She is one, not two. She only has one parent. Her mother. To whom she is genetically identical, I might add."

"What?"

"It always happens when they're 18. Married or not. In these times, she is unmarried, and at risk of being murdered by her own neighbors."

"Wait," he said, leaning back on the seat. He thought through it. "You're telling me she is parthenogenetically born."

"Yes."

"That's not possible."

"Yes, actually it is. Sharks and some reptiles and birds can do it. No other mammals that we know of can do it, though. It turns out there are several lines of wen, several lineages around the globe that can do this. Long ago, the Order identified some of these lines, and has moved to protect them from harm. We believe there are even more than we know of."

"Wow, that's some Secret." Then he asked, "Why didn't you tell me? You didn't trust me to keep The Secret?"

"It's not about trust. It's about need to know. I just proved to you that we trust you by telling you The Truth… Remember, it's about 'Need to Know', not Trust."

He paused again. "You're right," he shrugged. "Obviously, I didn't need to know."

She got a big grin on her face, grabbed his face with both hands, and pulled herself in for a big smooch. She loved this man, she thought to herself.

They sped north for more than an hour, Julius checking the onboard GPS and periodically making small course corrections with Nazeem. When they arrived at the coordinates stored on his phone they stopped. "Now we wait," Jennifer said in Arabic. Not moving except in the swell, Nadahlia got suddenly seasick, and threw up over the side. Nadeen held her hair until she finished.

Not long after they stopped, they heard a sound of rushing water and suddenly a ship was alongside. Not a ship, Nazeem saw, but a submarine. The conning tower loomed in the darkness, blotting out some of the stars. A man dressed in black was on the narrow deck. He called and tossed a line to Julius, who caught it, pulling the boat over, and made the line fast, securing the boat to the sub. Nazeem and Julius tossed the luggage over first. The man in black caught it and tossed it to another man in the top of the conning tower, who dropped it through the hatch to someone waiting below.

Luggage handled, Julius turned on a flashlight. Jennifer crossed over first, holding the hand of the man on the deck, to show Nadeen and Nadahlia how to do it. Nadeen, sucking in a breath, went next, Jennifer taking her to the ladder and helping her climb it to the arms of the second man. Nadahlia was next. Then Nazeem.

Julius went below deck and removed a small rectangular package from a pouch he'd left hanging from a hook near the deck above, clear plastic wrapping a whitish clay-like substance. He unwrapped it and inserted a detonator into the clay. He pushed the clay against the hull, below the waterline. Next, he removed a timer, an old analog kitchen timer strapped to a rectangular battery and attached the detonator wires. He set the clock for seven minutes. "Plenty of time," he said to himself. Last, he took a can of lighter fluid and squirted it on the hull and ceiling.

He went up on deck, undid the line and jumped across to the submarine, trailing the line behind him. He climbed the tower and lowered himself through the hatch. The men followed after, stowing the line. When the hatch closed, he turned and looked at the people around him. He was met first by a beautiful middle-aged wen.

She smiled, and smiled at them all, and said in Arabic, "Welcome, all of you. I am the Captain, the High Priestess Gutierrez. Make yourself comfortable. This is my ship, the Sea Squirt."

Jennifer, Julius and the Captain all looked at each other, smiling knowingly at the double entendre.

She turned and issued the command to dive. "Depth five meters. North by northeast, speed one knot." She turned and said to the man closest to her, her first mate, "Up periscope." She took the handles and swiveled until she could see the boat. She turned to Julius, "Want to watch?" He stepped forward and put his eyes to the glass. He could see the dark outline of the boat. There was a whumpf as the explosive blew, then a fire that engulfed the deck. The boat slowly sank, extinguishing the fire, and leaving no debris behind. He sighed and stepped back.

"Down periscope," the Captain said. "New depth, forty meters. Make yourselves comfortable, we've several hours to go. Set course for Kerkyra. Let's go home."

39

DRAGON ISLAND

Angelica and Meck had been invited to tour the facility at the Institute. She was very curious about the cave containing the submarine berth. The inspection proved as interesting as she thought it would. There was no room to turn the submarine around. Either the sub had to back in, or back out. She looked forward to meeting the Captain, whom she heard went by her last name—unusual in the Order, the custom serving as a protection for family members unaware of what a Member was doing. Then she realized that her family probably only knew that she worked for the Institute, maybe they knew she ran a submarine, but probably not.

While they were standing on the dock, the submarine surfaced. She was delighted and surprised. She could hear the hatch open and watched two crew members, one man, one wen, appear and descend the ladder, going in different directions on the deck and throwing lines to the men onshore to tie off. Then came two people who looked mixed African American, and then three people she believed of Middle Eastern descent. There was a young wen first, followed by someone who looked obviously like family, an elder wen she assumed was the mother. The younger moved slowly, hand under her belly. Angelica thought, "Pregnant," and said so to Meck, "Watch her. Make sure she's OK." Then followed perhaps the prettiest man she had ever seen, apparently also a relative. She stood at the end of the gangway and welcomed them, shaking their hands as if she had been appointed to be the formal greeter. Immediately behind her appeared someone she assumed was the formal greeter, appearing somewhat flustered, and smoothing her clothes. Angelica could smell the sex on her and looked around until she saw a man stepping out from behind some kind of motor house, pulling up his pants and buckling in. She smiled knowingly. She stepped back and let the greeter do her job.

She turned to Meck and said, "Can you take me to the dragon?"

"I'll find out where it is."

An hour later he returned to their room. She'd been waiting, sipping a glass of sparkling water, enjoying pretending to be a tourist and looking out over the sea. He said, "I have a car and there will be a boat waiting for us."

They drove in contented silence, she holding his hand, and occasionally, grinning, playing with whatever she could find in his lap. They took the coast road, coming down from the shoulder of a mountain and into a small town. They pulled into the parking lot of a hotel on the beach and signed in, their reservation having been made earlier by Meck. When they got to the room he mock-chastised her for teasing him the entire trip, making it hard to drive. "Hard to drive..." she said. "Bring that hard driver over here." She caressed him, then caused him to feed her, quickly. "Now, take me to the dragon."

They stood on the coast, looking at the massive rock island just past the outer limits of the harbor. "That's it," Meck said. She was stunned. She could see the outline of what had been the dragon, underlying what appeared to be heaps of stone. She could see its head, its forelegs, its spine and its tail. All in all, it looked to be over a quarter mile long. "Longer," Meck said, reading her mind.

"Stop it," she said, smiling

They walked across the street and onto the narrow beach, Meck going up to a young man standing there with papers in his hand. Behind him in the shallow water were six speed boats tied up to buoys. In short order the man waded out to a boat, untied it, started it up, and beached it, adroitly pulling the motor up as he ran into shallow water.

Meck and Angelica got on board and the young man pushed the boat out into deeper water. Meck dropped the motor, locked it in, and they took off.

Angelica said, "Take me all the way around it."

Meck slowed as they got close, drifting toward the rocks that were once, apparently, the dragon's right eye. He slowly turned to port, maintaining his distance, not sure how the rock lay under the surface. Slowly, with just enough headway to keep them off the rocks, he took them west along the side. Angelica held both hands up in the air, trying to sense anything, anything unusual. All the way around the rock they went, just away from the jagged edges.

There was no beach anywhere, just rock meeting the water. On the far side, just in front of what would have been the left shoulder she turned to Meck, face serious and said, "How close can you get me? Arm's length? I want to touch it."

"I'll try," was his response. "If I put a hole in it, how good a swimmer are you, anyway?"

With small thrusts forward and back, wheel turning the prop wash almost perfectly sideways, he got close. Angelica couldn't quite touch it. She stood on the gunwale, holding a mooring line, and leaned out.

She recalled what it was like to have a dragon inside her, the sensation, the taste. She recalled the imprint of the dragon egg she carried in her womb. She reached out and laid a palm on the rock.

There was a jolt of instant recognition.

The rock shuddered and there was a cracking sound over her head as a rock, a large rock the size of a small car, broke free and smashed into the water just off the bow. "That's enough," Meck said, "Get down in the boat." She did. He pulled away a safe distance and circled back so they could look at it.

"It responded to you. Responded to your touch," he said.

"Yes," she said.

"What did you feel?"

"Not so much feeling, more a sensation."

"What sensation, then?"

"An urge to scratch an itch, oddly enough."

"Where?"

"Up between my shoulder blades. I have to get up there."

"What?"

"Yes, take me around again. There has to be some place to land, even if I have to jump on a rock, and climb."

They came around the snout and traveled down along the south side again. The boulders were huge, sea slime slick, and impossible. The tail, even though it went low in the water, was surrounded by underwater rocks, and there was no close access. Angelica couldn't see herself clambering over slick and jagged rocks for even five feet, no less ten or fifteen, to pull herself out of the water.

They came around the snout again and stopped. They both looked down into the water. No rocks. Meck said, "I can get you close. Maybe five feet. You'll have to jump in and pull yourself up along the cracks. Can you do that?"

She shot him a look. "Twelve years of gymnastics. Four years of rock climbing. Asshole."

"Well," he said defensively. "Those aren't in your file. Thanks for telling me," he said, with just the slightest edge of sarcasm. "At least let me get you a wetsuit. And gloves and shoes. I don't want you freezing up top in a stiff breeze and a bikini."

"Deal," she said. And then she thought, "Anticipates my needs. Hmm. I want to suck his cock again." Then she said aloud, "OK. Just let me pay for it." Grinning, she pointed him away from the rocks, and toward shore.

40

STONEHAVEN TALK ON THE MYSTERY

"And so," Madeleine began, "we have talked about the Truth and Ecstasy, and Conscience. We point to phenomena that can serve as Absolutes in human experience, knowing the Absolute only, or at least almost always, in relative ways. We are not, ourselves, an Absolute, we are relative beings, but in our contemplation we can approach the Absolute and endeavor in our manifestations to bring the Absolute into the Relative.

"The Truth invites us to confront mental ambiguity.

"Ecstasy invites us to address the ambiguity by expanding our awareness, of not just the possible, but the real.

"Conscience invites us to confront the ambiguity and discern the most Beautiful, the most Good outcome to any ambiguous situation.

"The Ambiguity is unavoidable. Uncertainty is unavoidable. We live so far out in the Universe, and are subject to so many Natural Laws, the conflicts between these Laws of Relativity make it clear that Life here requires Indeterminacy. That which is not yet determined, and more particularly, that which is not yet Overdetermined, is the field in which we live and breathe.

"This makes Life Mysterious. It makes Life particularly more Mysterious when the improbable manifests in a repeatable way. I will show you what I mean."

She went quiet and settled into her meditative posture. She hummed, starting at a low growl. A circlet of blue flames appeared around her head. As the frequency of the hum increased in pitch, a violet flame appeared in the center of the circle, dancing upon the top of her head as the flames around the periphery flickered to the rhythm of the central cadence.

When she felt the manifestation stabilize, she spoke again. "You all can see this manifestation on my head. We don't know exactly what it is, although it is repeatable, and even though we have working hypotheses about it. We know how to do it, but we don't know why it is. We don't have a certain answer as to its significance, although we have a working hypothesis for the meaning of the phenomenon.

"We don't know. Therefore, we call it a Mystery. Moreover, it is an Esoteric Mystery. And there is another Mystery with which you are all familiar. We call it the Resonance of the Higher Heart."

She held out her arms, palm up, and called to the people nearest her to step forward. She called to people behind them to step forward and hold their hands. She instructed everyone to take the hands of the persons next to them. Then she told the man and the wen closest to her to take her hands.

The people felt a shock wave of bioelectricity run through them, causing a mild spasm and shifts in their posture, forward and back. After the initial contact, they all came to feel a heartbeat in the palms of their hands, which moved of its own accord up their arms and into their torsos, centering over their own hearts. After several beats it rose to their throats, then to the center of their heads. Next it came forward into their foreheads. The sensation became focused there and activated the sense of a ring of energy encircling their heads, much like the circlet crown on the Madeleine. They sat, resonating together.

Madeleine spoke, "This is the Resonance of the Higher Heart. It is a Mystery. In time, each of you will carry this yourselves. In time, each of you will overcome the consequences of the Kundalini buffer within you by this means, the activation of the Higher Heart. It will give you access to Higher Thought, Higher Sensation, and Higher Feeling. In this Higher Realm, in this field generated by this Higher Energy, many smaller Mysteries can be understood. But you must also understand this: A Higher Body requires a Higher Heart. The risk is that you may no longer be able to die a simple death, die once and forever and be done with it. What will happen to you will remain a Mystery until it happens. Your Fate remains—you must die. But your Destiny, to die that dead death, may no longer be the same. Your Destiny is malleable, even if it is inevitable."

As the contact continued into the ensuing silence some people sighed. Others moaned. Some began shaking, as if they were approaching orgasm. Suddenly the wall of blue flame spread out from Madeleine, encompassing everyone in the room. Small blue flamelets danced over each person's head. Madeleine herself became a pillar of violet flame.

Into this spreading ecstasy they each heard Madeleine's voice in their head.

"You can hear me. Say yes."

And the assembly answered her aloud, "Yes."

"This is a Mystery. Say yes."

They responded again, "Yes."

She said, "Mystery upon Mystery, the Gateway of Manifold Secrets."

The blue flames slowly receded, returning to Madeleine. Some wept openly. Madeleine herself became a smaller violet flame, a flame with two centers—one over her heart and one over her head. Eventually these merged into one, the heart flame rising to her crown.

"You know me. And I know you. Several of you received private messages from me."

Several in the group nodded their heads in affirmation.

"Act on the advice I gave you. Everyone else is to cultivate this power in themselves, and to assist each other in developing this power."

After a long pause, in which the people focused on keeping the sensation of the Higher Heart going in themselves, she said, "Are there any questions?"

Someone, a man, spoke. "I have never before seen the crown on a man. Just once I have seen the flame in the middle, and several times I have seen a kind of penumbra, a kind of cloud of light around a man's head. Why this difference?"

"The circlet is a symbol of the presence of She Who Comes, the

True Creator. The central flame is the manifestation of your True Self. It proves the opening of the Thousand Petalled Lotus. She Who Comes will only manifest through wen, not men. And the entry into a man of any entity will of necessity be of a lesser entity than She is. We do not allow it in our men to be possessed of a lesser entity than Her. Instead, we teach men to be worthy of Her manifestation to them and show men the path to their own Ecstasy thereby."

The man said, "I understand." And into his head he heard the voice of Madeleine say, "I know you do. I know you. Tonight, Consort, you will come to my chamber, and I will show you your Ecstasy."

As the Assembly dispersed, she said, "I expect you all to practice! Use your Ecstasy to Feed the World!"

41

Ah, So

Quinn found himself walking on a well-maintained path through a forest of Sequoia trees. He knew he was dreaming because She Who Comes was walking with him, holding his hand, and every time he looked at Her, She appeared to be a different person. He was talking, trying to figure something out.

"I have been thinking, trying to understand a dilemma I have carried with me throughout my Conscious Life. For most of it, I have not even been able to get clear about the parameters of the dilemma. And then, blessed by You," he looked and saw Regina, "I have had an 'Ah, so' moment. Ah, so that's what it's about…What I need versus what I ought."

She said to him, "So tell me."

"What I want is supposed to mediate between what I need and what I ought. At least that is what I used to think. Now I ask myself, 'But does it? Does it really? Or does what I want just distract me from the dilemma?

Since he knew he was dreaming he wasn't too surprised when he looked over at Regina and saw that it was Calley. So he asked, "How do you deal with it? How do you manage the forces of need, want, and ought?"

"I don't experience it like you. I don't experience need like you. I always get what I need, you don't. You are a part of the experiment, I am not, at least not in the same way. But my time among you, my time loving a mortal has given me some perspective. Perspective that She," She said, pointing a finger upward, "wanted me to have. Goddesses must Love, it is an imperative for us.

"She made us, we, who want for nothing, as the saying goes. Neither need nor want run through us like they do in you. And yet She gave us the capacity to put Ourselves in your place. It is one of the principal ways in which we learn."

"What if what I need is to die? Ought I? Probably not.

"What if what I ought to do is to die? Then maybe I need to.

"What if I don't want to?

"So what?," asked Quinn.

He felt the hand in his shift to another hand.

"We don't die as you do," Oshune laughed. "Your mortality, and the shortness of your life, make all that difficult for you. I would say, focus on the short term, but that is not what you need. So, focus on the next most obvious thing."

The hand in his shifted again.

"I used to believe it was possible to be impeccable," he said.

Salakta responded, "It doesn't work that way, Beloved. What you ought would normally be the mediator between what you need and what you want. But you have gone beyond that. What you ought is actually transcendent. It is the path to transcendence. For you, it is now the only path. It is the only way to find the impeccability you seek. Transcendence is the only way for you. One transcendence after another, until you are as far as you can go. And when you get there, there will be help waiting for you. If you want it."

He felt the hand in his change again. He looked over and saw it was Darvatiye, walking with Her free hand resting on Her belly. She looked up and smiled at him. "So you see, beloved, pursuing what you ought is the path forward. As well as upward. Remember this, the Alpha and the Omega. The Path runs from Aught to Ought. Not just from aught, Nothing, to Something, but from Nothing to The Thing. Aught to Ought. The path runs from Nothingness to what one Ought. And Ought Is the Omega of Life, it is where it ends, with Conscience. This is the true Alpha and Omega. The true beginning and the true end of all things."

42

THE DJINN IN KERKYRA

The next morning, Angelica and Meck drove to the capital to shop for a wet suit with shoes and gloves. There were spares at the Institute, but nothing fit properly: a wetsuit with a hood that would cover her head and hair, shoes that would withstand sharp corals, and gloves that would grip firmly on slippery surfaces, so they went to town.

Pleased with their purchases they returned to the village and parked near the shore, taking the clothes with them as they returned to the young man renting boats. They found him talking to a large, strangely built dark skinned man with flashing blue eyes and a shock of short spiky dark brown and white hair on top of his head. They stopped a short distance away, visible but allowing for the privacy of the others.

"No, no," the stranger said, waving his hands, in an accent that neither could place. "Yes, yes, I mean. Come over. I am here waiting for you."

Angelica took a step back and Meck stepped in front of her. "What do you want?" Meck asked steadily.

"No, no," the stranger said again, excitedly. "There's no need for that," commenting on Meck's defensive posture. "Good job, and all that, but I'm a friend. A friend of yours suggested that I might be of some help to you."

"Oh, yeah? Who?"

"I'm not sure what he is called now, but he introduced himself as Quinn."

"And who are you to me?"

"I am Regina's daughter's father. My name is Micah. And you are Angelica and Meck. Quinn told me I would find the two of you together. By all means, contact Regina and she will verify my story."

"And how can you help us?" Anglica asked over Meck's shoulder.

"Let's go get some lunch," he said, gesturing to the restaurant across the road. "And I'll tell you."

Angelica tapped Meck's shoulder. "It's OK. My intuition checked him out. No lies in what he's said."

"I agree," Meck said, stepping aside and pointing with his head across the street. "Let's go, Mr. Micah."

Micah's big grin dropped to a scowl. "No Mister, just Micah."

In the restaurant they sat at a table that Angelica knew offered the best view of the sunset, hoping they wouldn't be there that long. But Micah turned out to be a voluble and prolific speaker and storyteller.

After ordering drinks and before they ordered food he began talking in this manner: "I am not what you think I am. I am not human. I am half human, half mortal. My mother was mortal and my father was an Embla. And I am very old. Not yet tired of life, but very old. And I apologize for my appearance. This is not my normal form. I can't show it to you here, but I will, I promise."

His torso was big, perhaps bigger than any man Angelica had ever seen, resting on some of the skinniest legs she had ever seen. When he wasn't looking at her, she was of course curious. When he crossed his legs, she saw the sausage shape of his phallus running half-way down the inside of his pants leg. She stifled a gasp.

Of course, he noticed her glance. He said, quietly, "Yes. It's bigger than Thunder Cock the Rock Splitter's. Which I know you have seen. We are friends, and he told me so." Then he got a huge grin on his face and looked away from her. He continued, "Like many males with this condition it doesn't get much bigger when its hard, it just comes erect. My mother, though mortal, had Tree-spirit blood in her, and I inherited woodiness. I will show you my true form later, and you will see."

Meck said, "Enough."

Micah laughed. "Don't worry, she would never leave you for me."

Angelica, momentarily fascinated, asked "Why? Why wouldn't I leave him for you?"

"Because I am not in the Order. I am not a Consort. Even to them, I suspect I am an outcast. I am uncivilized and unpolished. If I am relating to you well, it is because I have a mission to help you. That keeps me focused. Otherwise, I don't think, and in fact I am pretty certain, that you would not like me."

Meck said, "I said enough. Now tell us why you're here. What is this 'mission'?"

Micah went quiet. Angelica could tell by watching his eyes that his thoughts were racing, a thousand images passing across his eyes, in the time of minutes.

Suddenly, knowing this place in herself, she felt a surge of sympathy, and put her hand on his arm. He didn't stop, but a tear rose in his eye, and trailed away down his cheek. He stopped his reverie and raised his other hand to wipe the tear away.

"Suffering," he said. "Goddamn suffering." He sighed, turned to her and said, "Thank you. I haven't felt sympathy in a long time."

Meck, hanging out in an utterly unsympathetic place, said, "What is your mission?"

Micah sighed and took a deep breath. "My mission is to help you wake the dragon."

"Why?"

"Because I know about dragons. I was around before the great spell-cast that turned the few left alive to stone. I even know this one's name. Moah. We fought together against the Embla, and the Dangla, more than once. You must understand that the spell turned even their memories to stone. Soon after the spell was cast, and we, the Djinn, lost them as allies, we were defeated in battle by the forces of De Murgos. He hated us, like he hated the dragons. He took my father's phallus before he killed him. Grabbed it and cut it off. I was there. I watched. All of the Embla who sired children on mortal women were treated the same way. And he would drink their blood and use it to track down their Djinn offspring."

Angelica felt the muscles in his forearm tighten. She stroked his arm.

"Stop it," he said.

"Yeah, stop it," Meck added.

"Because of my mother's mixed blood, I was able to change my shape in ways that allowed me to avoid the sword. I escaped because I couldn't be found. I can turn into wood, an old log, and since wood doesn't bleed red blood, he couldn't find me."

Angelica's mind, trying to distance itself from her sympathetic emotions, thought of a joke about morning wood, and she had to stifle her laugh as she removed her hand.

"Sorry," she said. "The improbability of you got to me."

"Trust me," he said. "I confront the improbability of my existence every day."

"Have you ever met Her?" Angelica asked.

"No, but I am certain She exists. Perhaps She will take me into her fold, now that I know how to help Her."

"Why hasn't She?" Meck wanted to know.

"Because I am a wild card. She doesn't know me well enough to trust me, and I am not beholden to Her." He looked slowly at both of them, in turn, and he said, "I am a free agent. There are no more of my kind. And She did not intervene to stop the slaughter."

After another pause Angelica said, "I know why."

Micah raised what passed for an eyebrow on his face, "Why, then? Why?"

"Because you carry the stain of the blood of De Murgos. It runs in your veins."

"I am my own man," he replied, through gritted teeth.

"Yes, that's it exactly. And hence unpredictable."

"Who the fuck wants to be predictable?"

"She does," Meck replied. He rolled his eyes back in his head, following the training he had received from the Madeleines. "She has witnessed the slaughter of hundreds of thousands of Her people Herself. That you are left alive, improbably, means that She cannot trust your uniqueness, nor your allegiance.

"I hate him."

"She cannot trust that either."

Angelica put her hand on his forearm again. "She will learn to. I am certain of this."

The intention she put in her hand flooded him with stillness.

"You can do that?" he asked, surprise and uncertainty on his face.

"Yes. It is what I used to quiet the dragon while he was inside me."

"If I had any people left you would be a legend among them."

"Perhaps your people left ghosts. We should ask Regina, or a Madeleine."

"I fear even their ghosts are long gone."

Angelica's vision flickered. It seemed that a large crowd of ghosts was assembling behind Micah. "Oh, I think not," she said. "If you can persist in this timeline, it makes sense that they can persist in another."

Micah turned and looked. Seeing nothing, he closed his eyes. Still nothing. He turned back to Angelica and shrugged. "If you can see them, perhaps I can learn to."

43

The Witness of Chantana and the Prophet

Chantana, gravid and in her eighth month, groaned as she rolled over in the bed at Regina's compound. The Prophet, lying next to her, snorted in his sleep. But she had to pee, and her bladder wouldn't hold it anymore, so she padded down the hall, squatted, and relieved herself into the hole in the floor. She stood up, holding her belly in her arms as if she was picking it up separately, kicked the lid over the hole, and pulled the cord from the tank on the wall that released a small amount of water into the tube. She washed her hands, and then her face in the sink. On her way back to bed, she stopped on the balcony and watched, curiously, as a large falling star streaked across the western sky, unusual in its green light. She felt the Prophet move up behind her and he looked at what she was looking at, catching just the tail end of it.

"Wow," he said, softly. Then in Nahasi he asked her, "All is well?"

She nodded, her face shining in the starlight. He leaned down and kissed the top of her head. It had been a difficult few months for her, since she announced to her Council of Healers and Priestesses at the Temple of Wasastami that she was pregnant and was going to marry the father, an off-islander. There was a lot of discontent and consternation. The women were gathered on the walls of the Temple, looking down when he appeared walking across the plaza in traditional clothing.

The Temple was back in the women's hands again, and its doors were open more often than not, the dragons on the steps awake now, and performing their duties as guardians, letting none pass who were unworthy. Their actions were invisible except to a few, and the unworthy would simply stop at the lowest step, unable to move forward as if they were at a wall, able only to move back. The assembled Healers and Priestesses watched to see what would happen.

He stopped at the bottom step, held up his hands and spoke to the dragons in Nahasi, although only a few heard his words of calming and good wishes. He laid his hands on their snouts and a moaning sound of pleasure rose from the stones beneath their feet. He was accepted, and life went on close to how it was intended to go.

Although the remodeling of her compound was finished, and she held audience there during the day, she usually left it to her family at night, spending the night instead with her husband at Regina's compound, where the security was better. It was said that roving bands of malice-filled Priests of the old Skreeva walked the back roads at night and disappeared into the jungle during the day, to hide in their camps. It was also rumored that some Meemons led squads of believers along the roads, ostensibly protecting their own, but really scouting to see the distribution and practices of their native neighbors, marking the locations of the devout, especially the Healers and Priestesses. She had arranged for security for these women herself, after there were several malicious crimes and two rapes committed against them. The malice remained, but the crimes stopped.

Chantana loved her mate, sometimes to her surprise. Every day he worked with the Queen Old Woman stone in the cabinet in Regina's meditation room. Sometimes he worked with the Stone under her audience platform. The work was to imbue the network of stones distributed around the island with the impulse of Conscience, so that the people behaved as they ought to behave. Crime had dropped all over the island, except for the capital, where the density of the Malice was greater there.

She loved the company of Onadaya, Tenara, and Napat but she missed Jasmine and her Consort Guiles, who were gone on a mission to install a Queen Old Woman Stone at the Temple to the Seven Sisters over on the mainland. They had been successful and were supposedly on the return journey. She watched the Prophet struggle a little at first, to establish contact with it from the network on the island. She had been told that this new installation would be close enough to enable connection with the other stones hidden all over the world.

She found herself amazed at the reach and power of the Order and its secrecy. She had never conceived of a network like the Order, never conceived of the curriculum they taught, and most of all she was amazed at the loyalty of the members. Finally, she was deeply impressed by their courage in dealing with the Molecules of Malice, and the consequences to those who had taken them into themselves, however unwittingly.

She was at home one morning preparing for an audience with several western women on a tour of the island when she heard shouting at the gate, demanding entry. Onadaya, who would accompany her along with the Prophet, went to the gate. She heard the gate open amid hurried conversation. She went to the raised platform from which she would pour her healing waters ritual and looked. Three men entered, two men holding a restrained fourth man, who was drooling and struggling against his restraints. She recognized the third man as one of her agents, men she hired to go round to the different main tourist destinations and identify people likely to come see her if invited. They dragged the restrained man over to the stone slab at the base of her ten-foot-tall ceremony tower and laid him on it. He was thrashing, occasionally screaming, but mostly growling and muttering gibberish.

"Something got into him," her agent was saying. "He started attacking people, mostly women. I know him, he is my cousin. This is not how he is normally. Something has happened. Please, Priestess, please heal him!"

"I shall try," she said. "Hold him down."

She prayed over the water, invoking the powers of healing in it, and ladled it onto him. He calmed but not completely, no longer thrashing but still rolling side to side, cursing.

The Prophet had been watching this. He stepped forward and looked up at his beloved, a question in his eyes? She nodded her assent and the Prophet knelt at his head and put his hands on either side. He called to the agent to kneel beside him and told him to hold his cousin's head, and to keep it from banging on the surface of the stone slab. He went to the man's midsection, holding both hands over his stomach and gut. Bumps started appearing on the surface of his skin, then disappearing back into his body. The Prophet's hands began to glow. Little bits of blackness emerged through the skin, drawn to the Prophet's hands and when they hit the glow, they burned out with a spark, leaving ash floating in the air. His abdomen was punctured from within, little blood trails running down his sides. The man stilled.

The Prophet signaled her to pour more water on the man. She prayed and did so, washing the blood away and closing the wounds. The Prophet stood up and the man farted sharply, soiling himself, the blackness of the stool oozing out from under his sarong and the stink of it filling the air. The man was breathing normally, apparently asleep.

The Prophet spoke to the agent. "This man has been somewhere bad. Someplace mean. He either inhaled or ate those black things you saw. They made him malicious. Find out where he went, let us know the location, and keep him away from there."

Chantana said, "You must clean this mess up. I have people coming." She pointed to a hose left behind by the construction crew and still attached to a faucet.

In the coolness of the present morning, she shivered at these memories. The Prophet pulled her close, and she felt his warmth and steadiness and let it fill her.

Today was a big day at Regina's compound. Regina had studied the Maithuna Ceremony held in Brazil, and the limited but supportive involvement by the local Pediments of Nature, as their local Shaman had called the deities. She decided it was time to hold Maithuna at her compound. Her primary goal was to strengthen the relationship with the local Pediments and the Spirits of the Land. It was always a struggle to balance these two with the force of the Spirits of the People. It was Chantana's forte and she had taught the Priestesses of the Order much about how to work with this three-part balancing act in order to keep the psychic world above the island from wobbling too much. The Order had stepped forward strongly in this regard, Priestesses being brought in from elsewhere to learn the rudiments then returning home to begin their Practice. All of this served to both strengthen Chantana and relieve her of some of her work, as her pregnancy progressed.

Chantana had never heard of Maithuna before, but in her dreams she had met Lee, the Prophet's sister and a Librarian in Shambhala. Lee traveled with her there and showed her where the books were, religious books she had mysteriously been able to access and quote from as a child. On her visit she had asked Lee about her childhood access. Lee told her, "Sometimes it happens. Children, especially those with the potential for power, were sometimes left with those doors and windows open, not overbearingly shut down by parents and schools. The older Librarians remember you coming here in your ghost body, but you were actually substantial enough to turn pages with your will alone. You were what, four? Or five?"

"Five and six," Chantana replied.

"Amazing. So here you are again," Lee smiled at her.

Chantana had looked deeply into the texts, focusing on the power of the sacred coupling to 'Feed the World'—the extension of the energy generated from the Ceremony to spread out into the neighboring countryside, not just enhancing the fecundity of the land, but the happiness of the people. She had been reading about the possibilities of the Director of Ceremony to gather the energy generated and direct it toward a specific place and accomplish a specific objective or outcome. Then she was awakened again, by that irrepressible urge to pee.

The inner courtyard was swept clean, and pillows were distributed in a 'V', two in each spot. There were now sixteen couples from the Order on the island, pairs of Priestesses and their Consorts. A pair of pillows was set out for each one, and a final pair of pillows just beyond the point of the 'V'.

Wooden frames on wheels were brought out and set just beyond the pillows at the point of the 'V' and at the open end of the 'V'. Hung from the frames were cloth paintings of Walleed at the closed end and Salakta at the open end. Salakta was the true creator, a form of She Who Comes. Her place was at the open end for Her to pour the blessings of the knowledge of what the Tantra could do, into the container set by the people. Walleed was Her Daughter, and a Goddess of Death, adorned by a necklace of human skulls. She was at the apex, in order to be in charge of where the energy might go, or that it go anywhere at all. She had the power to kill the collective charge. The paintings were rolled up and tied off in the frames, waiting until the right time. Napat prepared a place against the wall. She, Tenara, and Onadaya had been practicing ancient music. Her instrument was a sistrum, Tenara's a drum, and Onadaya would switch out between a small kithara and a flute.

Couples began to arrive in mid-afternoon, gathering around Regina's large dining table, lightly eating hors d'oeuvres and sipping wine, dressed in light linen clothes, the men all wearing sarongs that could fall open in the front, the wen all in draped linen dresses held closed by a belt. Many of the wen had done up their hair, holding it in place with various combs and clips. As the time approached Chantana and the Prophet climbed the observation tower and sat in chairs, choosing to witness rather than participate due to her condition.

As the last of the light fled up the tower and disappeared above the trees, Tenara took up the beater and sounded the big bass drum once. The portraits were unfurled and tied down. Each couple had received written instructions and had been practicing at home, and so knew the sequence of events as they assumed their seats, eight couples to a side, the men on the outside of the 'V', looking in, and the wen on the inside looking out.

They began by gazing at each other with love in their eyes. The music started and the Ceremony began with the wen leaning forward and opening the men's sarongs, gazing intensely with the same love on the phalli revealed before them. The wen leaned forward and engaged briefly in worship, activating the gland at the back of their throats that released the ambrosia, the men doing the same with their tongues against the roof of their mouths. The wen leaned back and opened their robes, the line of flesh from their throats to their phulvas revealed. They stood up, took a step forward, bringing their sex close to the face of their Consorts. The Consorts inhaled as one, and smiling, the Priestesses lowered themselves, sliding the sheath over the sword.

The music played a slow beat, the Priestesses matched it, rocking on the laps of the Consorts. At the apex of the V a cloud of silver light began to form, which then dimmed a little to show Regina, in her ghost body, an image of her at twenty, wearing nothing but a necklace of small animal and snake skulls, invoking her connection to Walleed, falling to her knees and bowing. The painting flapped lightly in a breeze no one could feel. From her knees, in a language no one else knew, she raised her voice, her upper body and arms raised in supplication.

Another cloud of light appeared, a golden cloud, and in it manifested a man, no, a god. It was Ketrak, God of War, holding a long javelin. He laid the javelin down and received worship from Regina before sitting on the pillow. Regina stood before him, then settled down on his phallus.

The music changed rhythm again, faster, the participants rocking in time. In short order, the crowns of flames appeared on the heads of Regina and the Priestesses, still riding their men. A golden glow surrounded the heads of the men. The rhythm increased again, the rocking increased and suddenly some of the Priestesses began raising their arms to the sky, hands spread, taking the energy from their sex and feeding it out into the world. Others cried out in ecstasy.

Then, at the walls of the compound appeared two rows of the Shining Ones of legend from the army of Ketrak, the masculine Devas standing along the wall, the feminine Devis sitting at their feet. Soon their weapons and clothes disappeared, the Devis turned as the Devas sat down. The Devis impaled themselves on the Devas, sitting on clouds of light.

Other music was heard, and human voices singing in ghostly melody. For nearly half an hour this continued until the Priestesses suddenly started crying out as one, raising their arms to feed the world as one, and the Devis did the same.

Then came a popping sound from all over the island as the Molecules of Malice burst into flashes of light. The Consorts shouted as one, coming as one, and the Priestesses did the same, feeding the world with every last drop of the generated energy.

The music slowed, Ketrak and Regina's ghost faded away, the Shining Ones faded away, and the Priestesses collapsed into the arms of their Consorts.

The drum and sistrum stopped. A last low note from Onadaya's flute echoed across the compound.

The Ceremony over, Chantana leaned into the Prophet's ear, "There is light all over the land."

The Prophet replied, "It is said that Love conquers Hate."

44

THE LAMA'S DEMISE

"One might think that one had paid enough, nay, eaten enough, if one was in your condition," She Who Comes said to the Lama's ghost.

And his condition was indeed dire. He had changed so much that She had struggled to trace his signature, as he passed through the hinterlands of the Hindu Kush collecting the scraps of the Molecules of Malice and doing all he knew to do with those scraps by eating them. She barely recognized him, all swollen and lumpy. She found him at sunset sitting on the bottom step of a long series of steps to a Temple high above.

"Even Shamans of old would take a break from drawing out poisons and go purge themselves," She said.

"I cannot digest them anymore. The poison has built up and I fear I shall become Malice itself. And I cannot purge them from fear that what is indigestible will spread the Malice again."

"I understand," She continued. "You did what you knew to do."

She reached forward and smoothed back his long stringy hair from his forehead. He winced as she brushed against one of the many lumps erupting from his skin. "And what do you propose to do about that, old friend?"

"I think I shall 'take the four', as we say. Come back as a four-legged."

"But you haven't killed. Your dharma will not allow it."

"Once I have killed, it will." He would not look at her.

She understood suddenly. "But you are already dead."

"Not dead enough," he replied.

"Since when does the dharma apply when it is not someone else that you will kill?"

"Until now. As you know, there is the Rule, the Exception to the Rule, and the Rule that governs the Exception to the Rule."

"Ah, I see. You are the Exception to the Rule, and the Lords of Dharma that govern the Exceptions have smiled upon you. Is it fixed how you will return?"

"Yes. As a very mean dog. It will not live long. When I return to two legs I shall seek you out."

"Good. I look forward to it. Perhaps you shall learn different Rules."

"That would be nice."

"Would you like me to stay with you?"

"Yes, that would be very nice. But undeserved."

"You are hardly in a position to discern what you deserve and what you don't deserve."

He laughed, a guttural laugh that ended in an explosive fit of coughing. He held his hands over his mouth and when a little flake of Malice escaped his lips, he sucked it back in. He let his hands hang over his knees and drooped his chin toward his chest. "Take care of my children, will you?"

"You know I shall."

She took one of his hands in Her own. Towards dawn he started to chant. As the chant continued, She started to feel heat build within him. As the sun rose and the light descended the steps behind them, the heat built. He sighed. "Thank you," he said. When the sunlight hit him he burst into flames.

Fire being an old friend of Hers, She did not withdraw Her hand until his fingers crumbled to ash in Her grasp. She let it fall and watched the wind carry it away.

45

TOUCHING THE DRAGON

The next day, Micah met Angelica and Meck on the beach at the boat rental. He was wearing sandals, shorts, and a Hawaiian print shirt, and high-tech reflector sunglasses. Meck carried Angelica's wetsuit. They piled into the boat and Meck motored around the rock. He kept twenty feet off while they slowly cruised the length. Near the shoulder hump he throttled down, keeping the boat steady while Angelica stripped down and put on the wetsuit. The Djinn regarded her nudity with a neutral eye. Meck was watching closely, and the Djinn appeared indifferent. He wasn't, but he was very good at appearing to be.

She donned her waterproof rock-climbing shoes and was pulling on her padded climbing gloves when Micah asked her, "Can you swim?"

She glanced sharply at him. "Of course."

"Not that you'll need to," he continued. "I will carry you over." Then he turned to Meck. "Where do you think we should land?"

Meck studied the slabs and chunks and cracks. "There's a place right over there, where some flat rock extends out just above the surface. If you could land her, there's a crack to the right that she should be able to get her hands and feet into and get above the rock on top of it."

"I see it," Micah said. "Do you?" he asked Angelica.

"Yes. What do you mean, you'll carry me?"

"Ready? Come on, I'll show you." He stripped off his clothes, phallus flopping, and jumped in the water. As she watched his torso became a log, a piece of wood, floating and incapable of sinking. "Climb on," he said.

She slid over the side and into the water. He sidled over to her and said, "On my back." She did and he breaststroked over to the flat rock rising a few inches above the surface. She scanned the surface and the crack, chose her path and climbed. Micah followed her. In five minutes, they were at the top of the shoulder. There was a large rock centered over where the spine would be, large enough for the both of them. They sat there, Angelica catching her breath for a moment, stilled herself so she could listen and feel. She tried not to steal glances at the monster tool the Djinn carried. She thought briefly of Regina, and her diminutive stature and wondered briefly how she did it. Then she shook her head to clear the image.

To the side and slightly behind her the Djinn smiled.

"Knock it off," she said, seriously.

"What?" the Djinn asked, smiling in mock innocence. "I wasn't doing anything."

She sighed, settling onto the rock, sitting cross-legged, her phulva resting on the stone. She extended her awareness down into the rock and felt—nothing. She lay belly down on it, face down, too, and extended her awareness through each of her chakras. She felt nothing until she checked through her forehead. There she saw an image of the water rising up to meet her, falling. She felt a flash of confusion. She sat up and turned to the Djinn. "Nothing but the memory of her falling into the water. Must be the last thing she saw."

Micah nodded. "She has been a rock for a long time. Millenia. She has known only sunlight and water and may no longer know even that. Be patient. If there is any awareness left in her, it will take it a while to come to her. And then longer to come to you."

So she sat again, phulva against the rock, focusing on the sensation of dragon in her womb, reasoning that she might respond to dragon before she would respond to human. Micah lay down on his back, folded his hands over his belly and apparently went to sleep, snoring lightly.

As the sun rose higher in the sky, the rock warmed around her and as long as she sat with her back to the wind, she stayed warm enough. She drifted into trance, following her mind but not interfering, watching to see where it went. Water, sunlight, wind, moonlight, endless alternation. Six hours went by, the Djinn stirred. Meck's voice was calling. "Time to go." Putting a hand on her shoulder, the Djinn brought Angelica back to the present. She felt the charge of his hand drop through her nipple to her root. She emerged into awareness angry. "I said, knock it off."

Micah shrugged. "I did." Then "Meck is calling, time to go."

"We'll be back," Angelica said, patting the rock.

When they got back into the boat Meck said, "We've got dinner with Byuteo tonight."

On the beach Micah demurred coming to dinner with them, saying he had his own plans. "I'll see you tomorrow." Micah had found an old grape arbor, loaded with grapes, with the leaves looking particularly delicious.

Byuteo returned to awareness of the present with her hand resting on her Queen Old Woman stone. She had been talking to Regina about the recent Maithuna Ceremony after seeing it through Chantana's memories, transmitted while sitting at her own stone. She paused her thinking about where and how to set it up, she had a dinner meeting with her new guests Nazeem, Nadahlia, and their mother Nadeen. She had arranged for the interpreter that had greeted them upon arrival to be in attendance. The interpreter, a young Consort by the name of Jacques and of French-Moroccan descent had spent the day with the younger ones, letting them tour the facility, bringing meals to their conjoined rooms. Nadeen had declined to go wandering. She was tired, she said when she refused to go with her children. Much to her surprise, room service was provided.

Byuteo had also arranged for each of them to have a guide, someone assigned to them individually to answer questions, as well as keep an eye on them. She had invited Jennifer and Julius, as familiar faces, and Angelica and Meck. Only two of her people spoke Arabic, one was on assignment, and she wanted to take advantage of Jennifer and Julius while they were still on the island. She had also found age and gender-appropriate companions for her guests, who would start their assignments in the morning. She had a suspicion that Nazeem would like his guide very much, given the intelligence about him that had come from the Market Queen. She picked a Priestess with a newborn for Nadahlia, and a wen from a Parthenoa lineage who happened to be in transit through the island for Nadeen.

Byuteo realized that the changes the family was going through would be profound, possibly involving some rejection about not being allowed to go back to their original lives. She had small doubt that the younger ones, brother and sister, would understand enough of their present situation to work at adapting. She hesitated about the mother, even knowing how different she was, that she may at least succumb to a mild depression. Her hope was that by pairing her with another wen from a similar lineage, Nadeen would come to accept her new life without much trouble. She decided it would be best if she assigned Jennifer to the two younger wen, and Julius to the older wen. He was solid and would not try to interfere unduly in their conversation. And he was in on the Secret. The reasoning was the same for assigning Jennifer to the two younger wen; her awareness of the Secret. Neither Jacques nor Nazeem's guide were aware, and she believed Nazeem would not speak of it without talking to his sister and mother first. The cover story, that they were friends of the Order, being given refuge for services rendered, was true enough.

In time, when their new papers were prepared, they would be given the option to be put on the Order's payroll and given jobs to do, even if they weren't invited to join the Order.

Byuteo could only hope that the Order's trust was not misplaced. The alternative was nigh on unthinkable. In the meantime, she would focus on being the gracious host and keeping them from knowing too much about what the Order was really up to.

46

Parting Company

Venge and Matthews had arrived back at the hotel overlooking the ferry dock in the predawn dark, landing silently on the balcony of their room and stepping through the open doors.

Their car was still in the parking lot below. The plan was for them to spend the day resting, then depart in the evening for Cairo and catch a commercial flight back to Italy in the morning. They were to return to the Towers of Marini together and debrief with the High Priestess Freya.

They had sex, slept, and had sex again. Venge was edgy but not talkative. Matthews knew why she was edgy—they would probably not be together much longer, now that the assignment was accomplished—but he decided he would say nothing until she brought it up. She stayed edgy but silent on the flight home. Matthews held her hand, filled with compassion for her suffering, and she fell asleep with a short sigh after Matthews told her how proud he was of her, how supportive she'd been, and what a good job she'd done.

She awoke in a strange state. As the plane was landing, she turned to Matthews and said, "Thank you." Then she said, "I haven't said that to anyone in a long time, except Her after she saved my worthless life."

He replied, "I don't know you well enough to know why you think your life was worthless."

She responded, "Yeah, but do you want to? Do you want to know me?"

He thought for a moment, understanding the fragility of the moment. "Yes. In the time we have left, I want to know you."

"I will think about where to start. Let's get home first."

Silent in the cab ride to the Towers of Marini, she reached over and took his hand. Through the contact, despite her unforgiving facial expression, he could feel her inner turmoil as her memories crossed her mind, trying to decide what to say and what not to say. In the end he felt her relax, surrendering to some thought or weight of feeling. Into that relaxation he said, "You can tell me anything. You can tell me everything. And if you want me to keep it secret I can do that."

Too comforted to speak she could only nod her head and smile at him with gratitude.

They arrived at the castle tower after dark. There was a new electric door over the auto entrance to the castle. When they pulled up to it there were two men acting as guards. The more senior man asked for their identification papers, and when he verified them, he told them "Freya sends her regards. She'll meet with you after breakfast in her office. You have the same rooms you had before. You can park over there," he said pointing to a space between two support columns for the massive weight above. Then he said, "Don't be late," and, smiling now, "Don't be late. I will tell you I have heard that she is pleased with your success, whatever that was."

Their rooms were on the third floor on opposite sides of the hallway. Pausing at the door she turned to him and said, "Give me a few minutes. I want to take a shower and change clothes. I'll knock on your door when I'm dressed, and we can go down to the kitchen and scrounge up something to eat."

He took in the softness in her eyes and in her shoulders. He said, "I'll be waiting." He showered and changed his clothes, too. While he was waiting, he opened a portal in his mind to Bree. He saw her sitting in the kitchen, a small fire in the background. He told her about the assignment, and what had happened. He told her about Venge, and the relationship, and what he wanted to do—stay a few days and spend the time listening to her story, maybe help her with acceptance of what she had become. Bree smiled at him and told him, "Yes, you have my blessing. Just don't bring her home. Yet."

He was lost in reverie when Venge knocked. Shaking his head, he said, "Come in."
She looked around. "Spartan, I see. Very Spartan."
"You're not?"
"Curtains, I like curtains."
"Keeps the birds from looking in the window while you practice in front of the mirror, eh?"
"Asshole."
"Yeah. You changed the braid in your hair. I like it."
"Yeah. It can be looser if I'm not gonna fly."
"You're not gonna fly?"
"Not tonight. I want to go back to the person I was, or at least how I felt, before this," she gestured toward her shoulders."
"How did you feel?"
She thought about it. "I guess that's not right. I used to be angry all the time. Now I'm not. I don't want to go back to that. I want to go back to something I maybe never was. Some baseline of normalcy that I never really had, maybe."
"So why don't we just go down and have a normal supper together?"
"Sounds good. I need to practice being normal, I'm certain. Maybe even feel normal, whatever that is. I don't just think so, I'm sure. I may never have felt normal."
"I'll be your barometer then. Normal pressure. But I want to make sure we start off with something normal."
"What's that?"
"The feeling that comes with knowing you did a good job and you did it well."
"You think?"
"Yeah, I think so." He'd finished pulling his boots on and stood up. He took her by the shoulders in both hands, leaned his head down so she would look at him. "Good job, partner. Mission's over, let's go digest it."

They left the room, he closed the door. Walking down the hall she put her arm in his and said, "OK, Mr. Barometer. Show me the road to Normalville."

"We're on it. I think we'll go in the back way. Less traffic."

She looked up at him and smiled. A normal smile.

They went to the canteen, the former nightclub between the towers and got a table. Venge showed her Order Identification and they got a nice table for two out of the way, with a view of the remains of sunset.

After they ordered, Matthews started off with the question, "So what's the first thing you remember."

"Start at the beginning? Like the story tellers say?"

"Yup."

"The first thing I remember is being angry and scared and alone. I'm maybe two, wearing a soiled diaper, sitting on the floor in the living room of my mother's apartment. I remember crying, and then when the anger at not getting a response passed, I became inconsolable. No one answered my cry." She paused, lost in the memory of her feelings.

After a pause to let her feel it, not wanting to rescue her and pull her out of it, he said, "That's what the True Creator felt."

"Whaat?"

"In the beginning it was just Her. She went round and round and did not weary. All things were in Her, Nothing was outside. Something happened, something moved within Her, and She cried out in pain. But there was no answer, not even an echo. She was inconsolable."

"What did She do?"

"She created the Universe, so there would always be an echo. Since everything that existed was inside Her, She gave away everything, keeping only as much for Herself as a stone."

Venge was silent, thinking and feeling her way into the story.

Into the silence Matthews said, "What will you create to end your inconsolability?"

Venge smiled hugely. "I will create a consolation prize. That is how I will think of you. For now. Let's go flying."

47

DE MURGOS AT THE RED STONE TEMPLE

The Embla, stationed at the Temple of the Stones to monitor the continuous flow of prayer energy that was used to feed De Murgos, were shocked when two winged beings appeared briefly on the circling Pilgrim Grounds and rescued a man who had caused a disturbance. The winged ones had been completely invisible to them up until the moment they revealed themselves. One of them had even been armed with an automatic rifle.

The report on the event, with an emphasis on the voice that issued from the stones, was sent up the line to De Murgos. He was already aware that there had been an interruption in the energy flow to him, and by the time the report got to him, the energy flow had not yet been restored.

He met first with the Embla on duty. He was surprised that the security cameras had been blown out by a lightning strike—it almost never rained there, and he was doubly surprised that it had just been lightning and thunder originating in what seemed to be a cloud of mist, but no rain. He asked what the wings looked like. He was told they were large compared to Embla wings. And dirty. They were brownish and speckled compared to the pure white of the Embla. Remembering the winged being from the encounter at the place called Stonehaven, he was convinced that one of the monsters was the same one he'd faced at the fight in the road between he and his agents against the residents.

He descended to the Temple, wanting to hear the Song of the Stones for himself. He realized that the voice he'd been hearing in the background, singing a single quiet high note was the Song that had been imbued by whatever the liquid was that had been poured onto it.

He'd known that there was another meteor in the foundation of the Temple, but he'd never paid attention to it, focused only on the devotional energy released when people would kiss the fragments of the Black Stone. He hadn't even known it was red, and that it was anciently called the Stone of Happiness.

The people moving past the Black Stone were quietly happy, smiling, whereas before they'd had fierce expressions on their faces, desperate to finish their circling and spiral rotations around the Temple to fulfill their obligations. But when he got within an arm's length of the Red Stone and reached out to touch it, sensing it even through the veneer, the volume amped up and the sweet sound became a scream that had everyone on the grounds holding their hands over their ears. People began to collapse, some screaming, some losing consciousness.

The sound increased in pitch slowly climbing the octaves to a point just audible and suddenly De Murgos felt the oddest sensation. His mind seemed to split. He put his hands on either side of his head and squeezed, trying to keep his head together. He lofted out of the Pilgrim Grounds, noting that his Emblas were also holding their heads. The volume of the sound diminished as he rose, but the note, the horrible note, stayed stuck in his brain.

He retreated to his cave on the far side of the moon. Finally, he could hear himself think, and the pain faded. He reviewed events and realized that he'd grown complacent about the automatic way in which the prayers and devotional energy of the people had been feeding him for all these centuries. He reviewed every detail of that encounter with the monsters, the winged being rising to meet him, telling him to get off the rock, remembering the abandonment by the Embla and Dangla in the face of the threat. He realized that he hadn't heard from the Embla since that day, and that, in his fever, he'd forgotten to look for either of them. He remembered the cylinder of black lightning-infused energy swirling around the man holding his agent. He remembered the rise of the dragon from the young woman covered in blood laying with her head in the lap of the axe-murdered woman, and the incineration of his agent. He remembered the wound he'd suffered from the handful of his psychic filaments thrown back at him by the burned-black man standing there naked and hairless.

He remembered that in his fever, he had forgotten to look for the burned man. Then he remembered the smell of the dragon and remembered where he'd encountered that smell a second time—On Wallid when the Temple was destroyed by the other Temple smashing into it.

He remembered all these things as his ability to think was restored in the aftermath of the Singing Stone.

He had searched Wallid, not finding the dragon, or the woman who had carried it. So he searched again, looking for both her and the burnt man. He found neither. So, he concluded that he had to return to Stonehaven, the place where it began. He assembled a squad of twenty Embla to accompany him, and he descended to the surface again.

Just as he was leaving, he received more reports of his houses of worship collapsing. He resolved to get to the bottom of it while he was on the surface.

48

SETTING UP STONEHAVEN

Stonewen was having fun. She would hang out in basements, or even under concrete slabs, putting her hand up to the floor and she would listen to the conversations above her, looking for signs of hypocrisy in a congregation's leadership. She'd given up listening to conversations of the congregants—they were mostly all hypocrites in one way or another. She'd decided this was a general weakness among humans, but she'd come to despise it in their religious leaders. She'd thought about some way she might leave a calling card, explaining why a particular house of worship was targeted, but she couldn't figure out how this might be done, so she contented herself with the knowledge that once a house collapsed, the people went elsewhere and eventually found themselves a house where the leadership was sincere. Mostly.

Then one day, when she was examining the foundation of a megachurch, she felt a different kind of presence above her, then two, then three. When she felt their footsteps move past her, she stuck her head up through the floor and immediately pulled it back down as she recognized the three as Embla by their mandorlas.

She felt trapped until she remembered that they couldn't move through rock and earth like she could. Then, working through her feelings of rage at them, an idea occurred to her that made her smile. Rather than collapse a corner, or an entire wall, she put both hands on the pad above her and shook the entire building. The concrete fractured, all the walls collapsed and the roof collapsed on the Embla before they could get out. She stuck her head up through the dust and saw all three forms lying prone. One started stirring. She knew she couldn't kill them through their shields, but she couldn't stop herself from cackling at them before she disappeared with a zipping sound, leaving just a hint of blue smoke behind her, dissipating in the dust.

Five hundred miles away, in a 'vacation rental' on the Upper Road, Diana sighed as she closed the laptop. She turned and jumped when she saw the cloud of golden light behind her. She bowed her head and said, "Your Highness."

She Who Comes laughed out loud. "Yes, but am I not also your Lowness? And it's alright Beloved. Raise your beautiful face to me."

Diana did, smiling. "I am my own Lowness, I suspect."

She Who Comes laughed again. "I am here with some delightful news. Delightful to me, certainly, and perhaps you as well."

"Tell me, do please tell me."

"De Murgos is here. With a whole squad of Embla!"

"And why does this delight You?"

"I think we should give him a show. Have you seen the reports from Brazil and Regina's compound on Wallid?"

"Yes. Do you wish to see the Ceremony happen here?"

"Yes. It will be antipathetic to him, and anathema. It will risk his wrath."

"Will he attack?"

"He might. He fears it. He fears sexuality. The liberation of sexual energy counters his repression of it—and you know the suffering that repression causes is a major source of his energy supply. If he does attack it will be from fear or rage, both of which weaken him."

"Yes, but what will he do to us? We cannot fight back against a squad of Embla."

"True. But I will want to add an element to the Ceremony that we've not used before. How much trouble is it to retrieve your Queen Old Woman Stone from under the foundation?"

"Some trouble, I admit. Where do you want it?"

"On the South Lawn. I will show you. Or Madeleine. Whom

would you like to conduct the Ceremony, you or she?"

"I think the honor belongs to her. She will conduct, at the apex, below the portrait of Walleed. I will serve as the channel, at the open end, below the portrait of Salakta."

"Have you been practicing the hymns of Invocation and Evocation to Her?"

"We have, but with limited competency so far. If it will not interfere with the energetics, we can move a sound system outside and use the recordings."

"It will not interfere. The recordings will produce a better result."

"And it will free up more people to participate."

"How many couples are there on site?"

"Only about thirty couples at the moment. How many do you want?"

"I see eighty. How long would it take to assemble them?"

"At least a week."

"Too long. His attention span shortens daily, and I want him here to see this."

"I can call in those that are close. They can be here tomorrow. That would give us forty."

"Twenty on a side should be enough. I shall stay here then, with you. May I abide in you?"

"For the Ceremony? Of course. And if you wish to go about anywhere incognita, I shall be happy to have you with me."

"Good. Then call Madeleine and let's get her involved. I will meet you down at the Mansion."

The Madeleine of Stonehaven was sitting at her altar, engaged in the meditation phase of the practice when she felt Diana's touch on her shoulder. She heard the words form in her mind, "She is here. We have Ceremony to plan."

Madeleine smiled. She stretched, creaking slightly and popping quietly in her shoulder joints. 'More chi gung,' she thought to herself. She was seventy-one now, and deeply grateful for the presence of She Who Comes in her life, and the decades of practice of the Alchemy and the Tantra. She reasserted the Devotion of Gratitude, with which she had started, and ended the sit with the Devotion of Love. As she rose and dressed, she found herself humming one of the mantras of the Hymns to Salakta, and smiling to herself, thinking of Crow, her new Consort. She sighed, looking at the rumpled bedding, reading the outline of his form. What she loved now about a younger Consort was his excess of enthusiasm over form. That, and licking the sweat from his brow before it dripped into her eyes. And she was yet still uncertain of the provenance of what he would do—did he respond to the imagery of what she wanted that she projected into his mind? Or was his intuition just that good?

49

Dragon Stirring

The next day Meck, Micah, and Angelica returned to the dragon rock. Micah, toying with Meck's emotions and pushing him to see how far he could be provoked, leered at Angelica as she stripped off her clothes and put on her wetsuit. He had stripped off his shorts and shirt quickly and sat on the bench seat scratching his pubes, his phallus swinging side to side between his legs in time with the swell. He grinned when Meck scowled.

"Knock it off," Meck growled.

Micah laughed. "I'm fuckin' with you. Trying to get a rise out of you, so to speak."

"I know," Meck said, still scowling. "Knock it off."

"I will, when you relax your shoulders," Micah said seriously. "I'm not your adversary."

Meck deliberately dropped his shoulders, Micah took his hand away from his pubes and stopped leering at Angelica, regarding her seriously.

Aware of what had been going on, and deliberately ignoring it, she suddenly turned to both of them, zipping up the suit, and said, "I don't understand. Dick measuring has always seemed a futile endeavor to me. Why do males do it?" After a quick pause she said, "Never mind. I know why males do it. I also know it doesn't improve anybody's odds of getting laid."

"Well, shit," Micah said. "I don't know about you Meck, but I certainly feel properly chastised."

"Go on, dick head. Get in the water," she said, going over to Meck and kissing him on the cheek.

Grinning broadly, Micah said, "I love it when you talk dirty to me." He slipped over the side.

Angelica jumped in and climbed up on his back. "Behave yourself," she said.

While Meck backed the boat away from the rocks Angelica climbed, Micah climbing after her, his fingers and toes growing into the cracks in the rock like tree roots seeking purchase.

Arriving at the top, Angelica removed her shoes and gloves and unzipped her wetsuit as far as it would go, exposing her belly. She lay down on the rock, putting her forehead on the stone as well.

Micah finished climbing up behind her and sat down on the edge of the rock, naked, breathing, meditating.

Angelica's mind established contact with the level of simple memory that she'd connected with the day before, rain and sunshine and moonlight. As she reconnected with the memory of the dragon falling into the water as the ancient spell had taken hold, the rock beneath her belly began to grow warm, warmer than the sun-exposed rock she felt under her hands.

Suddenly she knew what to do. She turned around to where Micah was sitting cross-legged. She picked up his phallus, marveling a little at its weight and girth, and stroked it into hardness with both hands. Micah regarded her through half closed eyes, saying nothing, sensing what she sensed, but not knowing what she planned.

She opened her mouth as wide as she could and slipped her lips over the head of it, feeling it against the roof of her mouth. Her mouth flooded with saliva as the recently underused gland released. She swallowed, shivering. Before he could orgasm, she turned around and stood up, dropping her wet suit below her knees, and inserted him with some exertion and slid shortly on him, the head of his huge phallus inside, arching her back, working it up and down against her good spot.

She used her skills to draw him quickly into orgasm, standing up as it sprayed out across the rocks between her feet. Working her clitoris, she quickly came to rain, raining on the ejaculate with her own. Suddenly the mixture started to sizzle and then smoke. She could feel the heat through her feet. Then the rock narrowly cracked open.

When the sizzling stopped, she lay down along the crack, and sent a voice down into it, whispering incantations Regina had taught her, rare and powerful words from the necromantic arts, and when she was finished, she sang down into the crack. She sang the dragon's name, "Moah, Moah," calling to it.

She felt it stir, and in its stirring rocks cracked off and fell from its sides, skittering and falling into water. Meck shouted to her. She heard Regina's voice in her head saying, "Enough. Too soon. Not yet," and she stopped singing.

The vibrations in the rock eased.

She thought to herself, nodding, "Yes…Life over and against Death."

Behind her Micah whistled low. "So that's how it's done."

50

Stonehaven Maithuna

The next day, just before she rose from her daily practice of devotions, prayers, blessings, meditations, and illuminations, Madeleine leaned forward, her fingertips touching the central conducting crystal. She was frozen by the contact, her mind opened, and a vision was transferred to her. It was a vision of Embla, dozens of Embla sitting in the trees around the property, watching the buildings and the land. Up near the Pine Eye she saw a white cloud with apparent white flames surrounding the cloud, waving gently.

When the vision ended, she cautiously extended her senses to the middle of the yard and watched as some branches moved out of sync with the light breeze that was blowing. The lighter limbs shook up and down slightly while other limbs bent with the wind. The Embla were, of course, invisible to her but the invisibility didn't change their mass. And some she had seen or been told about were massive. She'd seen the Slayer on his reconnaissance visit to Stonehaven, and he had been huge, a well-built solid form about eight feet tall.

She smiled to herself. They were going to get quite a show. She picked up the landline phone and called Security, asking them to find Craft and the current High Consort Mason, also the Head of Security, and ask them to come see her at the Mansion. Then she called Diana.

She answered, "Hey hon. It's early for you to be calling me.

What's up?"

"You may want to delay heading home for at least a day. We have company in the trees."

"I was going to stay and perform in the Ceremony. I think you should be Walleed and I'll be Salakta. Will that work for you?"

Relief in her voice, Madeleine said, "Thank you. By the way, that's how I saw it, too. And I've called Security and Craft and I'll bring them up to speed with what I saw. They're really there."

"What's there? Who I think?" Diana sent the word 'Embla' down the telepathic channel she and Madeleine maintained.

Madeleine said aloud into the phone, "Yes. A couple dozen, I think. More up in the Pine Eye." She had an image of De Murgos bent over, sniffing the air for traces of Calley and Alam.

She heard him say, "A mortal. And someone different, not the same, an immortal, an elemental I know this one from before. I smelled it at Wallid. And Wekka."

Madeleine shuddered.

"Good then. We'll get started with the set up after breakfast. I have a crew ready to set up the blue stone at the apex just in front of the backdrop painting."

The meeting with the Security squad was tense. The nature of Emblas, as well as Danglas, was academic to both men and wen. Only Craft had seen them, at the fight at the Gatehouse, and Madeleine had been present at the interrogation and destruction in the cistern of the pair sent to spy on Stonehaven.

She had not been impressed by them and the substantiality of their being, and consequently, her nonchalance was encouraging to her people. She said, "No one expects you to see the invisible. All you need to do is be close, and always scanning around you. When they appear, and that is the intention, to make them appear, just aim and shoot. And I want you to use these," she said, passing out short crossbow bolts, the heads of which were made of the same black metal inscribed with arcane sigils that were on the sword Halloran used to cut the arm off the Slayer at the dude ranch battle. Calley had brought the metal blanks with Her from the Invisible Lands, forged and finished by Alam, inscribed by the hand of She Who Comes.

Craft said, "We don't know if these will kill the Embla. But we are pretty sure they will hurt. We believe the Ceremony will make the Embla visible, but we don't know if the Ceremony will collapse their mandorlas, the vesica shaped container that surrounds them. But we're certain it will terrify them. And remember, they can't breathe without their mandorlas. So if you see a crack, make sure you aim for it.

"So, here's the plan. Before the couples seat themselves in the lawn on the south side, we'll exit on the north side through the servants' entrance. We'll split into A and B groups, A to the left, B to the right. Make straight for the woods. The camouflage should get us through the woods if we move silently. No running, there's lots of time to get into position. Take your positions back at least three trees from the edge, four would be better. I want you back-to-back with your partner, in case the Embla mount a defense. We know they have their own will, and that they can go to anger, even rage, if they choose, and they can be terrifying. No freezing. No freezing allowed. They will become partially visible all at once. Point and shoot. Reload and shoot again. Be prepared to defend yourself at close quarters. There is a rumor that your knife will penetrate the mandorla if you're very slow about it. Apparently, the substance of their shields is thixotropic. The faster you move the harder the shielding becomes. From what we know, the Slayer had to drop the shield of his mandorla to attempt to kill Quinn and our team at the dude ranch. What you need to remember is that he was stopped, first by Quinn, and then Halloran took his sword arm. They are not invulnerable. Look for where the branches move, but not from the wind."

The setup took most of the morning and more than half the afternoon. The Queen Old Woman Stone was taken out from under the stage in the tower and rolled carefully on a rubber-tired cart. They set it on the ground and covered it with a gold embroidered sky-blue cloth. The cloth paintings of the goddesses were hung from wooden frames and covered with a black cloth. Pillows were laid out paired in a 'V'. Madeleine and Diana inspected the setup, each sitting at their respective ends. A breeze lifted their hair, the wind chill on their necks.

"It will be cool here this evening," Diana said.

"Much cooler than Wallid," Madeleine agreed.

"Shall we lay fires, then?"

"Yes," Madeleine nodded her head.

Diana got out her walkie-talkie and gave the order, telling them to lay larger fires as the V-shape widened. After receiving instructions from Madeleine and Diana, shortly before sunset the lines of couples formed, emerging from the library and the music room, and descended the veranda steps. Priestesses and Consorts, High Priestesses and High Consorts, both men and wen dressed in sarongs and shawls. The music, played from speakers, started with an invocation Hymn to the Goddess. As prescribed, the wen kneeled and engaged briefly in phallus worship. The men sat down on the cushions cross-legged, sarongs open, and the wen lowered themselves while the men held themselves vertical.

Slowly settling, everyone sighed.

Then the music shifted slightly, and so did the motion of the self-impaled Priestesses.

Humans, like all prey animals, have almost all lost the instinct to look up for predators. It's why a hunter's tree stand works. Only training overcomes the lost instinct. And for the ground dwellers, up is the only place to look. The King of Salamanders sat on the central finger of the ridge behind the Mansion. He could see over the roof. He could see the Embla, like blazing lights in the trees.

Craft, since Quinn had left, had been practicing telepathy with the King. He had held back, focusing from the tree line behind the open end of the vortex. The woods were thinnest there. When the King opened the telepathic channel to his mind, Craft was struck so hard he almost faltered and fell. Almost. What the King showed him was the glistening whitish mandorla of De Murgos himself. Directly over his head. In the image, De Murgos was intently focused on the lawn. He didn't look down. Maybe he thought there were no predators below him. Craft slowly looked up and saw just the slightest column of white light above him. Taking almost a minute he slowly raised his crossbow toward the column.

On the lawn, mass synchrony was happening. The Priestesses began to moan. The Consorts began to tone solitary and singular sustained notes. The music changed rhythm again, and the Priestesses went from rocking to sliding, arms linked over the shoulders of their men. Flickers of flame began to appear around their heads.

Priestesses, on their knees, rode their Consorts.

A runner with a torch ran down the line of set fires, and they went off like lights on a landing strip. Diana raised her arms and her face to the sky and summoned Salakta. She waved her arms slightly and the slightest of breezes wafted down the V. When it arrived, Madeleine raised her arms and sent the breeze upward, redolent of the smell of forty couples having sex.

It fed Walleed. She smiled. Her portrait cloth shifted in a downward erotic speed-wave. The Priestesses felt it, and copied it, rocking, rolling downward energetically. The men groaned. The wen groaned again, still in synchrony, sliding down. There was a shout from a Priestess. Then another.

Then the music shifted again. In unison, the hips of each Priestess began to rise and fall.

The Queen Old Woman Stone began to glow. The Embla shifted, leaning forward.

Security saw it. They saw it in the incongruity of the branches of the trees, just like they'd been told. Even Craft, connected to the King of Salamanders, who saw it all and passed it to him... he focused on the shift forward of the small white column. He remembered to breathe. Quietly, very, very quietly.

The music changed again, winding down from its peak and the rhythm of the Priestesses slowed, they put their foreheads on the Consorts, stilling. They all took one rest breath, as the hymn ended, sighing again in unison as the Hymn of Invocation changed to a Hymn of Evocation.

As Madeleine rode her Consort, she sent the energy of rhythm to Diana, both of them slowed the pace, hands raised and grinning. Salakta in Diana sent it back and it raised up again to Walleed, Goddess of Death in her human skull necklace—Death feeding Life, Life feeding

Death, reciprocal and reciprocating, celebrating the Natural Order of Things, back and forth the energy flowed in the vortex.

This was a new thing, before now in the Ceremony it had been One Way or Another…now it was Both. Slowly, back and forth. Sometimes in clusters, the Crowns of Flame rose on the heads of the Priestesses. All of them.

The fires warmed, and then heated, the flames rose.

The flames rose. Within them Ecstasy verged.

The Emblas and De Murgos leaned forward again.

The Priestesses raised their arms to the sky, in a ripple, synchronous.

And then Sacred. Chronos time became Kairos time.

The Consorts groaned, groans rising to a shout.

The Queen Old Woman Stone lit up. Blue lines emanated from it, along the backs of all the Priestesses, their backs arching in unison. Then lines emanated from it, connecting to all the closer stones in the network. The Ecstasy fed the light.

Then, Diana catching a portion of those lines of blue energy fed them back to Madeleine. Hands forward, riding their Consorts, looking into each other's eyes across forty couples having sex in a Sacred Manner, every Priestess united as one Mind, arms raised, blue light feeding out into the world.

It was too much for the Embla. Shaking in the presence of ecstasy, the lines reminded them of feeding. They became visible. They became hungry, leaning forward, and shimmered into visibility, waiting for their commander, their creator, to allow them to feed.

And Security fired.
Embla shrieked.

Priestesses screamed.
Most of them orgasming,
The resonance vibrating the cross bolts.

Security fired again.
It became violent.
For a moment.

Craft was under the column.
He shot straight up.
Twice.
The light rose up.
There was screaming.

The Priestesses rose up, screaming, too.

The Embla rose up screaming.
Rage.
One fell.
Just one.

He had slipped from his perch, and ran off, bolts sparking off his shield.

Alas, the word, one word in their language in the song of Evocation.

"Alas..." Madeleine thought. "They all got away".

Miles away, Stonewen, resting in the wreckage of another church basement, woke when she started to glow blue. She saw the faint lines of the network of Queen Old Woman Stones, tying her back to Stonehaven.

Suddenly, all around her, she heard the popping noises of the Molecules of Malice as the Love that followed the lines exploded the particles of malice and hate. There was a small drift of Malice molecules in the corner opposite her. They lit up like small sparklers as they winked out. She smiled and went back to resting.

51

Dragon Wakes

Byuteo met with Angelica and Meck shortly after breakfast. "Today," she said, "You are to try and wake the dragon, but not all the way. We do not want it to fly today, but we need it to fly tomorrow. Do you think you can do that? Wake it up but keep it still?"

Angelica, thinking of the mysterious energetic imprint of the egg she carried in her womb, a gift left behind when the dragon she'd carried departed off the coast of Wallid, said "I don't know. I believe I can bring it to a twilight state and keep it dreaming."

"If you can't keep it in twilight, can you put it back to sleep?"

"I don't know how. I don't have that kind of power. Maybe the Djinn does."

"Djinn? What Djinn?"

"Oops. That just slipped out. Sorry."

"Answer the question," Byuteo said sharply.

"This one," Micah said, emerging from camouflage as the wood-paneled wall next to the door. "I came in when they did."

Byuteo was visibly shocked. She stood up from the chair behind her desk and bowed her head. "Your Highness," she said.

"Highness?" Meck asked with a contemptuous edge to his voice.

Micah smiled. "It's from the old days. We were considered Princes among men. No longer. And," he said, speaking to Byuteo, reading her mind, "Yes, I am the last one."

Byuteo, her physical body sitting down and falling asleep, remained standing, naked, in her ghost body. "My profound sympathy, your Highness."

"My thanks, child," Micah said, stepping forward, putting a finger under her chin, and raising her face. He looked her in the eyes. He saw only fearlessness and sympathy there. He inhaled deeply, feeding on both, then he smiled broadly. "My thanks," he said again.

"So, do you think you can help? Bring it only back as far as twilight sleep, waking it fully tomorrow?

"I can try. Angelica's power to call it is very strong. Easy to bring it back too fast. I know this one. Her name is Moah. We fought together. If I am there, she may remember my smell, and that should calm her down. It may be easier if we try to bring her back closer to real twilight. If it's full daylight, she may be inclined to come all the way back. If night falls while Angelica is doing the summoning, she will be more inclined to stay asleep, and dream."

"With his help, I think I can do it. I followed the sleep and dreaming states of the one I carried very closely. I know what it feels like in me."

"Good then. We must try," Byuteo said. "You go in the afternoon. I will go with you. And please do take one of the Institute's boats this time. I got the invoice yesterday from the boat renter."

They met at 3:00 on one of the Institute's docks. Micah rose up out of the wooden pier in front of them as they prepared to Board. Byuteo cracked a big smile. Meck groused that he was getting tired of that trick. Angelica smacked him on the arm.

The boat Byuteo chose was larger than the boat they'd been renting. It had two decks, the upper being the bridge. It was outfitted to look like a sport fishing boat and had the Institute's logo stenciled on both sides. Byuteo backed it out of the slip and piloted it through the small harbor. When she had it out in open water she headed west.

Meck, at her elbow learning the throttle, the trim tabs, and the instrumentation, asked, "Wrong direction?"

"We're heading away, out of sight of the town harbor, then we'll come around and approach the rock unseen on the far side. People in town noticed you before. They were wondering what you were doing on the rock."

Meck nodded his affirmative understanding and focused on the depth finder.

Once out of sight of land they turned east. Meck took over the wheel. Byuteo's ghost body stood next to him, giving him the appraising side-eye the entire time.

They approached the rock from the north, keeping it between the boat and the image of the town. They watched as Angelica put on her wet suit.

Byuteo called her over. She was holding a water-proof fanny pack with a web belt in one hand, and in the other she opened the hand revealing a crystal ball. She put it in Angelica's hand. "In depictions of these dragons, you often see that they are holding a ball in one hand, yes?

Angelica nodded.

Byuteo continued, "Do you know what it symbolizes?

Angelica shook her head.

"It is sometimes called 'The Pearl'. It is a symbol of the Diamond Body, the near-Immortal body that our Alchemical Practice is supposed to create. Look closely at this one," she said. "Look at the impurity in the middle."

There was a cloud encased in the sphere in the form of a lightning strike. "This is our awareness, inside and inhabiting the sphere of our Immortal Body. It is sometimes called 'The Irritant', much like a pearl requires an irritant lodged in its host in order to form around it. You are to keep this with you. Imbue it with your Spirit and Essence over the next twenty-four hours. Tomorrow, when it is time for you to fully wake Moah, drop it down into the crack you have made."

Angelica was surprised that Byuteo knew about the crack in the rock.

Byuteo read the surprise and, standing up, suddenly teleported to the top of rock where Angelica and Micah had broken it open. Standing there, she said, "Oh yes. Of course, I know about it. I have inspected it thoroughly and I agree with your approach. Quite brilliant, actually."

She held the crystal out in her hand, directly over what would be the crack. "I can feel it, I can feel the dragon longing for the Pearl. They keep them for us, you know." She teleported back to the deck of the boat. "They keep them for us, guard them for us, always looking, and always hating to look, to find someone worthy of the gift." She put the crystal into the pouch, zipped it up and said, "Keep this with you until tomorrow."

Angelica took it and fastened it around her waist, adjusting the belt for a snug fit. "I will," she said. As before, Micah ferried her over to the rock. She climbed off and up, now knowing the path. She arrived at the top, looked once at the boat, and sat down, waiting for Micah. Sitting down she could not be seen from the boat.

Byuteo went to Meck, his hand on the throttles, keeping the boat in position. "Back away from the rock," she said. Then, "What's the depth finder read out now?"

Meck answered, "Seven meters."

"Perfect," she said. "We have an anchor, and the cable is ten meters long. See the red button on the dash? Push it and the anchor will drop. Let's see if we can hook it on the bottom and stabilize our position. That way we can shut down the engine."

Meck pushed the button. There was a splash off the bow and the sound of cable unspooling from a drum. When it stopped Meck put the throttles in neutral, letting the boat drift in the swell. Shortly the boat stopped drifting, simply rising and falling. He shut down the engines.

"Good," she said. "Now come here." Meck stepped over to where she was sitting. "I am a High Priestess of the Order of the Fleur de Vie. You are a Consort. I am in need of your attentions." She opened her sarong and spread her legs. "Put your mouth on me," she said, smiling.

Meck looked at her hard, a serious expression on his face, wondering about what was happening up on the rock.

Gesturing with one hand that he should get on his knees, "Don't be so serious, Mechanic. Feed."

He had never touched a ghost before. Everywhere he touched she was warm and firm. Soon she was wet as well. And the edges of her skin became sparkly in his peripheral vision. She became a sparkly ghost. Then the sparkles started to buzz faintly. Soon the buzz became a soft growl deep in her throat.

The growl became a shout as she orgasmed. After catching her breath, she told Meck to stand up and she stood up. She undid his shorts, freeing his phallus, and she took it in hand, and led him below deck to the cabin.

Up on the dragon Angelica did not hear the shout, although Micah did, and it made him grin. Angelica was already laying down on the crack in the rock, feeling her way down into the mass and darkness below her. She was singing a song, a wordless lullaby that she had used to calm her own dragon when she was carrying it around.

Deeper into the rock her awareness sank. Suddenly she was stopped by something solid, more solid than even her perception of the rock she was laying on. She touched the dragon. Since the day before the crack widened all the way to the living being trapped there.

It wasn't breathing.

She withdrew, sliding up back into herself. She heard Byuteo's words, "Imbue it with your Spirit and your Essence." She suddenly knew what that meant. She stood up and unzipped the wetsuit, peeling it off. She took up the pouch holding the crystal and opened it, palming the stone in her hand. She looked at Micah. "It's important," she said. "Can you get hard without me touching you?"

He shrugged as if he didn't know. He said, "Probably," although he was certain he could. Just watching Angelica naked was enough to start that feeling between his legs.

She shrugged back at him. "We'll just see then." She reached down, spread herself, and slipped the crystal sphere inside herself. She lay back down on the crack. She dropped her ghost body back down, laying herself out on the dragon's back.

The crystal within her began to warm. "I have what you want. I have the Diamond Body within me." Then the crystal began to spin of its own accord, the lightning bound within it began to shoot little sparks within her. Those sensations she sent forward into the dragon.

Up laying on the crack, her body moaned as she could feel the orgasm building. She started to drip rain down into the crack.

Micah, who had never seen this level of the Sacred Erotic before, was fully hard, and it was all he could do to not touch himself. He got to his knees, putting his face right up behind Angelica, watching, drooling with thirst, and he did not touch her. He let the sensations build in him, he surrendered to the Beauty before him, and eyes narrowed, he groaned himself, ejaculating into the crack in the rock.

Angelica, her ghost body on the dragon's back felt the spatters of Micah on her back, on her backside, down the backs of her thighs. Enough landed between her legs that when her present body dripped rain onto the copious spread from Micah, the mixture began to sizzle as before, except now the heat of it reached into the dragon. The fire touched its heart and lit it up.

It beat once, then the entire island groaned, some stones falling away into the sea. The dragon huffed, breathing once, steam coming up from the water level with its nose.

"Sing it to sleep, Angelica," Micah said urgently. "Sing it back to sleep."

Angelica sighed, returning from her trance of continuous orgasm, breathing down into the rock, soothing the beast with songs of promise.

On the boat Meck groaned at the same time as the Dragon, his legs shaking like the rocks as he fed the ghost of the High Priestess before him.

She wiped the corner of her mouth, licking the last bit of him from her finger. Eyes closed, smiling, and in a ghostly echoing voice, said, "Good Consort."

Leaning on the bulkhead over her head, waiting for his legs to stop shaking so he could stand on them, he whispered hoarsely, "I'm honored."

52

On the Mountain

Angelica, dreaming on the crack, woke up and told Micah they were to spend the night on the Dragon Rock. Micah climbed down to the water and shouted to the boat. Meck shouted back to take care of Angelica and Micah said he would. Meck turned on the anchor cable spool and it pulled the anchor up, and the boat took off, going back the indirect way it came. All the way back to the dock, Byuteo stood next to him, brushing shoulders, bumping hips, stroking down the front of his shorts sometimes. They filled themselves with each other's minds, thinking only of what they would do to each other overnight.

Up on the rock, the Djinn being a Djinn, conjured food and drink, and as the sun set, he conjured a small fire, a fire that burned hotter than it looked, yet out of the sight lines to shore. He conjured a blanket for Angelica, and one for himself, although she suspected he didn't need one.

Angelica broke her silence. "In the trance just then, I had a vision of Regina, the Madeleine from Stonehaven and Byuteo in conversation with She Who Comes." She paused to shiver in ecstasy as the crystal moved within her. When it stopped, she grinned and said, "At first light, I am to drop the crystal into the crack to finish bringing the dragon back. We will leave immediately, you with me, and ride the dragon someplace we will have to fly to. I don't know where yet, they'll tell me in the morning." Angelica yawned and shuddered. "I'm so tired," she said, and lay down on her side. Micah watched her breathe until he was sure she was asleep. He turned to watch the sunset, his eyes seeing memories. When darkness settled in, he lay down beside her, spooning, shielding her from the wind.

"Where is he?" Regina wanted to know, so she sent the query to She Who Comes.

She Who Comes responded with, "He just left Wekka again. The sound from the singing stone had him holding his hands over his ears and his face was contorted in pain." Regina could feel the grin. "He has landed on one of his favorite mountains, Shinai. He has his entire cohort with him. It would be a good place for us to assemble."

"Let us go to Katra then. He can see us there from Shinai."

There are more than a hundred Sacred Mountains on the planet. Queen Old Woman Stones had been planted near the summits of each of them.

On Wallid, Jasmine had returned with Guiles the day before from her assignment to place a stone at the Temple of the Seven Sisters. She helped the Prophet roll the large Queen Old Woman Stone from the cabinet in Regina's meditation room. Guiles was upstairs guarding Regina's body with Tenara and Napat.

Chantana, heavy with child, reclined on her side on pillows behind the Prophet. She had noticed that when he did this kind of energetic work the muscles in his back would knot up, painfully twisting his ribs. She had discovered that all she had to do was push on the bump, and the muscles would relax.

The Prophet put his hands on the stone, muttering the mantra, "Be Good. Be Good. Be Good." Jasmine put her hands on the stone, and suddenly they both began to tingle. The stone lit up with a blue light. The light suddenly coalesced into lines that ran, they knew, to the other Stones hidden under Temples. The light spread to other stones on other islands, then to the mainland, spreading the light in a network, igniting and passing the mantra along with the light.

The Crown of Flames appeared over Jasmine's head, and her heart emitted a green light. The light sank to the level of her solar plexus.

She put her hands there, palms up, and a glowing green tetrahedron emerged. She took it and placed it in the air over the Queen Old Woman Stone, and it started to spin. Then it started to bounce slightly. The bounce rhythm entered into the blue light from the stone and made it pulse with the beat of the Higher Heart.

A golden nimbus appeared around the Prophet's head. In a few minutes, all the Stones around the world were networked, in many cases assisted by members of the Order, lending their souls and their energy to boost the network and keep it lit up.

In the courtyard of Regina's compound, the other Priestesses and Consorts on the island commenced a Maithuna ritual.

The same happened at Stonehaven, Kerkyra, Rimini, Bath, and other properties of the Order around the world. In places where a group could not be brought together, such as among the management staff at hotels across the planet, couples, and small groups of couples, also commenced with the Ceremony. Their energies were added to the energies of the Stones, and the pulse of the Higher Heart headed toward global manifestation.

On the mainland, in a chamber under one of his Temples, Quinn-Skreeva leaned over and kissed the very pregnant sleeping Darvatiye "Is it today then?" She rolled toward him, opening an eye.

"It is, my darling. Go back to sleep."

"Will you return to me then?"

"I think so," he said. And in his tightly sealed mind he thought to himself, "In one form or another."

Lee appeared and led him by the hand, following the vibrating rails of light connecting the Queen Old Woman stones as they changed direction. She disappeared as he emerged, standing out, the first on Katra, staring at the army of De Murgos across the open sky, his six arms and three heads, looking side to side, sharing this with his brothers. He found it mildly remarkable that he was completely unafraid.

Neither De Murgos nor his horde noticed the god-man standing there. Quinn grinned at the irony. "Still forgotten," he ruminated, smiling to himself.

While he was standing there, the blue light network came online visibly. In every place there was a stone, an image of the two mountains appeared, a holographic projection, focusing first on Quinn, then on the army on the other mountain looking around at the surrounding landscape. The projection was visible to anyone who looked in the direction of a Queen Old Woman Stone. The intention was to provide the opportunity for as many people as possible to witness what would happen on the mountains.

Ketrak appeared next, Regina at his side. He was naked, holding a long lance, Regina had a shield and a short sword. Suddenly, as if from nothing, a line of Devas and Devis, a line of Shining Ones a thousand strong appeared in a circle around the top of Mount Katra, wearing shoulder plates and golden helmets, carrying long lances like Ketrak.

The army of De Murgos finally noticed them then, and grouped themselves on that side of Shinai to see what was going on.

"Amateurs," Ketrak whispered to Regina.

Suddenly, the sun was darkened by a huge flying beast. It settled on the mountain top behind Quinn, Ketrak, and Regina, its upper body flashing red scales in the sunlight. Micah slid off the dragon, followed by Angelica. Micah joined the line of three to form four, just below the peak. His eyes glowed with power. He raised his hand and turned slowly in a circle. He found the Queen Old Woman stone buried near the peak and summoned it to himself. He stood there, holding it, while it glowed an electric blue color. Regina reached over and put her hand on it, becoming a blue glow herself.

She Who Comes appeared behind the four in a glistening mandorla of light that collapsed when Her feet touched the ground. Angelica stepped back as She Who Comes, smiling brilliantly at her, approached Moah and petted her snout, scratching her under her chin. "May I ride you?" She asked. "Will you carry me?"

Moah huffed at Her and She climbed up, floating in the air above the four and the circle of Shining Ones.

She handed Angelica a small cloth bag, closed by a drawstring. "Look for my signal then put these on."

De Murgos blanched, his gut contracting as if he was going to vomit. The monster, that was the Djinn, was bad. But it was the Harlot on the Beast of his nightmare. She rose in the air on the dragon and screamed at him, "Get off the rock! Get off me!"

Behind Her, the Harlot's daughter Calley raised a bank of thunderheads, firing lightning. The Harlot clapped her hands and in the Dragon's hands appeared the corpse of the Embla She'd taken the life of years before, kept frozen under the ice of Greenland. The dragon tossed the corpse and it slid down the mountain, bouncing off rocks and boulders, sliding to a clumsy halt near the bottom of the gorge between the two mountains.

The Embla, enraged and shouting, charged down the slope, feet just above the ground. Even the Dangla hiding in the rocks at the edge of the army shouted.

"Really?" Ketrak asked Regina. When she shrugged, he asked Micah, "Really? This is how he fights?"

Micah responded, "Killing isn't his forte. Making men kill for him is."

The wave of Embla reached the first of the Shining Ones' lances. Not stopping, hoping to overrun the line, every time a lance point engraved with sigils would touch an Embla they would burst into flame, some screaming, others falling in a pile of ash. In some places, the weight of the Embla overwhelmed the line and their swords felled Shining Ones. And where they fell another would emerge from the earth to take its place.

Ketrak whispered to Regina, "I can do this all day,"

She whispered back, "It is why you have never been defeated."

He grinned hugely.

No new Embla appeared to replace their casualties. The Embla had each been fashioned by their creator's hands, and that took time, time De Murgos did not have.

Moah held up the crystal ball of Immortality. It began to spin in her hand. In Wekka, the red stone in the foundation of the Temple began to sing louder, and then louder still. It reached the ears of De Murgos and wormed its way into his head. The pain in his head, the pitch made it feel like his head would split.

Everywhere there was a Queen Old Woman stone and a Priestess nearby, Maithuna was happening. Touching the stones brought power into the network, and the blue light began to pulse, and then hum.

Decades before, when he was twenty-one, Quinn had an extended encounter with the being on the next mountain. Then De Murgos left him, left the possession of Quinn's body. As he left, De Murgos tried to place his hand on the top of Quinn's head, telling Quinn to not look upon his face. Quinn, of course, was having none of it. He wrestled with De Murgos, trying to raise his face to see the being in front of him. Finally, he came up with a ruse to succeed in looking. He employed it and succeeded. The hand came down on his forehead, rather than on top of his head, and the immediate impact was that he could no longer see the being in front of him. In fact, it blinded his higher insight capacity, handicapping his psychic development.

Quinn now faced the same being. He knew this even though the being wore a mask. Quinn remembered when the being reappeared in front of him a few months later and commanded him to wait. He had waited more than thirty years, with no return or further reappearance of De Murgos. He had waited in every way he could think of, but nothing drew the being back to him. He felt he had wasted his life, obeying a higher being that never returned, never turned its face to him again.

Suddenly, decades of resentment rose up in him. He shivered with rage.

Impatient with it all, the god-man Quinn the Destroyer pointed his lance at De Murgos. "You! I want you!" and stepped forward into the air, leaving his brothers behind.

De Murgos held out his hand in a halting gesture and the god-man stopped as if he'd been frozen. Then a light in the shape of De Murgos' hand blazed forth from the god-man's forehead.

De Murgos was visibly shocked.

The god-man asked him, "Do you remember me? Do you remember me now?"

"Yes. You tricked me. You looked upon my face. You know what I truly look like. You cannot be allowed to live."

"You missed your chance, motherfucker." A golden whirlwind formed over him in strands that coalesced into a funnel, a vortex of golden light.

De Murgos threw a bolt of lightning at him.

Quinn separated himself from himself muttering, "I am nothing." He left his body, traveling upward, casting his awareness into the whirlwind. The bolt hit his body and it dissolved into black dust. Encapsulated in the golden whirlwind, he charged De Murgos. De

Murgos' eyes widened in fear and terror. Paralyzed, he didn't move as Quinn-Skreeva, the god of Destruction, encased in the golden whirlwind swept toward him and when Quinn was within arm's length he reached out and tore the mask from the face, shouting, "Get off this rock! De Murgos screamed and took off, aloft, leaving the rock.

The Embla and the Dangla all flew up, following their Master except for a small group of Dangla, who remained behind.

The whirlwind of golden light stayed, stopped in mid-air, the mask crumbled to dust in Quinn's hand.

53

Off the Rock

The global network of Priestesses and Consorts all orgasmed at the same moment, those near Queen Old Woman Stones, placed their hands on the stones and fed the network. Those not near a stone fed the world. The ecstatic power released transmitted itself to the stone Micah was holding. As the field of blue light expanded, Regina reached over and touched it with one hand, raising her other hand, palm open, fingers spread, to the sky. She Who Comes raised both arms. The power blew through Regina's ghost body, then through She Who Comes, and a blinding flash of light encompassed everyone.

When the flare died, the Embla were blind. The army of She Who Comes stood there, every one of them wearing sunglasses.

As they flew, De Murgos and all of his creations flew blindly into a silver white web with layered filaments that appeared when one of them touched it. Every one flashed out of existence, dying in a burst of light and a wealth of sighs. The best fireworks ever. The web was the gift of the First One, made by Her almost two thousand years ago when She, the First True Creator, heard the cries for help from She Who Comes. It just took a long time to get there from the center of the Universe.

The dragon carried She Who Comes over to Quinn, or rather, to what had been Quinn, floating in the air halfway between the peaks.

"You are Trismegistus now, thrice enlightened. What will you do?" She Who Comes asked him.

He answered, "The human in me was dying when the first Enlightenment came. I was dying again, the second time the Enlightenment came. I died yet again, just now in the third Enlightenment. Not my third death either, but my seventh. My human, my inner human was dying anyway, grown tired of all the suffering. Yet my awareness insists on surviving. I have died enough, I think, to be allowed to die, and perhaps, to be born again on the eighth step, the first note of the next octave. I know well that if suffering is inevitable, then choose the path with greater Beauty."

She Who Comes, floating in the air on the dragon, looked closely at the Beauty glowing from the man inside the whirlwind. Tears ran down her face. She said, "It worked. The strategy worked."

"They were your words, months ago. I just said them back to you. You said, 'Indeterminacy is the companion of Life, Overdeterminacy is the companion of Death'."

"Indeterminacy is the companion of Life. Life requires flexibility, leaning with the wind. I couldn't prevail in such an Indeterminate environment. There were always too many variables, too many options. Too many masks used by De Murgos. Too much chaos to break the people free from the Great Lie."

"He and his army became Overdetermined. They became too rigid to continue to live as they had. Their fear locked them in. The fear of the Trimerase, fear of the God of War and his Consort Regina's ghost, the Djinn and the Dragon almost paralyzed him. Then he saw you on the dragon. He thought he had no other option than up and out. They could not move, except in the direction they moved, to escape. There was no other path for them. Overdetermined, they die. They died like we die. It was inevitable."

"Still, thank you."

He nodded his head and asked, "Do I have your blessing then, to go? Remember, all phenomena are ephemeral. Please give my blessing to our son."

She nodded. "Thundercock the Rock Splitter. Bodhisattva of Assholes. Man-god Skreeva. My beloved. Father of my son. Yes, go. It will all be better here now."

He leaned forward and kissed her, then pulled away smiling.

The vortex turned into a column of light, and he could no longer be seen.

A great bellow of laughter rang from the column, then the column collapsed and disappeared.

Regina said, "He deserved to die laughing."

Micah leaned toward her. "He didn't die."

"What?"

"He isn't dead."

"Where is he, then?"

"Somewhere else," Micah said with a finality and turned from his former lover, so she wouldn't see the tear slip down his weathered and ancient face. And then he relented and looked into 'somewhere else'. "He is dancing," he said, and smiled.

54

RETURN TO KERKYRA

Angelica sat on a rock near the top of Katra. Ash was still falling from the burning of the Embla and the Dangla, most of whom had followed the Embla into the web, not wanting to be left behind. She watched as Lee appeared and took her father Micah's hand, disappearing into the Eternal World of Shambhala. Regina reached around Ketrak's body, hugging herself to him, then they too, along with the army of Shining Ones, disappeared.

Withdrawing her gaze from the distance, She Who Comes turned and slowly brought the dragon to Angelica's side, dismounted, and came and sat next to her.

Angelica's body felt embraced with warmth, and she realized, with Love emanating from the body of the Goddess. Barely breathing she asked, "Diosa, what happens now?"

"I return you to Kerkyra, if that's where you want to go." Diosa paused. "And I will make arrangements for your Initiation as a High Priestess. You will be the youngest in a long time. Youngest since Regina. You have seen and done enough to qualify."

"I don't know where I want to go. And I don't much want a Consort right now." She went quiet, then asked, "What will happen to him?" nodding toward the empty sky where Quinn had been.

"There are laws about these things, these rare things that sometimes happen. They are not as strict as Natural Laws, but determinations are made by a Council called the Lords of Dharma. We shall see what they say. There is a huge hole now in the fabric of human affairs. It needs to be filled by a New Mythology. The hole leaves the everyday people unprotected, their prayers mostly unheard and their devotion unreceived. And the Mystery needs a presence, a figurehead to replace the long-ago slain Hermes Trismegistus. And soon we will welcome the child who will replace Skreeva. It will not be long."

Angelica sighed. "I realize there are too many possibilities for you to give me a solid answer."

"Yes, beloved, too many. It is all very Indeterminate. That is why I asked you what you wanted."

"I want to stay with you. Or perhaps I should say I want you to stay with me," she whispered, tears running down her cheeks as the adrenaline faded.

"I think I know a place where that could happen."

Emmalia was out on the flat in front of the cabin. She had three days left in her sojourn before she returned to Stonehaven. She was staring westward, into the setting sun, drinking in the light with her eyes, fueling her Soul, so that she could alchemize the light into her Spirit. Suddenly before her flashed a huge moving shadow, as if from a cloud. She followed the cloud, turning around to watch it settle on the mountain behind the cabin. The shadow took the form of a dragon as it touched the earth, and two riders dismounted. She watched them descend the mountain toward her. She turned and sat facing the sun again.

The two sat beside her, and together they watched. When the last of Sola's orb was below the horizon, Emmalia spoke. "I know who you are. Diosa, I am uncertain as to how to respond to the Presence of your Grace, tell me how. And you, you are Angelica. I remember you. I was the attendant at the Gate House when you first arrived at Stonehaven."

The Goddess put a hand in the air over Emmalia's head. Her crown of flames burst into light. Emmalia almost swooned, rocking her torso in a circle. "It was all there," the Goddess said. "It just needed organizing. When you go, leave everything here for her to use. She will be your replacement."

Emmalia reached out on either side to steady herself, putting one hand on Angelica and one hand on Diosa. Both hands immediately resonated with the Higher Heart."

"That is yours now, make sure you take it with you."

And then, her hands on the arms of two people who had no barrier, no buffer to the suffering of the world, powered by the pulse of the Higher Heart, Emmalia overcame the consequences of the Kundalini buffer. The power rose up her spine in a vortex originating in her lower back.

She struggled to breathe. She panted, leaning forward, but refusing to let go of the arms she held. Then her eyes rolled back in her head, and she lost consciousness and fell over backward, her legs still crossed on the ground.

Angelica looked at Diosa, smiling slightly. "A new assignment?" she asked.

"Yes," Diosa smiled. "You are to her what Diana was to you. Can you do it?"

"Yes."

"The Order will send someone to pick her up in three days. Her time here is done. If she needs more, you can tell them to come back in a week. Are you good with this?"

Angelica thought. She'd realized that being thoughtful was a good way to be. She turned around and looked at the cabin, with its row of windows facing south, and thought of spending a whole night watching the Moon cross through each of them. "Yes," she said, looking out over the mountains below her. "I'm good. Thank you."

Diosa looked off into the distance with her. "There is only one bed here. Sometimes, when your nightmares were bad after your Release, Diana would sleep with you. Did you know that?"

"No, I did not."

"Sometimes the comfort of another's arms in sleep is the only thing that lets them know they are not alone."

"Mother, have you spent much time alone?"

"Eons."

"Then let me hold you."

Suddenly Diosa's form disappeared and then Angelica felt Diosa within herself. She spoke, "This is how I am not alone."

Angelica grinned then wrapped her arms around herself. "Then let me hold you this way," turning side to side.

Together, turning side to side, they both said simultaneously, "Mmm, mmmm."

Angelica smiled, thinking to herself, "She's just a girl after all."

Diosa laughed. "Come, let me help you carry her inside." Diosa's hand raised over Emmalia's prone form. Emmalia levitated. Angelica gasped

Diosa smiled. "Who do you think kept everyone off the ground at the fight?" Up the hill the dragon huffed. "Except him, of course," Diosa said apologetically.

Emmalia safely in bed, Angelica asked Diosa, "What am I to do here?

Diosa said, "Pray, meditate, practice the devotions, the blessings and the illuminations I will send you, and wait.

"Wait for what?"

"Waiting is its own challenge," Diosa said. "I must go."

"I love you."

"And I love you. Wait here for me until I return."

And then She was gone.

Angelica sat at the kitchen table, looking over at Emmalia, who occasionally whimpered in her sleep. There was an unopened bottle of wine on the table. She thought to herself, "If I'm gonna sleep with her I need to be really drunk." She went to the kitchen drawers, looking for a corkscrew.

55

Return to Bree

Matthews stood on the small hill just outside the boundary of the Invisible Lands. He knew someone would see him eventually. He thought back on the past few weeks in Marini. He'd waited until a Consort could be found and assigned to Venge. She didn't want one, but Freya thought it better that she not be alone. The Consort was counseled, "Love is patient." And left to his own chances to work on his impatience with behavior that did not conform to his expectations. Matthews thought those expectations, especially of Venge, would be on the chopping block shortly.

He'd figured out that if he had something he wanted to do with her, or for her, he had to make it appear that it was her idea. Really, she wanted no control over her behavior and choices except her self-control. Suggestions were mostly met with contempt. The guy was in for it. Before he left he told the man, whom Venge had compelled to watch them have sex, that the way to foster patience was to cultivate his capacity for indifference. And to remember that whenever she tried to make some issue about him, that it would always likely be about her.

She had enormous work on herself yet to do. But she had flight as her escape now, and she would take to it often.

Matthews sighed and shrugged, filling his mind with images of the Land behind the barrier of invisibility. Then images, and the memories of his sensations and feelings for Bree. He refused to think about the big issue of his mortality, with regard to Her immortality. He knew from talking to Alam, that time flowed differently in the Invisible Land, and that his mortality didn't seem too important to either him or Calley anymore. He'd been amazed when Alam told him he was three thousand years old.

Just on the other side of the barrier Bree stood, looking at him, evaluating him. She watched him leaving his recent past behind him, shedding it like a suit of old skins, and watched as he focused on where he was, watched and felt him begin to focus on Her. She wasn't sure about dropping the barrier until she felt a piercing longing arise in him for Her.

That was when she knew, knew that his longing would keep him true. She dropped the barrier, enjoying his surprise that She'd been standing right there, one arm cradling her belly, close enough to touch. Her hair lifted with a different breeze.

His eyebrows lifted when he saw how she was standing. He dropped to one knee, bowing his head. He released his wings and looked up at her. "Come fly with me," he smiled.

56

THE NEOMYTHIC AGE

She Who Comes knew that it would be a while before people would come to sense the absence of the being they'd been feeding with their devotion and prayers for millennia. She'd called a meeting of the High Council to discuss what should be done for the people, as they came to realize their world had changed. In the beginning, once She'd laid out the problem, the room devolved into a kind of raucous joy with shouts of:

"Let's teach men to cook."

"First teach them to do dishes and laundry."

"No, first teach them to clean the bathroom."

The Consorts behind the High Priestesses all smiled and laughed with them, confident because they all knew how to do these things.

When it settled down again, She told them Her beginnings of a plan.

"We are in a new time for the people, a New Age, the time of new stories about creation and the Creator. We are living in the Neomythic Age, and into that New Age we shall carry the four pediments of our principles: The Truth, Ecstasy, Conscience, and The Mystery."

First, the Order had to make sure that the Molecules of Malice had all been destroyed. Since the Maithuna Ceremony and its feeding of the Spirits of the Land had been shown to destroy the Molecules, the Ceremony would be conducted at all the enclaves of the Order around the world. Even if it was a solitary coupling the effect would be the same, just the radius, the effective distance of the feeding energy would be less, so the couple may be compelled to have sex in more than one location, close to but not in, some nearly public place. "Try not to get caught," she'd told them.

There was some laughter, but She said, "Seriously. Some of you will be working in places where the old attitudes still prevail. We are looking into extending the power of the Invisible Land to you for your protection. That is, you could do the Ceremony in a crowded plaza, just not in the center of it, where people would trip over you. There is still violence against wen that we must preclude."

The Council went quiet. She told them, "Look, just because the source of the hatred of the Feminine is gone from our skies, it doesn't mean that the attitudes of centuries will crumble to ash as our adversaries have.

She smiled, and they grinned back at Her. She continued, "The Men's Rebellion is not over. The men who led it, even though it was always disorganized, are still out there. I believe, speaking as the Harlot on the Beast, that it is time for a new Revelation. And that it shall be the Divine Feminine revealing itself to those who hate us.

"The Madeleines are beginning to work on a new training. We have recently had huge success with using the Ghost Body. This training will show more of you how to use it, how to project it into the private spaces of the Haters, and at little to no risk to yourselves, so long as your temporal body is protected, sleeping in safety somewhere under guard. The High Priestesses Regina, Byuteo, and Freya will be holding the first training in this art form in the immediate future at the Towers of Marini, then at our base in Kerkyra. Smaller trainings will be held at Stonehaven and in Brazil, as needed.

"In addition to mastering this magic of projecting your ghost, you will all have to memorize the content of The New Revelation. Some of this content will form the basis of the New Mythology that must replace the Mythologies promoted by our oppressors. These are the topics of the new Myths:

"The Antecedence of the Feminine, and the Consequence of the

Masculine. By which I mean The Truth, the Ecstasy, the Conscience, and the Mystery.

"The Feminine and the Masculine shall be equal except in one regard, and that is the True Idea, the True Myth, the Neomyth, that the Feminine came first. The Masculine shall treat the Feminine as its Antecedent, and in all things give the Feminine the respect it deserves.

"The next Myth will be the Tree of Life and the Circle of Life, our individuality and our relatedness to all things.

"Finally, we shall teach the Practice of Life, including Sex over and against Death and the fostering of Indeterminacy as the basis of Freedom in Human Affairs.

"When these subjects and the art form are mastered, you will be set free to practice on the men.

"You will enjoy it, I promise, even if they don't."

Shouts of joy and triumph filled the Council Hall. She Who Comes grinned, clapped her hands together, and disappeared.

57

THREE PRIME NUMBERS

Lulu had gone quiet as the time passed on her ride from the airport in Baltimore to Stonehaven. She'd been met by a couple in a nice car. The woman's name was Theresa and she'd introduced the man with her as her partner in crime, Carlos. He'd smiled hugely at the introduction, looking at Theresa with genuine affection. He loaded the luggage, closed the trunk and got into the back seat, telling Lulu to take the front.

Into her quietude, Lulu remembered how pleased she'd been by the invitation to come study at the yoga school at Stonehaven. The invitation had come from her teacher Diana, and it solved a huge problem in her life—she couldn't find a boyfriend willing to practice the techniques of the Order she'd been taught. As she had become more powerful and adept, the man she'd taken as a practice partner had become more uncooperative. She thought the class would be a good break from him, and maybe she would use it as an opportunity to break it off completely.

She'd run out of questions about the same time Theresa had run out of answers. She knew she'd be staying in the Mansion, on the fourth floor. She'd seen pictures of the Mansion on the website, and it would be the grandest place she had ever slept. Theresa had given her the daily schedule and made clear the expectation that she was to be at every function on her schedule unless she felt ill. To her surprise, she was told that her work share requirement would be modified when she was on her period. Theresa said that time was meant to serve primarily as an opportunity for reflection and rest. She didn't know what the duties would be, but she would be relieved of kitchen and food preparation responsibilities. "Almost a day off," Theresa said. She said she'd been glad of it, once she adjusted her attitude. She'd come to Stonehaven subject to bad cramping, and the yoga, the change in diet, and some herbal supplements had helped her tremendously. It wasn't a problem that Lulu had often, but she found the idea of treatment somehow relieving.

She started to wonder about what the rules around sex were. She was surprised that before she could formulate the question her mind was filled with images of couples in the first position, and then even more surprised that she found herself in that position herself, looking down at the top of a man's head, a face she couldn't see. She felt a tingling in her root and moved her hand to her lap.

Theresa, driving, glanced over at her. "Thinking about sex?" she asked.

Lulu looked up and saw her profile with a wicked grin. "How'd you know?"

"Intuition. That, and there is a scent that has changed in the car."

"Oh, no," Lulu stuttered. "How embarrassing. I'm so sorry."

"Oh no, don't worry about it, you're fine. I just have a very sensitive nose. There's no hard and fast rule about it. They recommend that you wait a week before you hook up with anyone. Your energy, the fields that surround you should be given time to lose all the ick it's been interacting with. You'll probably want to use the steam bath down at the Barn before you do any of that. And don't be surprised if you get turned down. A lot of the men here are already hooked in with the wen, excuse me women. We use that word here though, to describe ourselves. Wen. Anyway, I think you'll probably want to give it a break for a few days. I did."

After a pause she continued, "You'll want to check that all out with your mentor. Do you know who that is yet?"

"No. Diana invited me, I thought it might be her."

"Maybe, but Diana is really busy, she's high up in running this place. So it may be a few days before the Staff watches you enough to tell who would be good for you."

From the back seat Carlos said, "Staff? Did you say staff? I've got your staff right here."

And as creepy as the intrusion could have been, Theresa pealed with laughter, infectiously making Lulu grin herself.

"We shall see, then," she said.

"Yes, we shall," Theresa said. "Yes, we shall."

And she added, "You can always ask me."

58

BITER

A month after De Murgos was driven off the rock and into the arms of the True Creator, the Lama was reincarnated expeditiously by the Lords of Dharma, as a dog.

The dog distinguished itself shortly after birth by kicking the other pups in the litter away from the teat. Those that didn't starve, he fought with and crushed their throats before he was weaned. There was no play in this puppy.

Shortly after being weaned, the dog bit the hand that fed him, leading to the name Biter.

The owner raised dogs for the purpose of pit fighting.

The owner waited a year before pitting the dog. He won heavily in the betting on the first two fights.

Before the third fight, Biter bit whoever was close. The owner drugged the dog's food in order to render it unconscious so he could muzzle the dog.

When the dog came to from anesthesia it became apparent that in order to remove the muzzle so the dog could fight, the risk of getting bitten was high. And it was too expensive to keep knocking the dog out in order to muzzle it and then take the muzzle off.

So the owner resolved to shoot the dog between its hate-filled eyes.

In the second before the owner pulled the trigger, the dog's face melted into an expression of gratitude so clear and powerful that the owner had a moment of felt-sense shock and almost hesitated pulling the trigger, but his finger was already in the unconsciously automatic mode of pull.

The Lords of Dharma smiled.

August 18, 2024

Acknowledgments

In the sixteen years since I first told the story of *American Siddhi* and began writing it all down, including the notes and outlines for the subsequent novels in the series *The Siddhi Wars*, I have been blessed by the support and encouragement of many friends and readers, especially those who suffered through me reading sections and chapters to them aloud. Those close to me know who they are, and I will spare them the mild embarrassment of listing them all by name.

However, I wish to thank particularly my editors, AH and BR. Hopefully, they were tougher on me than I was on them.

As far as I know this book, *Antecedence of the Feminine*, is the last in this series. I have an idea for a follow up, *Tales from the Neomythic*, which looks like a collection of short stories, perhaps a novella, that focus on some of the characters created whose trajectories are not covered. I liked all the characters of the resistance, and it should be fun when I get to it after a couple of other projects.

It has been a blessing also to get to experience the joys of writing, and I hope that joy comes through for you, the reader.

www.ingramcontent.com/pod-product-compliance
Lightning Source LLC
Chambersburg PA
CBHW050327010526
44119CB00050B/709